Software Engineering: Theory and Practice

Software Engineering: Theory and Practice

Cersei Page

www.willfordpress.com

Published by Willford Press,
118-35 Queens Blvd., Suite 400,
Forest Hills, NY 11375, USA

ISBN: 978-1-68285-746-5

Cataloging-in-Publication Data

Software engineering : theory and practice / Cersei Page.
p. cm.
Includes bibliographical references and index.
ISBN 978-1-68285-746-5
1. Software engineering. 2. Computer engineering. I. Page, Cersei.
QA76.758 .S64 2019
005.1--dc23

For information on all Willford Press publications
visit our website at www.willfordpress.com

Contents

Preface

Software is the collection of data and instructions that drives the working of the computer. Software is usually written in high-level programming languages, which are then translated into machine language via a compiler or interpreter. Computer software can be classified into application software, system software and malicious software. The development of software through the application of scientific and technological methods is under the scope of software engineering. It is a vast subject that branches out into a number of significant sub-domains such as software requirements, software design, software testing, software construction, software development process, etc. This book explores all the important aspects of software engineering in the present day scenario. It is an upcoming field that has undergone rapid development over the past few decades. For all those who are interested in this domain, this textbook can prove to be an essential guide.

A foreword of all chapters of the book is provided below:

Chapter 1- Software is a set of instructions that guide the working of a computer. It includes computer programs, computer libraries and non-executable data. This chapter will introduce briefly all the significant aspects of software and its varied types, such as application, system and malicious software;

Chapter 2- The application of engineering for the development of software is under the scope of software engineering. This chapter has been carefully written to provide an introduction to software engineering through a detailed discussion of software design, software construction, software testing and software maintenance ;

Chapter 3- Software development refers to the process of designing, programming, testing and debugging in the creation and maintenance of software components. The aim of this chapter is to explore the fundamentals of software development, which includes software development process, lean software development, incremental funding methodology, rapid application development, spiral model, waterfall model, V-model, etc.;

Chapter 4- A variety of tools and techniques are used in software development for creating high-quality software products. The topics elaborated in this chapter will help in developing a better perspective about the different software development tools such as graphical user interface builder and integrated development environment, etc.;

Chapter 5- Software designing primarily involves problem solving and planning software solutions. The complex structures of a software system are referred to as software architecture. This chapter closely examines the key concepts of software design and architecture, through an analysis of software architectural model, software architectural style, software architecture description and software architecture analysis method, besides many others;

Chapter 6- The modification of a software or software product for improvement of performance or correction of faults is known as software maintenance. In order to completely understand software maintenance, it is necessary to understand the processes related to it. The following chapter elucidates the varied processes and mechanisms associated with this area of study, such as backporting, software maintenance model, legacy modernization, etc.;

Chapter 7- User interface design refers to the design of user interfaces for software and machines, such as computers, appliances and electronic devices for optimizing usability and the user experience. This chapter discusses in detail about GUI, graphic control elements, HTML, cascading style sheets, client-side scripting, etc. for a deeper understanding of user interface design;

Chapter 8- Software requirements is an area of software engineering concerned with the establishment of the needs of the user that can be solved by software. It involves activities that can be grouped under analysis, elicitation, specification and management. The varied aspects of software requirements have been introduced in this chapter, such as requirement gathering, requirement analysis and software requirements specification.

At the end, I would like to thank all the people associated with this book devoting their precious time and providing their valuable contributions to this book. I would also like to express my gratitude to my fellow colleagues who encouraged me throughout the process.

Cersei Page

Software and its Types

Software is a set of instructions that guide the working of a computer. It includes computer programs, computer libraries and non-executable data. This chapter will introduce briefly all the significant aspects of software and its varied types, such as application, system and malicious software.

Software is a general term for the various kinds of programs used to operate computers and related devices. (The term hardware describes the physical aspects of computers and related devices).

Software can be thought of as the variable part of a computer and hardware the invariable part. Software is often divided into application software (programs that do work users are directly interested in) and system software (which includes operating systems and any program that supports application software). The term middleware is sometimes used to describe programming that mediates between application and system software or between two different kinds of application software (for example, sending a remote work request from an application in a computer that has one kind of operating system to an application in a computer with a different operating system).

An additional and difficult-to-classify category of software is the utility, which is a small useful program with limited capability. Some utilities come with operating systems. Like applications, utilities tend to be separately installable and capable of being used independently from the rest of the operating system.

Applets are small applications that sometimes come with the operating system as "accessories." They can also be created independently using the Java or other programming languages.

Software can be purchased or acquired as shareware (usually intended for sale after a trial period), liteware (shareware with some capabilities disabled), freeware (free software but with copyright restrictions), public domain software (free with no restrictions), and open source (software where the source code is furnished and users agree not to limit the distribution of improvements).

Software is often packaged on CD-ROMs and diskettes. Today, much purchased software, shareware, and freeware is downloaded over the Internet. A new trend is software that is made available for use at another site known as an application service provider.

Some general kinds of application software include:

- Productivity software, which includes word processors, spreadsheets, and tools for use by most computer users.

- Presentation software.

- Graphics software for graphic designers.

- CAD/CAM software.

- Specialized scientific applications.

- Vertical market or industry-specific software (for example, for banking, insurance, retail, and manufacturing environments).

Application Software

Application software, also known as applications, or apps for short, cover a whole range of programs that can run on almost any device, from your desktop computer and your laptop to your smartphone and tablet. Really, an application is pretty much anything that runs on a device to complete a task.

Application software is generally more intuitive than full-blown software, with a simple user interface (UI) and crucially, built with the end user's best interests at heart.

The programs can be used for a vast array of different purposes, from managing social media, to productivity software for creating and editing documents or a web browser to navigate the internet, all the way up to more sophisticated use cases, such as enabling you to add entries into a database. Simpler apps with only one function are things like a device's pre-installed calendar.

What's important to note is that although the line between software and applications is blurred, there's one major difference between how the two work. Application software doesn't use the computer's core running system like utilities or maintenance programs that are normally preinstalled on a computer or device do. Applications run completely independently and thus, they don't rely on the computer's core to provide them with information.

Application Software Types

Desktop Applications

Desktop applications are 'installed' on a user's computer. They are normally pretty high-powered software that uses the computer's memory directly to carry out an action. Other characteristics include that they allow people to manipulate datasets, graphics or numbers to create an output. Examples of desktop applications include productivity applications such as a word processor, a music player or video player.

Web-based Applications

While most application software can be installed directly to a machine, many allow users to access tools through web browsers and some only exist in web format. Not only do these services free up space on a user's hard drive or network, being web-based means they can be accessed from anywhere in the world at any time, with data being stored in the cloud. This also means the application is kept up-to-date automatically, without the risk of a user running an insecure version.

This has given rise to software-as-a-service (SaaS), in which users agree to a subscription in exchange for application services, often provided through a web browser. Salesforce, Oracle, and Adobe Creative Cloud are some of the most widely used SaaS application suites.

Application Suites

While applications can be stand-alone products, it's far more common that programs will be bundled together as a suite, offering various solutions to any problems you may encounter.

Packages are often themed around a specific environment and are able to communicate with each other to provide greater value. For example, in an enterprise setting, this may involve a provider offering a package that includes database management tools, an HR application, and customer relationship management software.

Smaller suites, or those used predominantly by SMBs or in the home, tend to offer more general purpose applications, such as Microsoft Office that covers word processing and presentation software.

Utility applications, such as anti-virus software, offer the same basic functions regardless of the user, but pile on additional services depending on their needs. For these applications, the number of users dictates what additional features may be required, such as password management for personal subscriptions, or protections for file servers on business accounts.

System Software

System software is software on a computer that is designed to control and work with computer hardware. The two main types of system software are the operating system and the software installed with the operating system, often called utility software. The operating system and utility software typically depend on each other to function properly.

Some system software is used directly by users and other system software works in the background. System software can allow users to interact directly with hardware functionality, like the Device Manager and many of the utilities found in the Control Panel.

There are five types of systems software, all designed to control and coordinate the procedures and functions of computer hardware. They also enable functional interaction between hardware, software and the user.

Systems software carries out middleman tasks to ensure communication between other software and hardware to allow harmonious coexistence with the user.

Systems software can be categorized under the following:

- Operating system: Harnesses communication between hardware, system programs, and other applications.

- Device driver: Enables device communication with the OS and other programs.

- Firmware: Enables device control and identification.

- Translator: Translates high-level languages to low-level machine codes.

- Utility: Ensures optimum functionality of devices and applications.

Operating System

The operating system is a type of system software kernel that sits between computer hardware and end user. It is installed first on a computer to allow devices and applications to be identified and therefore functional.

System software is the first layer of software to be loaded into memory every time a computer is powered up.

Suppose a user wants to write and print a report to an attached printer. A word processing application is required to accomplish this task. Data input is done using a keyboard or other input devices and then displayed on the monitor. The prepared data is then sent to the printer.

In order for the word processor, keyboard, and printer to accomplish this task, they must work with the OS, which controls input and output functions, memory management, and printer spooling.

Today, the user interacts with the operating system through the graphical user interface (GUI) on a monitor or touchscreen interface. The desktop in modern OSs is a graphical workspace, which contains menus, icons, and apps that are manipulated by the user through a mouse-driven cursor or the touch of a finger. The disk operating system (DOS) was a popular interface used in the 1980s.

Windows 8.1 graphical desktop is a component of Windows opertaing system type

Types of Operating Systems

- Real-Time OS: Is installed in special purpose embedded systems like robots, cars, and modems.

- Single-user and single-task OS: Are installed on single-user devices like phones.

- Single-user and multitask OS: Are installed on contemporary personal computers.

- Multi-user OS: Is installed in network environments where many users have to share resources. Server OSs are examples of multi-user operating systems.

- Network OS: Is used to share resources such as files, printers in a network setup.

- Internet/Web OS: Is designed to run on the browser that is online.

- Mobile OS: Is designed to run on mobile phones, tablets and other mobile devices.

Functions of Operating Systems

- They provide the interface between the user and hardware through GUI.

- Manages and allocates memory space for applications.

- Processes the management of applications, input/output devices, and instructions.

- Configures and manages internal and peripheral devices.

- Manages single or multi-user storage in local and network computers.

- Security management of files and applications.

- Manages input and output devices.

- Detects, installs, and troubleshoots devices.

- Monitors system performance through Task Manager and other tools.

- Produce error messages and troubleshooting options.

- Implement interface for network communication.

- Manages printers in single or multi-user systems.

- Internal or network file management.

Examples of Operating Systems

Popular OSs for computers are:

- Windows 10

- Mac OS X

- Ubuntu

Popular network/server OSs are:

- Ubuntu Server

- Windows Server

- Red Hat Enterprise

Popular internet/web OSs are:

- Chrome OS

- Club Linux

- Remix OS

Popular mobile OSs are:

- iPhone OS
- Android OS
- Windows Phone OS

Device Drivers

Driver software is a type of system software which brings computer devices and peripherals to life. Drivers make it possible for all connected components and external add-ons perform their intended tasks and as directed by the OS. Without drivers, the OS would not assign any duties.

Examples of devices which require drivers:

- Mouse
- Keyboard
- Soundcard
- Display card
- Network card
- Printer

Usually, the operating system ships with drivers for most devices already in the market. By default, input devices such as the mouse and keyboard will have their drivers installed. They may never require third-party installations.

If a device is newer than the operating system, the user may have to download drivers from manufacturer websites or alternative sources.

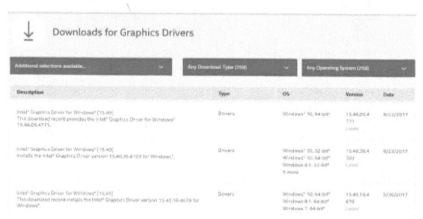

Intel driver page.

Firmware

Firmware is the operational software embedded within a flash, ROM, or EPROM memory chip for the OS to identify it. It directly manages and controls all activities of any single hardware.

Traditionally, firmware used to mean fixed software as denoted by the word firm. It was installed on non-volatile chips and could be upgraded only by swapping them with new, preprogrammed chips.

This was done to differentiate them from high-level software, which could be updated without having to swap components.

Today, firmware is stored in flash chips, which can be upgraded without swapping semiconductor chips.

BIOS chip in a desktop motherboard.

BIOS and UEFI

The most important firmware in computers today is installed by the manufacturer on the motherboard and can be accessed through the old BIOS (Basic Input/Output System) or the new UEFI (Unified Extended Firmware Interface) platforms.

It is the configuration interface which loads first when the computer is powered up and is going through POST (Power On Self Test).

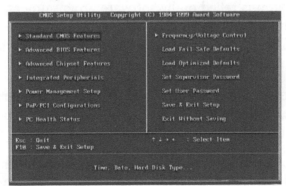

BIOS setup utility.

The motherboard firmware starts by waking up all the hardware and ensures that components like the processor, memory, and disk drives are operational. If all the crucial components are fine, it will run the bootloader, which will load the operating system. If the random-access memory is faulty, the BIOS will not allow the computer to boot up.

The user can change the BIOS and UEFI settings by pressing special keys (a function key, delete, or the esc key) at boot-up to load the configuration page. The user can configure security, boot order, time, and other options in the page that pops up.

Though they work differently, firmware compliments drivers in a few ways. Both give identity to hardware devices, with the latter making the operating system see the device.

The major difference between the two is that firmware will always reside within devices while drivers will install within the operating system.

UEFI setup utility.

Firmware upgrades come from the device manufacturer (not the OS manufacturer). They're necessary if the user wants computer hardware to receive new hardware and software support. Firmware will make it possible for devices to work better with old and new operating systems and applications.

Almost all devices and peripherals are embedded with firmware. Network card, TV tuner, router, scanner, or monitor and examples of devices which have firmware installed on them.

Programming Language Translators

These are intermediate programs relied on by software programmers to translate high-level language source code to machine language code. The former is a collection of programming languages that are easy for humans to comprehend and code (i.e., Java, C++, Python, PHP, BASIC). The latter is a complex code only understood by the processor.

Popular translator languages are compilers, assemblers, and interpreters. They're usually designed by computer manufacturers. Translator programs may perform a complete translation of program codes or translate every other instruction at a time.

Machine code is written in a number system of base-2, written out in 0 or 1. This is the lowest level language possible. While seemingly meaningless to humans, the zeros and ones are actually sequenced intelligently by the processor to refer to every conceivable human code and word.

Besides simplifying the work of software developers, translators help in various design tasks. They;

- Identify syntax errors during translation, thus allowing changes to be made to the code.

- Provide diagnostic reports whenever the code rules are not followed.

- Allocate data storage for the program.

- List both source code and program details.

Utilities

Utilities are types of system software which sits between system and application software. These are programs intended for diagnostic and maintenance tasks for the computer. They come in handy to ensure the computer functions optimally. Their tasks vary from crucial data security to disk drive defragmentation.

Most are third-party tools but they may come bundled with the operating system. Third-party tools are available individually or bundled together such as with Hiren Boot CD, Ultimate Boot CD, and Kaspersky Rescue Disk.

Examples and features of utility software include:

- Antivirus and security software for the security of files and applications, e.g., Malware-bytes, Microsoft Security Essentials, and AVG.

- Disk partition services such as Windows Disk Management, Easeus Partition Master, and Partition Magic.

- Disk defragmentation to organize scattered files on the drive. Examples include Disk De-fragmenter, Perfect Disk, Disk Keeper, Comodo Free Firewall, and Little Snitch.

- File Compression to optimize disk space such as WinRAR, Winzip, and 7-Zip.

- Data backup for security reasons, e.g., Cobian, Clonezilla, and Comodo.

- Hardware diagnostic services like Hard Disk Sentinel, Memtest, and Performance Monitor.

- Data recovery to help get back lost data. Examples include iCare Data Recovery, Recuva, and EaseUs Data Recovery Wizard.

- Firewall for protection against external threats, e.g., Windows Firewall.

The HIREN CD bundles several types of system software for troublesshooting purposes

Malicious Software or Malware

Malware is shorthand for malicious software. It is software developed by cyber attackers with the intention of gaining access or causing damage to a computer or network, often while the victim remains oblivious to the fact there's been a compromise. A common alternative description of malware is 'computer virus' although are big differences between these types malicious programs.

Types of Malware

Like traditional software, malware has evolved over the years and comes equipped with different functions depending on the goals of the developer

Malware authors will sometimes combine the features of different forms of malware to make an attack more potent - such as using ransomware as a distraction to destroy evidence of a Trojan attack.

Computer Virus

At its core, a computer virus is a form of software or code that is able to copy itself onto computers. The name has become associated with additionally performing malicious tasks, such as corrupting or destroying data.

While malicious software has evolved to become far more diverse than just computer viruses there are still some forms of traditional viruses like the 15-year-old Conficker worm which can still cause problems for older systems. Malware, on the other hand is designed to provide the attackers with many more malicious tools.

Trojan Malware

One of the most common forms of malware the Trojan horse is a form of malicious software which often disguises itself as a legitimate tool that tricks the user into installing it so it can carry out its malicious goals.

Its name of course comes from the tale of ancient Troy, with the Greeks hidden inside a giant wooden horse, which they claimed was a gift to the city of Troy. Once the horse was inside the city walls, a small team of Greeks emerged from inside the giant wooden horse and took the city.

Just as the Greeks used a Trojan Horse to trick Troy into letting troops into the city, Trojan malware disguises itself in order to infiltrate a system.

Trojan malware operates in much the same way, in that it sneaks into your system often disguised as a legitimate tool like an update or a Flash download then, once inside your system, it begins its attacks.

Once installed in the system, depending on its capabilities a Trojan can then potentially access and capture everything logins and passwords, keystrokes, screenshots, system information, banking details, and more and secretly send it all to the attackers. Sometimes a Trojan can even allow attackers to modify data or turn off anti-malware protection.

The power of Trojan horses makes it a useful tool for everyone from solo hackers, to criminal gangs to state-sponsored operations engaging in full-scale espionage.

Spyware

Spyware is software which monitors the actions that are carried out on a PC and other devices. That might include web browsing history, apps used, or messages sent. Spyware might arrive as a Trojan malware or may be downloaded onto devices in other ways.

For example, someone downloading a toolbar for their web browser may find it comes packed with spyware for the purposes of monitoring their internet activity and computer use, or malicious adverts can secretly drop the code onto a computer via a drive-by download.

In some cases, spyware is actively sold as software, designed for purposes such as parents monitoring their child's internet use and is designed to explicitly be ignored by antivirus and security software. However, there are various instances of such tools being used by employers to spy on the activity of employees and people using spyware to spy on their spouses.

- Android malware spies on smartphones users and runs up their phone bill too.

- Hacking group used Facebook lures to trick victims into downloading Android spyware.

- Hackers are using hotel Wi-Fi to spy on guests, steal data.

Ransomware

While some forms of malware rely on being subtle and remaining hidden for as long as possible, that isn't the case for ransomware.

Often delivered via a malicious attachment or link in a phishing email, ransomware encrypts the infected system, locking the user out until they pay a ransom - delivered in bitcoin or other cryptocurrency in order to get them back.

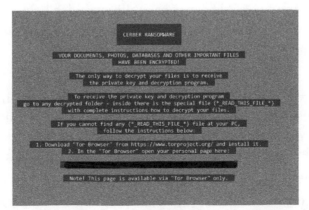

Ransomware demands a payment in return for returning encrypted files.

It might sound simple, but ransomware works: Cybercriminals pocketed over $1 billion from ransomware attacks during 2016 alone, and a Europol report describes it as having "eclipsed" most other global cybercriminal threats in 2017.

Wiper Malware

Wiper malware has one simple goal: To completely destroy or erase all data from the targeted computer or network. The wiping could take place after the attackers have secretly removed target data from the network for themselves, or it could could be launched with the pure intention of sabotaging the target.

One of the first major forms of wiper malware was Shamoon, which targeted Saudi energy companies with the aim of stealing data then wiping it from the infected machine. More recent instances of wiper attacks include StoneDrill and Mamba, the latter of which doesn't just delete files, but renders the hard driver unusable.

One of the most high profile wipers of recent times was Petya ransomware. The malware was initially thought to be ransomware. However, researchers found that not only was there no way for victims retrieve their data via paying the ransom, but also that the goal of Petya was to irrecoverably destroy data.

Computer Worm

A worm is a form of malware that is designed to spread itself from system to system without the actions by the users of those systems.

Worms often exploit vulnerabilities in operating systems or software, but are also capable of distributing themselves via email attachments in cases where the worm can gain access to the contact book on an infected machine.

It might seem like a basic concept, but worms are some of the most successful and long-lived forms of malware out there. The 15-year-old SQL slammer worm is still causing issues by powering DDoS attacks, while the 10-year-old Conficker worm still ranks among the most common cyber infections.

Recently, Wannacry ransomware outbreak infected over 300,000 computers around the world - something it did thanks to the success of worm capabilities which helped it quickly spread through infected networks and onto unpatched systems.

Adware

The ultimate goal of many cybercriminals is to make money - and for some, adware is just the way to do it. Adware does exactly what it says on the tin - it's designed to maliciously push adverts onto the user, often in such a way that the only way to get rid of them is to click through to the advert. For the cybercriminals, each click brings about additional revenue.

In most cases, the malicious adverts aren't there to steal data from the victim or cause damage to the device, just sufficiently annoy the user into repeatedly clicking on pop-up windows. However, in the case of mobile devices, this can easily lead to extreme battery drain or render the device unusable due to the influx of pop-up windows taking up the whole screen.

Adware displays intrusive pop-up adverts which won't disappear until they're clicked on.

Botnet

A botnet short for robot network involves cybercriminals using malware to secretly hijack a network of machines in numbers, which can range from a handful to millions of compromised devices. While it is not malware in itself these networks are usually built by infecting vulnerable devices.

Each of the machines falls under the control of a single attacking operation, which can remotely issue commands to all of the infected machines from a single point.

By issuing commands to all the infected computers in the zombie network, attackers can carry out coordinated large-scale campaigns, including DDoS attacks, which leverage the power of the army of devices to flood a victim with traffic, overwhelming their website or service to such an extent it goes offline.

Other common attacks carried out by botnets include spam email attachment campaigns - which can also be used to recruit more machines into the network - and attempts to steal financial data, while smaller botnets have also been used in attempts to compromise specific targets.

Botnets are designed to stay quiet to ensure the user is completely oblivious that their machine is under the control of an attacker.

As more devices become connected to the internet, more devices are becoming targets for botnets. The infamous Mirai botnet - which slowed down internet services in late 2016 - was partially powered by Internet of Things devices which could easily be roped into the network thanks to their inherently poor security and lack of malware removals tools.

Cryptocurrency Miner Malware

The high profile of the rise of bitcoin has helped push cryptocurrency into the public eye. In many instances, people aren't even buying it, but are dedicating a portion of the computing power of their computer network or website to mine for it.

While there are plenty of instances of internet users actively engaging in this activity on their terms - it's so popular the demand has helped to push up the price of PC gaming graphics cards - cryptocurrency mining is also being abused by cyber attackers.

There's nothing underhanded or illegal about cryptocurrency mining in itself, but in order to acquire as much currency - be it bitcoin, Monero, Etherium or something else - some cybercriminals are using malware to secretly capture PCs and put them to work in a botnet, all without the victim being aware their PC has been compromised.

One of the largest cybercriminal cryptocurrency networks, the Smominru botnet, is thought to consist of over 500,000 systems and to have made its operators at least $3.6 million dollars.

Typically, a cryptocurrency miner will deliver malicious code to a target machine with the goal of taking advantage of the computer's processing power to run mining operations in the background.

The problem for the user of the infected system is that their system can be slowed down to almost a complete stop by the miner using big chunks of its processing power - which to the victim looks as if it is happening for no reason.

The rise of cryptocurrency has led to a rise in criminals
using malware to mine it via compromised systems.

PCs and Window servers can be used for cryptocurrency mining, but Internet of Things devices are also popular targets for compromising for the purposes of illicitly acquiring funds. The lack of security and inherently connected nature of many IoT devices makes them attractive targets for cryptocurrency miners - especially as the device in question is likely to have been installed and perhaps forgotten about.

Analysis by Cisco Talos suggests a single system compromised with a cryptocurrency miner could make 0.28 Monero a day. It might sound like a tiny amount, but an enslaved network of 2000 systems could add the funds up to $568 per day - or over $200,000 a year.

Methods of Delivering Malware

In the past, before the pervasive spread of the World Wide Web, malware and viruses would need to be manually, physically, delivered, via floppy disc or CD Rom.

In many cases, malware is still delivered by using an external device, although nowadays it is most likely to be delivered by a flash drive or USB stick. There are instances of USB sticks being left in car parks outside targeted organizations, in the hope that someone picks one up out of curiosity and plugs it into a computer connected to the network.

However, more common now is malware that is delivered in a phishing email with payloads distributed as an email attachment.

The quality of the spam email attempts vary widely - some efforts to deliver malware will involve the attackers using minimal effort, perhaps even sending an email containing nothing but a randomly named attachment.

In this instance, the attackers are hoping to chance on someone naive enough to just go ahead and click on email attachments or links without thinking about it - and that they don't have any sort of malware protection installed.

A slightly more sophisticated form of delivering malware via a phishing email is when attackers send large swathes of messages, claiming a user has won a contest, needs to check their online bank account, missed a delivery, needs to pay taxes, or even is required to attend court - and various other messages which upon first viewing may draw the target to instantly react.

For example, if the message has an attachment explaining (falsely) that a user is being summoned to court, the user may click on it due to the shock, opening the email attachment - or clicking a link - to get more information. This activates the malware, with the likes of ransomware and trojans often delivered in this way.

If the attackers have a specific target in mind, the phishing email can be specifically tailored to lure in people within one organization, or even just an individual. It's this means of delivering malware which is often associated with the most sophisticated malware campaigns.

However, there are many other ways for malware to spread that do not require action by the end user - through networks and through other software vulnerabilities.

Fileless Malware

As traditional malware attacks are being slowed by prevention tactics including the use of robust anti-virus or anti-malware system, and users are becoming cautious of unexpected emails and strange attachments, attackers are being forced to find other ways to drop their malicious payloads.

One increasingly common means of this is via the use of fileless malware. Rather than relying on a traditional method of compromise like downloading and executing malicious files on a computer - which can often be detected by anti-virus software solutions - the attacks are delivered in a different way.

Instead of requiring execution from a dropped file, fileless malware attacks rely on leveraging zero-day exploits or launching scripts from memory, techniques which can be used to infect endpoints without leaving a tell-tale trail behind.

This is achieved because the attacks uses a system's own trusted system files and services to obtain access to devices and launch nefarious activity - all while remaining undetected because anti-virus doesn't register wrongdoing.

Exploiting the infrastructure of the system in this way allows the attackers to create hidden files and folders or create scripts they can use to compromise systems, connect to networks and eventually command and control servers, providing a means of stealthily conducting activity.

The very nature of fileless malware means not only is it difficult to detect, but difficult to protect against by some forms of antivirus software. But ensuring that systems are patched, up to date, and restricted users from adopting admin privileges can help.

References

- Software: searchmicroservices.techtarget.com, Retrieved 21 May 2018

- What-is-application-software, business-operations-30331, Retrieved 11 April 2018

- Systsoft, jargon: computerhope.com, Retrieved 28 April 2018

- The-Five-Types-of-System-Software: turbofuture.com, Retrieved 26 March 2018

- What-is-malware-everything-you-need-to-know-about-viruses-trojans-and-malicious-software: zdnet.com, Retrieved 16 May 2018

Introduction to Software Engineering

The application of engineering for the development of software is under the scope of software engineering. This chapter has been carefully written to provide an introduction to software engineering through a detailed discussion of software design, software construction, software testing and software maintenance.

Software is more than just a program code. A program is an executable code, which serves some computational purpose. Software is considered to be collection of executable programming code, associated libraries and documentations. Software, when made for a specific requirement is called software product.

Engineering on the other hand, is all about developing products, using well-defined, scientific principles and methods.

Software engineering is an engineering branch associated with development of software product using well-defined scientific principles, methods and procedures. The outcome of software engineering is an efficient and reliable software product.

Software Evolution

The process of developing a software product using software engineering principles and methods is referred to as software evolution. This includes the initial development of software and its maintenance and updates, till desired software product is developed, which satisfies the expected requirements.

Evolution starts from the requirement gathering process. After which developers create a proto-type of the intended software and show it to the users to get their feedback at the early stage of software product development. The users suggest changes, on which several consecutive updates and maintenance keep on changing too. This process changes to the original software, till the desired software is accomplished.

Even after the user has desired software in hand, the advancing technology and the changing requirements force the software product to change accordingly. Re-creating software from scratch and to go one-on-one with requirement is not feasible. The only feasible and economical solution is to update the existing software so that it matches the latest requirements.

Software Evolution Laws

Lehman has given laws for software evolution. He divided the software into three different categories:

- S-type (static-type): This is a software, which works strictly according to defined specifications and solutions. The solution and the method to achieve it, both are immediately understood before coding. The s-type software is least subjected to changes hence this is the simplest of all. For example, calculator program for mathematical computation.

- P-type (practical-type): This is a software with a collection of procedures. This is defined by exactly what procedures can do. In this software, the specifications can be described but the solution is not obvious instantly. For example, gaming software.

- E-type (embedded-type): This software works closely as the requirement of real-world environment. This software has a high degree of evolution as there are various changes in laws, taxes etc. in the real world situations. For example, online trading software.

E-Type Software Evolution

Lehman has given eight laws for E-Type software evolution -

- Continuing change: An E-type software system must continue to adapt to the real world changes, else it becomes progressively less useful.

- Increasing complexity: As an E-type software system evolves, its complexity tends to increase unless work is done to maintain or reduce it.

- Conservation of familiarity: The familiarity with the software or the knowledge about how it was developed, why was it developed in that particular manner etc. must be retained at any cost, to implement the changes in the system.

- Continuing growth: In order for an E-type system intended to resolve some business problem, its size of implementing the changes grows according to the lifestyle changes of the business.

- Reducing quality: An E-type software system declines in quality unless rigorously maintained and adapted to a changing operational environment.

- Feedback systems: The E-type software systems constitute multi-loop, multi-level feedback systems and must be treated as such to be successfully modified or improved.

- Self-regulation: E-type system evolution processes are self-regulating with the distribution of product and process measures close to normal.

- Organizational stability: The average effective global activity rate in an evolving E-type system is invariant over the lifetime of the product.

Software Paradigms

Software paradigms refer to the methods and steps, which are taken while designing the software. There are many methods proposed and are in work today, but we need to see where in the software engineering these paradigms stand. These can be combined into various categories, though each of them is contained in one another:

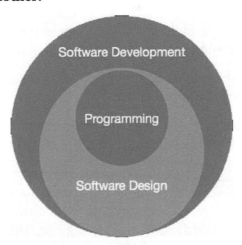

Programming paradigm is a subset of Software design paradigm which is further a subset of Software development paradigm.

Software Development Paradigm

This Paradigm is known as software engineering paradigms where all the engineering concepts pertaining to the development of software are applied. It includes various researches and requirement gathering which helps the software product to build. It consists of:

- Requirement gathering

- Software design
- Programming

Software Design Paradigm

This paradigm is a part of Software Development and includes –

- Design
- Maintenance
- Programming

Programming Paradigm

This paradigm is related closely to programming aspect of software development. This includes –

- Coding
- Testing
- Integration

Need of Software Engineering

The need of software engineering arises because of higher rate of change in user requirements and environment on which the software is working.

- Large software: It is easier to build a wall than to a house or building, likewise, as the size of software become large engineering has to step to give it a scientific process.

- Scalability: If the software process were not based on scientific and engineering concepts, it would be easier to re-create new software than to scale an existing one.

- Cost: As hardware industry has shown its skills and huge manufacturing has lower down he price of computer and electronic hardware. But the cost of software remains high if proper process is not adapted.

- Dynamic Nature: The always growing and adapting nature of software hugely depends upon the environment in which user works. If the nature of software is always changing, new enhancements need to be done in the existing one. This is where software engineering plays a good role.

- Quality Management: Better process of software development provides better and quality software product.

Characteristics of Good Software

A software product can be judged by what it offers and how well it can be used. This software must satisfy on the following grounds:

- Operational

- Transitional
- Maintenance

Well-engineered and crafted software is expected to have the following characteristics:

Operational

This tells us how well software works in operations. It can be measured on:

- Budget
- Usability
- Efficiency
- Correctness
- Functionality
- Dependability
- Security
- Safety

Transitional

This aspect is important when the software is moved from one platform to another:

- Portability
- Interoperability
- Reusability
- Adaptability

Maintenance

This aspect briefs about how well a software has the capabilities to maintain itself in the ever-changing environment:

- Modularity
- Maintainability
- Flexibility
- Scalability

In short, Software engineering is a branch of computer science, which uses well-defined engineering concepts required to produce efficient, durable, scalable, in-budget and on-time software products.

Software Design

Once the requirements document for the software to be developed is available, the software design phase begins. While the requirement specification activity deals entirely with the problem domain, design is the first phase of transforming the problem into a solution. In the design phase, the customer and business requirements and technical considerations all come together to formulate a product or a system.

The design process comprises a set of principles, concepts and practices, which allow a software engineer to model the system or product that is to be built. This model, known as design model, is assessed for quality and reviewed before a code is generated and tests are conducted. The design model provides details about software data structures, architecture, interfaces and components which are required to implement the system.

Software design is a phase in software engineering, in which a blueprint is developed to serve as a base for constructing the software system. Software design is 'both a process of defining, the architecture, components, interfaces, and other characteristics of a system or component and the result of that process.'

In the design phase, many critical and strategic decisions are made to achieve the desired functionality and quality of the system. These decisions are taken into account to successfully develop the software and carry out its maintenance in a way that the quality of the end product is improved.

Principles of Software Design

Developing design is a cumbersome process as most expansive errors are often introduced in this phase. Moreover, if these errors get unnoticed till later phases, it becomes more difficult to correct them. Therefore, a number of principles are followed while designing the software. These principles act as a framework for the designers to follow a good design practice.

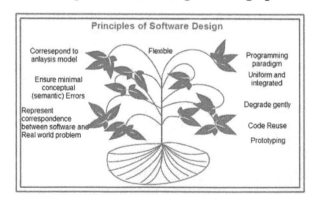

Some of the commonly followed design principles are as following:

1. Software design should correspond to the analysis model: Often a design element corresponds to many requirements, therefore, we must know how the design model satisfies all the requirements represented by the analysis model.

2. Choose the right programming paradigm: A programming paradigm describes the structure of the software system. Depending on the nature and type of application, different programming paradigms such as procedure oriented, object-oriented, and prototyping paradigms can be used. The paradigm should be chosen keeping constraints in mind such as time, availability of resources and nature of user's requirements.

3. Software design should be uniform and integrated: Software design is considered uniform and integrated, if the interfaces are properly defined among the design components. For this, rules, format, and styles are established before the design team starts designing the software.

4. Software design should be flexible: Software design should be flexible enough to adapt changes easily. To achieve the flexibility, the basic design concepts such as abstraction, refinement, and modularity should be applied effectively.

5. Software design should ensure minimal conceptual (semantic) errors: The design team must ensure that major conceptual errors of design such as ambiguousness and inconsistency are addressed in advance before dealing with the syntactical errors present in the design model.

6. Software design should be structured to degrade gently: Software should be designed to handle unusual changes and circumstances, and if the need arises for termination, it must do so in a proper manner so that functionality of the software is not affected.

7. Software design should represent correspondence between the software and real-world problem: The software design should be structured in such away that it always relates with the real-world problem.

8. Software reuse: Software engineers believe on the phrase: 'do not reinvent the wheel'. Therefore, software components should be designed in such a way that they can be effectively reused to increase the productivity.

9. Designing for testability: A common practice that has been followed is to keep the testing phase separate from the design and implementation phases. That is, first the software is developed (designed and implemented) and then handed over to the testers who subsequently determine whether the software is fit for distribution and subsequent use by the customer. However, it has become apparent that the process of separating testing is seriously flawed, as if any type of design or implementation errors are found after implementation, then the entire or a substantial part of the software requires to be redone. Thus, the test engineers should be involved from the initial stages. For example, they should be involved with analysts to prepare tests for determining whether the user requirements are being met.

10. Prototyping: Prototyping should be used when the requirements are not completely defined in the beginning. The user interacts with the developer to expand and refine the requirements as the development proceeds. Using prototyping, a quick 'mock-up' of the system can be developed. This mock-up can be used as a effective means to give the users a feel of what the system will look like and demonstrate functions that will be included in the developed system. Prototyping also helps in reducing risks of designing software that is not in accordance with the customer's requirements.

Note that design principles are often constrained by the existing hardware configuration, the implementation language, the existing file and data structures, and the existing organizational practices. Also, the evolution of each software design should be meticulously designed for future evaluations, references and maintenance.

Software Design Concepts

Every software process is characterized by basic concepts along with certain practices or methods. Methods represent the manner through which the concepts are applied. As new technology replaces older technology, many changes occur in the methods that are used to apply the concepts for the development of software. However, the fundamental concepts underlining the software design process remain the same, some of which are described here.

Abstraction

Abstraction refers to a powerful design tool, which allows software designers to consider components at an abstract level, while neglecting the implementation details of the components. IEEE defines abstraction as 'a view of a problem that extracts the essential information relevant to a particular purpose and ignores the remainder of the information.' The concept of abstraction can be used in two ways: as a process and as an entity. As a process, it refers to a mechanism of hiding irrelevant details and representing only the essential features of an item so that one can focus on important things at a time. As an entity, it refers to a model or view of an item.

Each step in the software process is accomplished through various levels of abstraction. At the highest level, an outline of the solution to the problem is presented whereas at the lower levels, the solution to the problem is presented in detail. For example, in the requirements analysis phase, a solution to the problem is presented using the language of problem environment and as we proceed through the software process, the abstraction level reduces and at the lowest level, source code of the software is produced.

There are three commonly used abstraction mechanisms in software design, namely, functional abstraction, data abstraction and control abstraction. All these mechanisms allow us to control the complexity of the design process by proceeding from the abstract design model to concrete design model in a systematic manner.

1. Functional abstraction: This involves the use of parameterized subprograms. Functional abstraction can be generalized as collections of subprograms referred to as 'groups'. Within these groups there exist routines which may be visible or hidden. Visible routines can be used within the containing groups as well as within other groups, whereas hidden routines are hidden from other groups and can be used within the containing group only.

2. Data abstraction: This involves specifying data that describes a data object. For example, the data object window encompasses a set of attributes (window type, window dimension) that describe the window object clearly. In this abstraction mechanism, representation and manipulation details are ignored.

3. Control abstraction: This states the desired effect, without stating the exact mechanism of control. For example, if and while statements in programming languages (like C and C++)

are abstractions of machine code implementations, which involve conditional instructions. In the architectural design level, this abstraction mechanism permits specifications of sequential subprogram and exception handlers without the concern for exact details of implementation.

Architecture

Software architecture refers to the structure of the system, which is composed of various components of a program or system, the attributes (properties) of those components and the relationship amongst them. The software architecture enables the software engineers to analyze the software design efficiently. In addition, it also helps them in decision-making and handling risks. The software architecture does the following.

- Provides an insight to all the interested stakeholders that enable them to communicate with each other.

- Highlights early design decisions, which have great impact on the software engineering activities (like coding and testing) that follow the design phase.

- Creates intellectual models of how the system is organized into components and how these components interact with each other.

Currently, software architecture is represented in an informal and unplanned manner. Though the architectural concepts are often represented in the infrastructure (for supporting particular architectural styles) and the initial stages of a system configuration, the lack of an explicit independent characterization of architecture restricts the advantages of this design concept in the present scenario.

Note that software architecture comprises two elements of design model, namely, data design and architectural design.

Patterns

A pattern provides a description of the solution to a recurring design problem of some specific domain in such a way that the solution can be used again and again. The objective of each pattern is to provide an insight to a designer who can determine the following:

1. Whether the pattern can be reused.

2. Whether the pattern is applicable to the current project.

3. Whether the pattern can be used to develop a similar but functionally or structurally different design pattern.

Types of Design Patterns

Software engineer can use the design pattern during the entire software design process. When the analysis model is developed, the designer can examine the problem description at different levels of abstraction to determine whether it complies with one or more of the following types of design patterns.

1. Architectural patterns: These patterns are high-level strategies that refer to the overall structure and organization of a software system. That is, they define the elements of a software system such as subsystems, components, classes, etc. In addition, they also indicate the relationship between the elements along with the rules and guidelines for specifying these relationships. Note that architectural patterns are often considered equivalent to software architecture.

2. Design patterns: These patterns are medium-level strategies that are used to solve design problems. They provide a means for the refinement of the elements (as defined by architectural pattern) of a software system or the relationship among them. Specific design elements such as relationship among components or mechanisms that affect component-to-component interaction are addressed by design patterns. Note that design patterns are often considered equivalent to software components.

3. Idioms: These patterns are low-level patterns, which are programming-language specific. They describe the implementation of a software component, the method used for interaction among software components, etc., in a specific programming language. Note that idioms are often termed as coding patterns.

Modularity

Modularity is achieved by dividing the software into uniquely named and addressable components, which are also known as modules. A complex system (large program) is partitioned into a set of discrete modules in such a way that each module can be developed independent of other modules. After developing the modules, they are integrated together to meet the software requirements. Note that larger the number of modules a system is divided into, greater will be the effort required to integrate the modules.

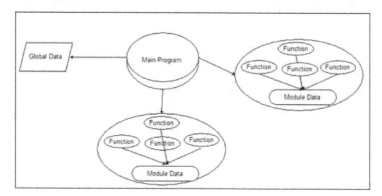

Modularizing a design helps to plan the development in a more effective manner, accommodate changes easily, conduct testing and debugging effectively and efficiently, and conducts maintenance work without adversely affecting the functioning of the software.

Information Hiding

Modules should be specified and designed in such a way that the data structures and processing details of one module are not accessible to other modules. They pass only that much information to each other, which is required to accomplish the software functions. The way of hiding unnecessary details is referred to as information hiding. IEEE defines information hiding as 'the technique of encapsulating software design decisions in modules in such a way that the module's interfaces reveal as little as possible about the module's inner workings; thus each module is a 'black box' to the other modules in the system.

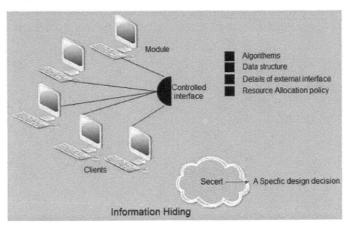

Information hiding is of immense use when modifications are required during the testing and maintenance phase. Some of the advantages associated with information hiding are listed below:

1. Leads to low coupling.

2. Emphasizes communication through controlled interfaces.

3. Decreases the probability of adverse effects.

4. Restricts the effects of changes in one component on others.

5. Results in higher quality software.

Stepwise Refinement

Stepwise refinement is a top-down design strategy used for decomposing a system from a high level of abstraction into a more detailed level (lower level) of abstraction. At the highest level of abstraction, function or information is defined conceptually without providing any information about the internal workings of the function or internal structure of the data. As we proceed towards the lower levels of abstraction, more and more details are available.

Software designers start the stepwise refinement process by creating a sequence of compositions for the system being designed. Each composition is more detailed than the previous one and contains more components and interactions. The earlier compositions represent the significant interactions within the system, while the later compositions show in detail how these interactions are achieved.

To have a clear understanding of the concept, let us consider an example of stepwise refinement. Every computer program comprises input, process, and output.

1. Input

- Get user's name (string) through a prompt.

- Get user's grade (integer from 0 to 100) through a prompt and validate.

2. Process

3. Output

This is the first step in refinement. The input phase can be refined further as given here.

1. INPUT

Get user's name through a prompt.

Get user's grade through a prompt.

While (invalid grade)

Ask again:

2. PROCESS

3. OUTPUT

Note: Stepwise refinement can also be performed for PROCESS and OUTPUT phase.

Refactoring

Refactoring is an important design activity that reduces the complexity of module design keeping its behaviour or function unchanged. Refactoring can be defined as a process of modifying a software system to improve the internal structure of design without changing its external behavior. During the refactoring process, the existing design is checked for any type of flaws like redundancy, poorly constructed algorithms and data structures, etc., in order to improve the design. For example, a design model might yield a component which exhibits low cohesion (like a component performs four functions that have a limited relationship with one another). Software designers may decide to refactor the component into four different components, each exhibiting high cohesion. This leads to easier integration, testing, and maintenance of the software components.

Structural Partitioning

When the architectural style of a design follows a hierarchical nature, the structure of the program can be partitioned either horizontally or vertically. In horizontal partitioning, the control modules are used to communicate between functions and execute the functions. Structural partitioning provides the following benefits:

- The testing and maintenance of software becomes easier.

- The negative impacts spread slowly.

- The software can be extended easily.

Besides these advantages, horizontal partitioning has some disadvantage also. It requires to pass more data across the module interface, which makes the control flow of the problem more complex. This usually happens in cases where data moves rapidly from one function to another.

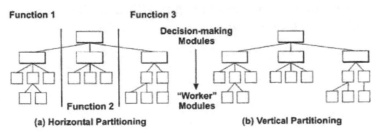

Horizontal and Vertical Partitioning

In vertical partitioning, the functionality is distributed among the modules-in a top-down manner. The modules at the top level called control modules perform the decision-making and do little processing whereas the modules at the low level called worker modules perform all input, computation and output tasks.

Concurrency

Computer has limited resources and they must be utilized efficiently as much as possible. To utilize these resources efficiently, multiple tasks must be executed concurrently. This requirement makes concurrency one of the major concepts of software design. Every system must be designed to allow multiple processes to execute concurrently, whenever possible. For example, if the current process is waiting for some event to occur, the system must execute some other process in the mean time.

However, concurrent execution of multiple processes sometimes may result in undesirable situations such as an inconsistent state, deadlock, etc. For example, consider two processes A and B and a data item Q1 with the value '200'. Further, suppose A and B are being executed concurrently and firstly A reads the value of Q1 (which is '200') to add '100' to it. However, before A updates es the value of Q1, B reads the value of Q1 (which is still '200') to add '50' to it. In this situation, whether A or B first updates the value of Q1, the value of would definitely be wrong resulting in an inconsistent state of the system. This is because the actions of A and B are not synchronized with each other. Thus, the system must control the concurrent execution and synchronize the actions of concurrent processes.

One way to achieve synchronization is mutual exclusion, which ensures that two concurrent processes do not interfere with the actions of each other. To ensure this, mutual exclusion may use locking technique. In this technique, the processes need to lock the data item to be read or updated. The data item locked by some process cannot be accessed by other processes until it is unlocked. It implies that the process, that needs to access the data item locked by some other process, has to wait.

Developing a Design Model

To develop a complete specification of design (design model), four To develop a complete specification of design (design model), four design models are needed. These models are listed below.

1. Data design: This specifies the data structures for implementing the software by converting data objects and their relationships identified during the analysis phase. Various studies suggest that design engineering should begin with data design, since this design lays the foundation for all other design models.

2. Architectural design: This specifies the relationship between the structural elements of the software, design patterns, architectural styles, and the factors affecting the ways in which architecture can be implemented.

3. Component-level design: This provides the detailed description of how structural elements of software will actually be implemented.

4. Interface design: This depicts how the software communicates with the system that interoperates with it and with the end-users.

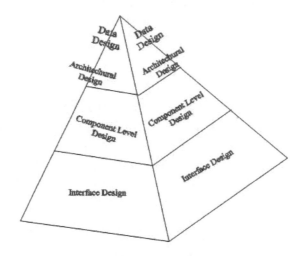

Design Model and its Elements

Design Document

A design doc, also known as a technical spec is a description of how you plan to solve a problem. It is the most useful tool for making sure the right work gets done.

The main goal of a design doc is to make you more effective by forcing you to think through the design and gather feedback from others. People often think the point of a design doc is to teach others about some system or serve as documentation later on. While those can be beneficial side effects, they are not the goal in and of themselves.

As a general rule of thumb, if you are working on a project that might take 1 engineer-month or more, you should write a design doc. But don't stop there a lot of smaller projects could benefit from a mini design doc too.

Things to be Included in a Design Doc

A design doc describes the solution to a problem. Since the nature of each problem is different, naturally you'd want to structure your design doc differently.

To start, the following is a list of important aspects that you should at least consider including in your next design doc:

Title and People

The title of your design doc, the author(s) (should be the same as the list of people planning to work on this project), the reviewer(s) of the doc, and the date this document was last updated.

Overview

A high level summary that every engineer at the company should understand and use to decide if it's useful for them to read the rest of the doc. It should be 3 paragraphs max.

Context

A description of the problem at hand, why this project is necessary, what people need to know to assess this project, and how it fits into the technical strategy, product strategy, or the team's quarterly goals.

Goals and Non-Goals

The goals should include:

- Describing the user-driven impact of your project where your user might be another engineering team or even another technical system

- Specifying how to measure success using metrics bonus points if you can link to a dashboard that tracks those metrics

Non-Goals are equally important to describe which problems you won't be fixing so everyone is on the same page.

Milestones

A list of measurable checkpoints, so your PM and your manager's manager can skim it and know roughly when different parts of the project will be done. I encourage you to break the project down into major user-facing milestones if the project is more than 1 month long.

Use calendar dates so you take into account unrelated delays, vacations, meetings, and so on. It should look something like this:

Start Date: June 7, 2018

Milestone 1-New system MVP running in dark-mode: June 28, 2018

Milestone 2 - Retire old system: July 4th, 2018

End Date: Add feature X, Y, Z to new system: July 14th, 2018

Add an Update subsection here if the ETA of some of these milestone changes, so the stakeholders can easily see the most up-to-date estimates.

Current Solution

In addition to describing the current implementation, you should also walk through a high level example flow to illustrate how users interact with this system or how data flow through it.

A user story is a great way to frame this. Keep in mind that your system might have different types of users with different use cases.

Proposed Solution

It include aspects of Technical Architecture. Again, try to walk through a user story to concretize this. Feel free to include many sub-sections and diagrams.

Provide a big picture first, then fill in lots of details. Aim for a world where you can write this, then take a vacation on some deserted island, and another engineer on the team can just read it and implement the solution as you described.

Alternative Solutions

What else did you consider when coming up with the solution above? What are the pros and cons of the alternatives? Have you considered buying a 3rd-party solution or using an open source one that solves this problem as opposed to building your own?

Monitoring and Alerting

People often treat this as an afterthought or skip it all together, and it almost always comes back to bite them later when things break and they have no idea how or why.

Cross-Team Impact

- How will this increase on call and dev-ops burden?
- How much money will it cost?
- Does it cause any latency regression to the system?
- Does it expose any security vulnerabilities?
- What are some negative consequences and side effects?
- How might the support team communicate this to the customers?

Discussion

Any open issues that you aren't sure about, contentious decisions that you'd like readers to weigh in on, suggested future work, and so on.

Detailed Scoping and Timeline

This part is mostly going to be read only by the engineers working on this project, their tech leads, and their managers. Hence this part is at the end of the doc.

Essentially, this is the breakdown of how and when you plan on executing each part of the project.

Ways to Write It

Now that we've discussed about what goes into a good design doc, let's discuss about the style of writing.

Write as Simply as Possible

Don't try to write like the academic papers you've read. They are written to impress journal reviewers. Your doc is written to describe your solution and get feedback from your teammates. You can achieve clarity by using:

- Simple words
- Short sentences
- Bulleted lists or numbered lists
- Concrete examples, like "User Alice connects her bank account, then."

Add Lots of Charts and Diagrams

Charts can often be useful to compare several potential options, and diagrams are generally easier to parse than text. You can use Google Drawing for creating diagrams.

Include Numbers

The scale of the problem often determines the solution. To help reviewers get a sense of the state of the world, include real numbers like # of DB rows, # of user errors, latency—and how these scale with usage .

Try to be Funny

A spec is not an academic paper. Also, people like reading funny things, so this is a good way to keep the reader engaged. Don't over do this to the point of taking away from the core idea though.

Do the Skeptic Test

Before sending your design doc to others to review, take a pass at it pretending to be the reviewer. What questions and doubts might you have about this design? Then address them preemptively.

Do the Vacation Test

If you go on a long vacation now with no internet access, can someone on your team read the doc and implement it as you intended?

The main goal of a design doc is not knowledge sharing, but this is a good way to evaluate for clarity so that others can actually give you useful feedback.

Photo by SpaceX on Unsplash

Process

Design docs help you get feedback before you waste a bunch of time implementing the wrong solution or the solution to the wrong problem. There's a lot of art to getting good feedback. For now, let's just talk specifically about how to write the design doc and get feedback for it.

First of all, everyone working on the project should be a part of the design process. It's okay if the tech lead ends up driving a lot of the decisions, but everyone should be involved in the discussion and buy into the design.

Secondly, the design process doesn't mean you staring at the whiteboard theorizing ideas. Feel free to get your hands dirty and prototype potential solutions. This is not the same as starting to write production code for the project before writing a design doc. Don't do that. But you absolutely should feel free to write some hacky throwaway code to validate an idea. To ensure that you only write exploratory code, make it a rule that none of this prototype code gets merged to master.

After that, as you start to have some idea of how to go about your project, do the following:

1. Ask an experienced engineer or tech lead on your team to be your reviewer. Ideally this would be someone who's well respected and familiar with the edge cases of the problem.

2. Go into a conference room with a whiteboard.

3. Describe the problem that you are tackling to this engineer (this is a very important step, don't skip it).

4. Then explain the implementation you have in mind, and convince them this is the right thing to build.

Doing all of this before you even start writing your design doc lets you get feedback as soon as possible, before you invest more time and get attached to any specific solution. Often, even if the implementation stays the same, your reviewer is able to point out corner cases you need to cover, indicate any potential areas of confusion, and anticipate difficulties you might encounter later on.

Then, after you've written a rough draft of your design doc, get the same reviewer to read through it again, and rubber stamp it by adding their name as the reviewer in the Title and People section of the design doc. This creates additional incentive and accountability for the reviewer.

On that note, consider adding specialized reviewers (such as SREs and security engineers) for specific aspects of the design.

Once you and the reviewer(s) sign off, feel free to send the design doc to your team for additional feedback and knowledge sharing. We suggest time-bounding this feedback gathering process to about 1 week to avoid extended delays. Commit to addressing all questions and comments people leave within that week.

Lastly, if there's a lot of contention between you, your reviewer, and other engineers reading the doc, We strongly recommend consolidating all the points of contention in the Discussion section of your doc. Then, set up a meeting with the different parties to talk about these disagreements in person.

Whenever a discussion thread is more than 5 comments long, moving to an in-person discussion tends to be far more efficient. Keep in mind that you are still responsible for making the final call, even if everyone can't come to a consensus.

Once you've done all the above, time to get going on the implementation! For extra brownie points, treat this design doc as a living document as you implement the design. Update the doc every time you learn something that leads to you making changes to the original solution or update your scoping. This way you don't have to explain things over and over again to all your stakeholders.

Finally, How do we evaluate the success of a design doc?

A design doc is successful if the right ROI of work is done. That means a successful design doc might actually lead to an outcome like this:

- You spend 5 days writing the design doc, this forces you to think through different parts of the technical architecture.

- You get feedback from reviewers that X is the riskiest part of the proposed architecture.

- You decide to implement X first to de-risk the project.

- 3 days later, you figure out that X is either not possible, or far more difficult than you originally intended.

- You decide to stop working on this project and prioritize other work instead.

Software Construction

An important part of software engineering is to make a rational choice of development style for a given software project.

Software construction is linked to all other Knowledge Areas (KAs, perhaps most strongly to Design, and Testing. This is because the construction process consumes the output of the Design process (KA3) and itself provides one of the inputs to the Testing process (KA5).

Software construction is a fundamental act of software engineering: the construction of working, meaningful software through a combination of coding, validation, and testing (unit testing) by a programmer. Far from being a simple mechanistic "translation" of good design into working software, software construction burrows deeply into difficult issues of software engineering. It requires the establishment of a meaningful dialog 1 between a person and a computer – a "communication of intent" that must reach from the slow and fallible human to a fast and unforgivingly literal computer. Such a dialog requires that the computer perform activities for which it is poorly suited, such as understanding implicit meanings and recognizing the presence of nonsensical or incomplete statements. On the human side, software construction requires that developers be logical, precise, and thorough so that their intentions can be accurately captured and understood by the computer. The relationship works only because each side possesses certain capabilities that the other lacks. In the symbiosis that is software construction, the computer provides astonishing reliability, retention, and (once the need has been explained) speed of performance. Meanwhile, the human being provides creativity and insight into how to solve new, difficult problems, plus the ability to express those solutions with sufficient precision to be meaningful to the computer.

Software Construction and Software Design

Software construction is closely related to software design see Knowledge Area Description for Software Design. Software design analyzes software requirements in order to produce a description of the internal structure and organization of a system that will serve as a basis for its construction. Software design methods are used to express a global solution as a set of smaller solutions and can be applied repeatedly until the resulting parts of the solution are small enough to be handled with confidence by a single developer. It is at this point – that is, when the design process has broken the larger problem up into easier-to- handle chunks – that software construction is generally understood to begin. This definition also recognizes the distinction that while software construction necessarily produces executable software, software design does not necessarily produce any executable products at all.

In practice, however, the boundary between design and construction is seldom so clearly defined. Firstly, software construction is influenced by the scale or size of the software product being constructed. Very small project which the design problems are already "construction s may neither require nor need an explicit design phase, very large projects may require a much more interacted relationship between design and construction as different prototyping alternatives are proposed, tested, and discard or used. Secondly, many of the techniques of software design also apply to software construction, since dividing problems into smaller parts is just as much a par construction as it is design. Thirdly, effective de techniques always contain some degree of guessing approximation in how they define their sub-problems few of the resulting approximations will turn out to wrong, and will require corrective actions during software construction. (While another seemingly obvious solution would be to remove guessing and approximation altogether from design methods, that would contradict the problem that the original problem was too large and complex to solved in one step. Effective design techniques ins acknowledge risk, work to reduce it, and help make that effective alternatives will be available when so choices eventually prove wrong).

Design and construction both require sophisticated problem solving skills, although the two activities have somewhat different emphases. In design the emphasis is on how partition a complex problem effectively, while construction the emphasis is on finding a complete executable solution to a problem. When software construction techniques do become so well-defined they can be applied mechanistically, the proper route the software engineer is to automate those techniques move on to new problems, ones whose answers are no well defined. This trend toward automation of well-defined tasks began with the first assemblers and compilers, an has continued unabated as new generations of tools computers have made increasingly powerful levels construction automation possible. Projects that do con highly repetitive, mechanistic software construction s should examine their designs, processes, and tools more closely for ways to automate such needle repetitive steps out of existence.

The Role of Tools in Construction

In software engineering, a tool is a hardware or software device that is used to support performing a process. Effective tool is one that provides significant improvement in productivity and quality. This is a very inclusive definition, however, since it encompasses general-purpose hardware devices such as computers and peripherals are part of an overall software-engineering environment Software construction tools are a more specific category tools that are both software-based and used prima within the construction process. Common examples software construction tools include compilers, version control systems, debuggers, code generators, special editors, tools for path and coverage analysis, test scaffolding and documentation tools. The best software construction tools bridge the gap between methodical computer efficiency and forgetful human creativity. Such tools allow creative minds to express their thoughts easily, but also enforce an appropriate level of rigor. Good tools also improve software quality by allowing people to avoid repetitive or precise work for which a computer is better suited.

The Role of Integrated Evaluation in Construction

Another important theme of software engineering is the evaluation of software products. This includes such diverse activities as per review of code and test plan, testing, software quality assurance, and measures Integrated evaluation means that a process (in this case a development process) includes explicit continuous or periodic internal checks to ensure that it is still working correctly. These checks usually consist of evaluations of intermediate work products such as documents, designs, source code, or compiled modules, but they may also look at characteristics of the development process itself. Examples of product evaluations include design reviews, module compilations, and unit tests. An example of process-level evaluation would be periodic re-assessment of a code library to ensure its accuracy, completeness, and self-consistency.

Integrated evaluation in software engineering has yet to reach the stage achieved in hardware engineering where the evaluation is built into the components themselves, e.g. integrated self-test logic and built-in error recovery in complex integrated circuits. Such features were first added to integrated circuits when it was realized the circuits had become so complex that the assumption of perfect start to finish reliability was no longer tenable. As with integrated circuits, the purpose of integrated checking in software processes is to ensure that they can operate for long periods without generating nonsensical or hazardously misleading answers.

Historically, software construction has tended to be one of the software engineering steps in which developers were particularly prone to omitting checks on the process. While nearly all developers practice some degree of informal evaluation when constructing software, it is all too common for them to skip needed evaluation steps because they are too confident about the reliability and quality of their own software constructions. Nonetheless, a wide range of automated, semi-automated, and manual evaluation methods have been developed for use in the software construction phase.

The simplest and best-known form of software construction evaluation is the use of unit testing after completion of e well-defined software unit. Automated techniques such compile-time checks and run-time checks help verify basic integrity of software units, and manual technique such as code reviews can be used to search for m abstract classes of errors. Tools for extract measurements of code quality and structure can also used during construction, although such measurement t are more commonly applied during integration of la suites of software units. When collecting measurement is important that the measurements collected be relevant the goals of the development process.

The Role of Standards in Construction

All forms of successful communication require a common language. Standards are in many ways best understood agreements by which both concepts and technologies become part of the shared "language" of a bro community of users. In many cases, standards are selected by a customer or by an organization. Project managers should consider the use of additional standards selected be suitable to the specific characteristics of the project.

Software construction is particularly sensitive to selection of standards, which directly affects s construction-critical issues as programming language databases, communication methods, platforms, and to Although such choices are often made before construction begins, it is important that the overall software development process take the needs of construction account when standards are selected.

Manual and Automated Construction/Spectrum of Construction Techniques

Manual Construction

Manual construction means solving complex problems language that a computer can execute. Practitioners manual construction need a rich mix of skills that includes the ability to break complex problems down into smaller parts, a disciplined formal-proof-like approach to problem analysis, and the ability to "forecast" how construct will change over time. Expert manual construction sometimes use the skills of advanced logicians; they always need to apply the skills they have within a comp changing environment such as a computer or network.

It would be easy to directly equate manual construction coding in a programming language, but it would also b incomplete definition. An effective manual construction process should result in code that fully and correctly processes data for its entire problem space, anticipates handles all plausible (and some implausible) classes errors, runs efficiently, and is structured to be resilient easy-to-change over time. An inadequate ma construction process will in contrast result in code like amateurish painting, with critical details missing and the entire construction stitched together poorly.

Automated Construction

While no form of software construction can be fully automated, much or all of the overall coordination of the software construction process can be moved from people to the computer – that is, overall control of the construction process can be largely automated. Automated construction thus refers to software construction in which an automated tool or environment is primarily responsible for overall coordination of the software construction process. This removal of overall process control can have a large impact on the complexity of the software construction process, since it allows human contributions to be divided up into much smaller, less complex "chunks" that require different problem solving skills to solve. Automated construction is also reuse-intensive construction, since by limiting human options it allows the controlling software to make more effective use of its existing store of effective software problem solutions. Of course, automated construction is not necessarily low cost; sometimes the cost of setting up the machinery is higher than the cost saved in its use.

In its most extreme form, automated construction consists of two related but distinct activities:

(1) configuring a baseline system, which means configuring a predefined set of options that provide a workable solution in a typical business context and

(2) implementing exceptions in the context of the product's usage.

This may include resetting parameters, constructing additional software chunks, building interfaces, and moving data from existing legacy systems and other data sources to the new system. For example, an accounting application for small businesses might lead users through a series of questions that will result in a customized installation of the application. When compared to using manual construction for the same type of problem, this form of automated construction "swallows" huge chunks of the overall software engineering process and replaces them with automated selections that are controlled by the computer. Toolkits provide a less extreme example in which developers still have a great deal of control over the construction process, but that process has been greatly constrained and simplified by the use of predefined components with well-defined relationships to each other.

Automated construction is necessarily tool-intensive construction, since the objective is to move as much of the overall software development process as possible away from the human developer and into automated processes. Automated construction tools tend to take the form of program generators and fully integrated environments that can more easily provide automated control of the construction process. To be effective in coordinating activities, automated construction tools also need to have easy, intuitive interfaces.

An important goal of software engineering is to move construction continually towards higher levels of automation. That is, when selection from a simple set of options is all that is really required to make software work for a business or system, then the goal of software engineers should continually be to make their systems come as close to that level of simplicity as possible. This not only makes software more accessible, but also makes it safer and more reliable by removing opportunities for error.

The concept of moving towards higher levels of construction automation permeates nearly every aspect of software construction. When simple selections from a list of options will not suffice, software engineers often can still develop application specific tool kits (that is, sets of reusable parts designed to work with each other easily) to provide a somewhat lesser level of control. Even fully manual construction reflects the theme of automation, since many coding techniques and good programming practices are intended to make code modification easier and more automated. For example, even a concept as simple as defining a constant at the beginning of a software module reflects the automation theme, since such constants "automate" the appropriate insertion of new values for the constant in the event that changes to the program are necessary. Similarly, the concept of class inheritance in object-oriented programming helps automate and enforce the conveyance of appropriate sets of methods into new, closely related or derived classes of objects.

Synthesis

The figure that follows combines the four principles of organization with the three styles of construction. Read the diagram by columns to see the principles, by rows to the styles.

Reduction in Complexity

Linguistic Construction Methods

The main technique for reducing complexity in linguistic construction is to make short, semantically "intuitive" text strings and patterns of text stand in for the much more complex underlying software that "implement" the intuitive meanings. Techniques that reduce complexity in linguistic construction include:

- Design patterns

- Software templates

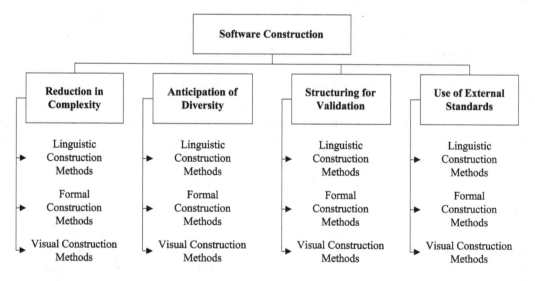

- Functions, procedures, and code blocks

- Objects and data structures

- Encapsulation and abstract data types

- Objects
- Component libraries and frameworks
- Higher-level and domain-specific languages
- Physical organization of source code
- Files and libraries
- Formal inspections

Formal Construction Methods

As is the case with linguistic construction methods, formal construction methods reduce complexity by representing complex software constructions as simple text strings. The main difference is that in this case the text strings follow the more precisely defined rules and syntax of formal notations, rather than the "fuzzier" rules of natural language. The reading, writing, and construction of such expressions requires generally more training, but once mastered, the use of formal constructions tends to keep the ambiguity of what is being specified to an absolute minimum. However, as with linguistic construction, the quality of a formal construction is only as good as its underlying implementation. The advantage is that the precision of the formal definitions usually translates into a more precise specification for the software beneath it.

- Traditional functions and procedures
- Functional programming
- Logic programming
- Concurrent and real-time programming techniques
- Spreadsheets
- Program generators
- Mathematical libraries of functions

Visual Construction Methods

Especially when compared to the steps needed to build a graphical interface to a program using text-oriented linguistic or formal construction, visual construction can provide drastic reductions in the total effort required. It can also reduce complexity by providing a simple way to select between the elements of a small set of choices.

- Object-oriented programming
- Visual creation and customization of user interfaces
- Visual programming (e.g., visual C++)
- "Style" (visual formatting) aspects of structured programming
- Integrated development environments supporting source browsing

Anticipation of Diversity

Linguistic Construction Methods

Linguistic construction anticipates diversity both by permitting extensible definitions of "words," and also by supporting flexible "sentence structures" that allow many different types of intuitively understandable statements to be made with the available vocabulary. An excellent example of using linguistic construction to anticipate diversity is the use of human-readable configuration files to specify software or system settings. Techniques and methods that help anticipate diversity include:

- Information hiding
- Embedded documentation (commenting)
- "Complete and sufficient" method sets
- Object-oriented methods
- Creation of "glue languages" for linking legacy components
- Table-driven software
- Configuration files, internationalization
- Naming and coding styles
- Reuse and repositories
- Self-describing software and hardware (e.g., plug and play)

Formal Construction Methods

Diversity in formal construction is handled in terms of precisely defined sets that can vary greatly in size. While mathematical formalizations are capable of very flexible representations of diversity, they require explicit anticipation and preparation for the full range of values that may be needed. A common problem in software construction is to use a formal technique – e.g., a fixed-length vector or array – when what is really needed to accommodate future diversity is a more generic solution that anticipates future growth – e.g., an indefinite variable-length vector. Since more generic solutions are often harder to implement and harder to make efficient, it is important when using formal construction techniques to try to anticipate the full range of future versions.

- Functional parameterization
- Macro parameterization
- Generics
- Objects
- Error handling
- Extensible mathematical frameworks

Provided that the total sets of choices are not overly large, visual construction methods can provide a good way to configure or select options for software or a system. Visual construction methods are analogous to linguistic configuration files in this usage, since both provide easy ways to specify and interpret configuration information.

- Object classes

- Visual configuration specification

- Separation of GUI design and functionality implementation

Structuring for Validation

Linguistic Construction Methods

Because natural language in general is too ambiguous to allow safe interpretation of completely free-form statements, structuring for validation shows up primarily as rules that at least partially constrain the free use of natural expressions in software. The objective is to make such constructions as "natural" sounding as possible, while not losing the structure and precision needed to ensure consistent interpretations of the source code by both human users and computers.

- Modular design

- Structured programming

- Style guides

- Stepwise refinement

Formal Construction Methods

Since mathematics in general is oriented towards proof of hypothesis from a set of axioms, formal construction techniques provide a broad range of techniques to help validate the acceptability of a software unit. Such methods can also be used to "instrument" programs to look for failures based on sets of preconditions.

- Assertion-based programming (static and dynamic)

- State machine logic

- Redundant systems, self-diagnosis, and fail-safe methods

- Hot-spot analysis and performance tuning

- Numerical analysis

Visual Construction Methods

Visual construction can provide immediate, active validation of requests and attempted configurations when the visual constructs are "instrumented" to look for invalid feature combinations and warn users immediately of what the problem is:

- "Complete and sufficient" design of object-oriented class methods

- Dynamic validation of visual requests in visual languages

External Standards

Linguistic Construction Methods

Traditionally, standardization of programming languages was one of the first areas in which external standards appeared. The goal was (and is) to provide standard meanings and ways of using "words" in each standardized programming language, which makes it possible both for users to understand each other's software, and for the software to be interpreted consistently in diverse environments:

- Standardized programming languages (e.g., Ada 95, C++, etc.)

- Standardized data description languages (e.g., XML, SQL)

- Standardized alphabet representations (e.g., Unicode)

- Standardized documentation (e.g., JavaDoc)

- Inter-process communication standards (e.g., COM, CORBA

- Component-based software

- Foundation classes (e.g., MFC, JFC)

Formal Construction Methods

For formal construction techniques, external standards generally address ways to define precise interfaces and communication methods between software systems and the machines they reside on.

- POSIX standards

- Data communication standards

- Hardware interface standards

- Standardized mathematical representation languages (e.g., MathML)

- Mathematical libraries of functions

Visual Construction Methods

Standards for visual interfaces greatly ease the total burden on users by providing familiar, easily understood "look and feel" interfaces for those users.

- Object-oriented language standards

- Standardized screen widgets

- Visual Markup Languages

Software Testing

Software testing is an activity to check whether the actual results match the expected results and to ensure that the software system is Defect free. It involves execution of a software component or system component to evaluate one or more properties of interest.

Software testing also helps to identify errors, gaps or missing requirements in contrary to the actual requirements. It can be either done manually or using automated tools. Some prefer saying Software testing as a white box and Black Box Testing.

Importance of Software Testing

Testing is important because software bugs could be expensive or even dangerous. Software bugs can potentially cause monetary and human loss, history is full of such examples:

- In April 2015, Bloomberg terminal in London crashed due to software glitch affected more than 300,000 traders on financial markets. It forced the government to postpone a 3bn pound debt sale.

- Nissan cars have to recall over 1 million cars from the market due to software failure in the airbag sensory detectors. There has been reported two accident due to this software failure.

- Starbucks was forced to close about 60 percent of stores in the U.S and Canada due to software failure in its POS system. At one point store served coffee for free as they unable to process the transaction.

- Some of the Amazon's third party retailers saw their product price is reduced to 1p due to a software glitch. They were left with heavy losses.

- Vulnerability in Window 10. This bug enables users to escape from security sandboxes through a flaw in the win32k system.

- In 2015 fighter plane F-35 fell victim to a software bug, making it unable to detect targets correctly.

- China Airlines Airbus A300 crashed due to a software bug on April 26, 1994, killing 264 innocent live.

- In 1985, Canada's Therac-25 radiation therapy machine malfunctioned due to software bug and delivered lethal radiation doses to patients, leaving 3 people dead and critically injuring 3 others.

- In April of 1999, a software bug caused the failure of a $1.2 billion military satellite launch, the costliest accident in history.

- In may of 1996, a software bug caused the bank accounts of 823 customers of a major U.S. bank to be credited with 920 million US dollars.

Types of Software Testing

Functional testing types include:

- Unit testing
- Integration testing
- System testing
- Sanity testing
- Smoke testing
- Interface testing
- Regression testing
- Beta/Acceptance testing

Non-functional testing types include:

- Performance Testing
- Load testing
- Stress testing
- Volume testing
- Security testing
- Compatibility testing
- Install testing
- Recovery testing
- Reliability testing
- Usability testing
- Compliance testing
- Localization testing

1) Alpha Testing

It is the most common type of testing used in the Software industry. The objective of this testing is to identify all possible issues or defects before releasing it into the market or to the user. Alpha testing is carried out at the end of the software development phase but before the Beta Testing. Still, minor design changes may be made as a result of such testing. Alpha testing is conducted at the developer's site. In-house virtual user environment can be created for this type of testing.

2) Acceptance Testing

An acceptance test is performed by the client and verifies whether the end to end the flow of the system is as per the business requirements or not and if it is as per the needs of the end user. Client accepts the software only when all the features and functionalities work as expected. It is the last phase of the testing, after which the software goes into production. This is also called as User Acceptance Testing (UAT).

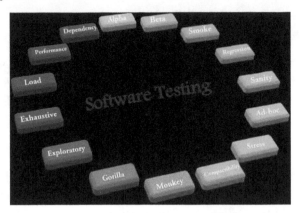

3) Ad-hoc Testing

The name itself suggests that this testing is performed on an ad-hoc basis i.e. with no reference to test case and also without any plan or documentation in place for such type of testing. The objective of this testing is to find the defects and break the application by executing any flow of the application or any random functionality.

Ad-hoc testing is an informal way of finding defects and can be performed by anyone in the project. It is difficult to identify defects without a test case but sometimes it is possible that defects found during ad-hoc testing might not have been identified using existing test cases.

4) Accessibility Testing

The aim of accessibility testing is to determine whether the software or application is accessible for disabled people or not. Here disability means deaf, color blind, mentally disabled, blind, old age and other disabled groups. Various checks are performed such as font size for visually disabled, color and contrast for color blindness etc.

5) Beta Testing

Beta Testing is a formal type of software testing which is carried out by the customer. It is performed in Real Environment before releasing the product to the market for the actual end users. Beta testing is carried out to ensure that there are no major failures in the software or product and it satisfies the business requirements from an end-user perspective. Beta testing is successful when the customer accepts the software.

Usually, this testing is typically done by end-users or others. It is the final testing done before releasing an application for commercial purpose. Usually, the Beta version of the software or product released is limited to a certain number of users in a specific area. So end user actually uses the software and shares the feedback to the company. Company then takes necessary action before releasing the software to the worldwide.

6) Back-end Testing

Whenever an input or data is entered on front-end application, it stores in the database and the testing of such database is known as Database Testing or Backend testing. There are different databases like SQL Server, MySQL, and Oracle etc. Database testing involves testing of table structure, schema, stored procedure, data structure and so on.

In back-end testing GUI is not involved, testers are directly connected to the database with proper access and testers can easily verify data by running a few queries on the database. There can be issues identified like data loss, deadlock, data corruption etc during this back-end testing and these issues are critical to fixing before the system goes live into the production environment.

7) Browser Compatibility Testing

Browser Compatibility Testing is performed for web applications and it ensures that the software can run with the combination of different browser and operating system. This type of testing also validates whether web application runs on all versions of all browsers or not.

8) Backward Compatibility Testing

It is a type of testing which validates whether the newly developed software or updated software works well with older version of the environment or not.

Backward Compatibility Testing checks whether the new version of the software works properly with file format created by older version of the software; it also works well with data tables, data files, data structure created by older version of that software. If any of the software is updated then it should work well on top of the previous version of that software.

9) Black Box Testing

Internal system design is not considered in this type of testing. Tests are based on the requirements and functionality.

10) Boundary Value Testing

This type of testing checks the behavior of the application at the boundary level.

Boundary value Testing is performed for checking if defects exist at boundary values. Boundary value testing is used for testing a different range of numbers. There is an upper and lower boundary for each range and testing is performed on these boundary values.

If testing requires a test range of numbers from 1 to 500 then Boundary Value Testing is performed on values at 0, 1, 2, 499, 500 and 501.

11) Branch Testing

It is a type of white box testing and is carried out during unit testing. Branch Testing, the name itself suggests that the code is tested thoroughly by traversing at every branch.

12) Comparison Testing

Comparison of a product's strength and weaknesses with its previous versions or other similar products is termed as Comparison Testing.

13) Compatibility Testing

It is a testing type in which it validates how software behaves and runs in a different environment, web servers, hardware, and network environment. Compatibility testing ensures that software can run on a different configuration, different database, different browsers and their versions. Compatibility testing is performed by the testing team.

14) Component Testing

It is mostly performed by developers after the completion of unit testing. Component Testing involves testing of multiple functionalities as a single code and its objective is to identify if any defect exists after connecting those multiple functionalities with each other.

15) End-to-End Testing

Similar to system testing, end-to-end testing involves testing of a complete application environment in a situation that mimics real-world use, such as interacting with a database, using network communications, or interacting with other hardware, applications, or systems if appropriate.

16) Equivalence Partitioning

It is a testing technique and a type of Black Box Testing. During this equivalence partitioning, a set of group is selected and a few values or numbers are picked up for testing. It is understood that all values from that group generate the same output. The aim of this testing is to remove redundant test cases within a specific group which generates the same output but not any defect.

Suppose, application accepts values between -10 to +10 so using equivalence partitioning the values picked up for testing are zero, one positive value, one negative value. So the Equivalence Partitioning for this testing is: -10 to -1, 0, and 1 to 10.

17) Example Testing

It means real-time testing. Example testing includes the real-time scenario, it also involves the scenarios based on the experience of the testers.

18) Exploratory Testing

Exploratory Testing is an informal testing performed by the testing team. The objective of this testing is to explore the application and looking for defects that exist in the application. Sometimes it may happen that during this testing major defect discovered can even cause system failure.

During exploratory testing, it is advisable to keep a track of what flow you have tested and what activity you did before the start of the specific flow.

An exploratory testing technique is performed without documentation and test cases.

20) Functional Testing

This type of testing ignores the internal parts and focuses only on the output to check if it is as per the requirement or not. It is a Black-box type testing geared to the functional requirements of an application.

21) Graphical User Interface (GUI) Testing

The objective of this GUI testing is to validate the GUI as per the business requirement. The expected GUI of the application is mentioned in the Detailed Design Document and GUI mockup screens.

The GUI testing includes the size of the buttons and input field present on the screen, alignment of all text, tables and content in the tables.

It also validates the menu of the application, after selecting different menu and menu items, it validates that the page does not fluctuate and the alignment remains same after hovering the mouse on the menu or sub-menu.

22) Gorilla Testing

Gorilla Testing is a testing type performed by a tester and sometimes by developer the as well. In Gorilla Testing, one module or the functionality in the module is tested thoroughly and heavily. The objective of this testing is to check the robustness of the application.

23) Happy Path Testing

The objective of Happy Path Testing is to test an application successfully on a positive flow. It does not look for negative or error conditions. The focus is only on the valid and positive inputs through which application generates the expected output.

24) Incremental Integration Testing

Incremental Integration Testing is a Bottom-up approach for testing i.e continuous testing of an application when a new functionality is added. Application functionality and modules should be independent enough to test separately. This is done by programmers or by testers.

25) Install/Uninstall Testing

Installation and uninstallation testing is done on full, partial, or upgrade install/uninstall processes on different operating systems under different hardware or software environment.

26) Integration Testing

Testing of all integrated modules to verify the combined functionality after integration is termed as Integration Testing. Modules are typically code modules, individual applications, client and server applications on a network, etc. This type of testing is especially relevant to client/server and distributed systems.

27) Load Testing

It is a type of non-functional testing and the objective of Load testing is to check how much of load or maximum workload a system can handle without any performance degradation.

Load testing helps to find the maximum capacity of the system under specific load and any issues that cause the software performance degradation. Load testing is performed using tools like JMeter, LoadRunner, WebLoad, Silk performer etc.

28) Monkey Testing

Monkey testing is carried out by a tester assuming that if the monkey uses the application then how random input, values will be entered by the Monkey without any knowledge or understanding of the application. The objective of Monkey Testing is to check if an application or system gets crashed by providing random input values/data. Monkey Testing is performed randomly and no test cases are scripted and it is not necessary to

Monkey Testing is performed randomly and no test cases are scripted and it is not necessary to be aware of the full functionality of the system.

29) Mutation Testing

Mutation Testing is a type of white box testing in which the source code of one of the program is changed and verifies whether the existing test cases can identify these defects in the system. The change in the program source code is very minimal so that it does not impact the entire application, only the specific area having the impact and the related test cases should able to identify those errors in the system.

30) Negative Testing

Testers having the mindset of "attitude to break" and using negative testing they validate that if system or application breaks. A negative testing technique is performed using incorrect data, invalid data or input. It validates that if the system throws an error of invalid input and behaves as expected.

31) Non-Functional Testing

It is a type of testing for which every organization having a separate team which usually called as Non-Functional Test (NFT) team or Performance team.

Non-functional testing involves testing of non-functional requirements such as Load Testing, Stress Testing, Security, Volume, Recovery Testing etc. The objective of NFT testing is to ensure whether the response time of software or application is quick enough as per the business requirement.

It should not take much time to load any page or system and should sustain during peak load.

32) Performance Testing

This term is often used interchangeably with 'stress' and 'load' testing. Performance Testing is done to check whether the system meets the performance requirements. Different performance and load tools are used to do this testing.

33) Recovery Testing

It is a type of testing which validates that how well the application or system recovers from crashes or disasters.

Recovery testing determines if the system is able to continue the operation after a disaster. Assume that application is receiving data through the network cable and suddenly that network cable has been unplugged. Sometime later, plug the network cable; then the system should start receiving data from where it lost the connection due to network cable unplugged.

34) Regression Testing

Testing an application as a whole for the modification in any module or functionality is termed as Regression Testing. It is difficult to cover all the system in Regression Testing, so typically automation testing tools are used for these types of testing.

35) Risk-Based Testing (RBT)

In Risk Based Testing, the functionalities or requirements are tested based on their priority. Risk-based testing includes testing of highly critical functionality, which has the highest impact on business and in which the probability of failure is very high. The priority decision is based on the business need, so once priority is set for all functionalities then high priority functionality or test cases are executed first followed by medium and then low priority functionalities.

The low priority functionality may be tested or not tested based on the available time. The Risk-based testing is carried out if there is insufficient time available to test entire software and software needs to be implemented on time without any delay. This approach is followed only by the discussion and approval of the client and senior management of the organization.

36) Sanity Testing

Sanity Testing is done to determine if a new software version is performing well enough to accept it for a major testing effort or not. If an application is crashing for the initial use then the system is not stable enough for further testing. Hence a build or an application is assigned to fix it.

37) Security Testing

It is a type of testing performed by a special team of testers. A system can be penetrated by any hacking way.

Security Testing is done to check how the software or application or website is secure from internal and external threats. This testing includes how much software is secure from the malicious program, viruses and how secure and strong the authorization and authentication processes are.

It also checks how software behaves for any hackers attack and malicious programs and how software is maintained for data security after such a hacker attack.

38) Smoke Testing

Whenever a new build is provided by the development team then the software testing team validates the build and ensures that no major issue exists. The testing team ensures that build is stable and a detailed level of testing is carried out further. Smoke Testing checks that no show stopper defect exists in the build which will prevent the testing team to test the application in detail.

If testers find that the major critical functionality is broken down at the initial stage itself then testing team can reject the build and inform accordingly to the development team. Smoke Testing is carried out to a detailed level of any functional or regression testing.

39) Static Testing

Static Testing is a type of testing which is executed without any code. The execution is performed on the documentation during the testing phase. It involves reviews, walkthrough, and inspection of the deliverables of the project. Static testing does not execute the code instead of the code syntax, naming conventions are checked.

The static testing is also applicable for test cases, test plan, design document. It is necessary to perform static testing by the testing team as the defects identified during this type of testing are cost-effective from the project perspective.

40) Stress Testing

This testing is done when a system is stressed beyond its specifications in order to check how and when it fails. This is performed under heavy load like putting large number beyond storage capacity, complex database queries, continuous input to the system or database load.

41) System Testing

Under System Testing technique, the entire system is tested as per the requirements. It is a Blackbox type testing that is based on overall requirement specifications and covers all the combined parts of a system.

42) Unit Testing

Testing of an individual software component or module is termed as Unit Testing. It is typically done by the programmer and not by testers, as it requires a detailed knowledge of the internal program design and code. It may also require developing test driver modules or test harnesses.

43) Usability Testing

Under Usability Testing, User-friendliness check is done. Application flow is tested to know if a new user can understand the application easily or not, Proper help documented if a user gets stuck at any point. Basically, system navigation is checked in this testing.

44) Vulnerability Testing

The testing which involves identifying of weakness in the software, hardware and the network is known as Vulnerability Testing. Malicious programs, the hacker can take control of the system, if it is vulnerable to such kind of attacks, viruses, and worms.

So it is necessary to check if those systems undergo Vulnerability Testing before production. It may identify critical defects, flaws in the security.

45) Volume Testing

Volume testing is a type of non-functional testing performed by the performance testing team.

The software or application undergoes a huge amount of data and Volume Testing checks the system behavior and response time of the application when the system came across such a high volume of data. This high volume of data may impact the system's performance and speed of the processing time.

46) White Box Testing

White Box testing is based on the knowledge about the internal logic of an application's code.

It is also known as Glass box Testing. Internal software and code working should be known for performing this type of testing. Under this tests are based on the coverage of code statements, branches, paths, conditions etc.

Software Maintenance

Software maintenance is widely accepted part of SDLC now a days. It stands for all the modifications and updations done after the delivery of software product. There are number of reasons, why modifications are required, some of them are briefly mentioned below:

- Market Conditions: Policies, which changes over the time, such as taxation and newly introduced constraints like, how to maintain bookkeeping, may trigger need for modification.

- Client Requirements: Over the time, customer may ask for new features or functions in the software.

- Host Modifications: If any of the hardware or platform (such as operating system) of the target host changes, software changes are needed to keep adaptability.

- Organization Changes: If there is any business level change at client end, such as reduction of organization strength, acquiring another company, organization venturing into new business, need to modify in the original software may arise.

Types of Maintenance

In a software lifetime, type of maintenance may vary based on its nature. It may be just a routine maintenance tasks as some bug discovered by some user or it may be a large event in itself based on maintenance size or nature. Following are some types of maintenance based on their characteristics:

- Corrective Maintenance: This includes modifications and updations done in order to correct or fix problems, which are either discovered by user or concluded by user error reports.

- Adaptive Maintenance: This includes modifications and updations applied to keep the software product up-to date and tuned to the ever changing world of technology and business environment.

- Perfective Maintenance: This includes modifications and updates done in order to keep the software usable over long period of time. It includes new features, new user requirements for refining the software and improve its reliability and performance.

- Preventive Maintenance: This includes modifications and updations to prevent future problems of the software. It aims to attend problems, which are not significant at this moment but may cause serious issues in future.

Cost of Maintenance

Reports suggest that the cost of maintenance is high. A study on estimating software maintenance found that the cost of maintenance is as high as 67% of the cost of entire software process cycle.

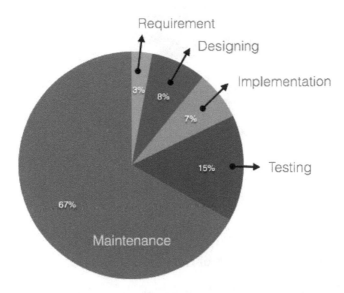

On an average, the cost of software maintenance is more than 50% of all SDLC phases. There are various factors, which trigger maintenance cost go high, such as:

Real-world Factors Affecting Maintenance Cost

- The standard age of any software is considered up to 10 to 15 years.

- Older softwares, which were meant to work on slow machines with less memory and storage capacity cannot keep themselves challenging against newly coming enhanced softwares on modern hardware.

- As technology advances, it becomes costly to maintain old software.

- Most maintenance engineers are newbie and use trial and error method to rectify problem.

- Often, changes made can easily hurt the original structure of the software, making it hard for any subsequent changes.

- Changes are often left undocumented which may cause more conflicts in future.

Software-end Factors Affecting Maintenance Cost

- Structure of Software Program
- Programming Language
- Dependence on external environment
- Staff reliability and availability

Maintenance Activities

Here is a framework for sequential maintenance process activities. It can be used in iterative manner and can be extended so that customized items and processes can be included.

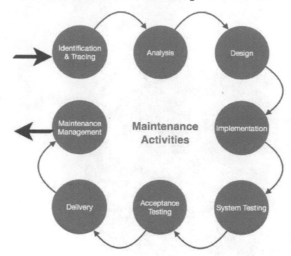

These activities go hand-in-hand with each of the following phase:

- Identification & Tracing: It involves activities pertaining to identification of requirement of modification or maintenance. It is generated by user or system may itself report via logs or error messages. Here, the maintenance type is classified also.

- Analysis: The modification is analyzed for its impact on the system including safety and security implications. If probable impact is severe, alternative solution is looked for. A set of required modifications is then materialized into requirement specifications. The cost of modification/maintenance is analyzed and estimation is concluded.

- Design: New modules, which need to be replaced or modified, are designed against requirement specifications set in the previous stage. Test cases are created for validation and verification.

- Implementation: The new modules are coded with the help of structured design created in the design step. Every programmer is expected to do unit testing in parallel.

- System Testing: Integration testing is done among newly created modules. Integration testing is also carried out between new modules and the system. Finally the system is tested as a whole, following regressive testing procedures.

- Acceptance Testing: After testing the system internally, it is tested for acceptance with the help of users. If at this state, user complaints some issues they are addressed or noted to address in next iteration.

- Delivery: After acceptance test, the system is deployed all over the organization either by small update package or fresh installation of the system. The final testing takes place at client end after the software is delivered.

    Training facility is provided if required, in addition to the hard copy of user manual.

- Maintenance management: Configuration management is an essential part of system maintenance. It is aided with version control tools to control versions, semi-version or patch management.

Software Re-engineering

When we need to update the software to keep it to the current market, without impacting its functionality, it is called software re-engineering. It is a thorough process where the design of software is changed and programs are re-written.

Legacy software cannot keep tuning with the latest technology available in the market. As the hardware become obsolete, updating of software becomes a headache. Even if software grows old with time, its functionality does not.

For example, initially Unix was developed in assembly language. When language C came into existence, Unix was re-engineered in C, because working in assembly language was difficult.

Other than this, sometimes programmers notice that few parts of software need more maintenance than others and they also need re-engineering.

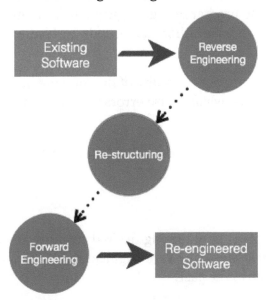

Re-engineering Process

- Decide what to re-engineer. Is it whole software or a part of it?
- Perform Reverse Engineering, in order to obtain specifications of existing software.
- Restructure Program if required. For example, changing function-oriented programs into object-oriented programs.
- Re-structure data as required.
- Apply Forward engineering concepts in order to get re-engineered software.

There are few important terms used in Software re-engineering:

Reverse Engineering

It is a process to achieve system specification by thoroughly analyzing, understanding the existing system. This process can be seen as reverse SDLC model, i.e. we try to get higher abstraction level by analyzing lower abstraction levels.

An existing system is previously implemented design, about which we know nothing. Designers then do reverse engineering by looking at the code and try to get the design. With design in hand, they try to conclude the specifications. Thus, going in reverse from code to system specification.

Program Restructuring

It is a process to re-structure and re-construct the existing software. It is all about re-arranging the source code, either in same programming language or from one programming language to a different one. Restructuring can have either source code-restructuring and data-restructuring or both.

Re-structuring does not impact the functionality of the software but enhance reliability and maintainability. Program components, which cause errors very frequently can be changed, or updated with re-structuring.

The dependability of software on obsolete hardware platform can be removed via re-structuring.

Forward Engineering

Forward engineering is a process of obtaining desired software from the specifications in hand which were brought down by means of reverse engineering. It assumes that there was some software engineering already done in the past.

Forward engineering is same as software engineering process with only one difference – it is carried out always after reverse engineering.

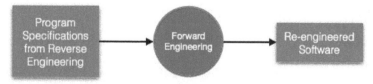

Component Reusability

A component is a part of software program code, which executes an independent task in the system. It can be a small module or sub-system itself.

Example

The login procedures used on the web can be considered as components, printing system in software can be seen as a component of the software.

Components have high cohesion of functionality and lower rate of coupling, i.e. they work independently and can perform tasks without depending on other modules.

In OOP, the objects are designed are very specific to their concern and have fewer chances to be used in some other software.

In modular programming, the modules are coded to perform specific tasks which can be used across number of other software programs.

There is a whole new vertical, which is based on re-use of software component, and is known as Component Based Software Engineering (CBSE).

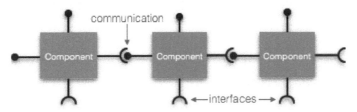

Re-use can be done at various levels:

- Application level: Where an entire application is used as sub-system of new software.

- Component level: Where sub-system of an application is used.

- Modules level: Where functional modules are re-used.

Software components provide interfaces, which can be used to establish communication among different components.

Reuse Process

Two kinds of method can be adopted: either by keeping requirements same and adjusting components or by keeping components same and modifying requirements.

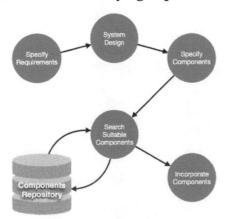

- Requirement Specification - The functional and non-functional requirements are specified, which a software product must comply to, with the help of existing system, user input or both.

- Design - This is also a standard SDLC process step, where requirements are defined in terms of software parlance. Basic architecture of system as a whole and its sub-systems are created.

- Specify Components - By studying the software design, the designers segregate the entire system into smaller components or sub-systems. One complete software design turns into a collection of a huge set of components working together.

- Search Suitable Components - The software component repository is referred by designers to search for the matching component, on the basis of functionality and intended software requirements..

- Incorporate Components - All matched components are packed together to shape them as complete software

References

- Principles-of-software-design-and-concepts, software-engineering: ecomputernotes.com, Retrieved 21 April 2018

- How-to-write-a-good-software-design-document-66: medium.freecodecamp.org, Retrieved 30 March 2018

- Software-Construction-237658594: researchgate.net, Retrieved 11 June 2018

- Software-testing-introduction-importance: guru99.com, Retrieved 19 July 2018

- Types-of-software-testing: softwaretestinghelp.com, Retrieved 21 July 2018

- Software-maintenance-overview, software-engineering: tutorialspoint.com, Retrieved 28 May 2018

Software Development

Software development refers to the process of designing, programming, testing and debugging in the creation and maintenance of software components. The aim of this chapter is to explore the fundamentals of software development, which includes software development process, lean software development, incremental funding methodology, rapid application development, spiral model, waterfall model, V-model, etc.

Software development is the collective processes involved in creating software programs, embodying all the stages throughout the systems development life cycle (SDLC).

SDLC methodologies support the design of software to meet a business need, the development of software to meet the specified design and the deployment of software to production. A methodology should also support maintenance, although that option may or may not be chosen, depending on the project in question.

The waterfall model, the original SDLC method, is linear and sequential, generally following these stages in order:

1) Identification of required software

2) Analysis of the software requirements

3) Detailed specification of the software requirements

4) Software design

5) Programming

6) Testing

7) Maintenance

The waterfall and similar models are considered predictive methodologies, in contrast to adaptive models such as agile software development (ASD), rapid application development (RAD), joint application development (JAD), the fountain model, the spiral model, build and fix and synchronize-and-stabilize. Frequently, several models are combined into some sort of hybrid methodology as is the case with open source software development (OSSD).

Software Development Process

A software development process or life cycle is a structure imposed on the development of a software product. There are several models for such processes, each describing approaches to a variety of tasks or activities that take place during the process.

Processes

More and more software development organizations implement process methodologies.

The Capability Maturity Model (CMM) is one of the leading models. Independent assessments can be used to grade organizations on how well they create software according to how they define and execute their processes.

There are dozens of others, with other popular ones being ISO 9000, ISO 15504, and Six Sigma.

The process of software development services goes through a series of stages in stepwise fashion that almost every developing company follows. Known as the 'software development life cycle,' these six steps include planning, analysis, design, development & implementation, testing & deployment and maintenance.

1. Planning: Without the perfect plan, calculating the strengths and weaknesses of the project, development of software is meaningless. Planning kicks off a project flawlessly and affects its progress positively.

2. Analysis: This step is about analyzing the performance of the software at various stages and making notes on additional requirements. Analysis is very important to proceed further to the next step.

3. Design: Once the analysis is complete, the step of designing takes over, which is basically building the architecture of the project. This step helps remove possible flaws by setting a standard and attempting to stick to it.

4. Development and Implementation: The actual task of developing the software starts here with data recording going on in the background. Once the software is developed, the stage of implementation comes in where the product goes through a pilot study to see if it's functioning properly.

5. Testing: The testing stage assesses the software for errors and documents bugs if there are any.

6. Maintenance: Once the software passes through all the stages without any issues, it is to undergo a maintenance process wherein it will be maintained and upgraded from time to time to adapt to changes.

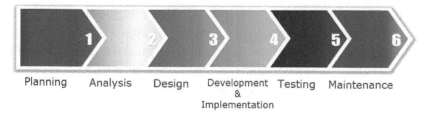

Process Activities/Steps

Software Engineering processes are composed of many activities, notably the following:

- Requirements Analysis

  Extracting the requirements of a desired software product is the first task in creating it.

While customers probably believe they know what the software is to do, it may require skill and experience in software engineering to recognize incomplete, ambiguous or contradictory requirements.

- Specification

Specification is the task of precisely describing the software to be written, in a mathematically rigorous way. In practice, most successful specifications are written to understand and fine-tune applications that were already well-developed, although safety-critical software systems are often carefully specified prior to application development. Specifications are most important for external interfaces that must remain stable.

- Software architecture

The architecture of a software system refers to an abstract representation of that system. Architecture is concerned with making sure the software system will meet the requirements of the product, as well as ensuring that future requirements can be addressed.

- Implementation

Reducing a design to code may be the most obvious part of the software engineering job, but it is not necessarily the largest portion.

- Testing

Testing of parts of software, especially where code by two different engineers must work together, falls to the software engineer.

- Documentation

An important task is documenting the internal design of software for the purpose of future maintenance and enhancement.

- Training and Support

A large percentage of software projects fail because the developers fail to realize that it doesn't matter how much time and planning a development team puts into creating software if nobody in an organization ends up using it. People are occasionally resistant to change and avoid venturing into an unfamiliar area, so as a part of the deployment phase, its very important to have training classes for the most enthusiastic software users (build excitement and confidence), shifting the training towards the neutral users intermixed with the avid supporters, and finally incorporate the rest of the organization into adopting the new software. Users will have lots of questions and software problems, which lead to the next phase of software.

- Maintenance

Maintaining and enhancing software to cope with newly discovered problems or new requirements could take far more time than the initial development of the software. Not only may it be necessary to add code that does not fit the original design but also just determining how software works at some point after it is completed may require significant effort by a software engineer. About 60% of all software engineering work is maintenance, but this statistic can be misleading. A small part of that is fixing bugs. Most maintenance is extending systems to do new things, which in many ways can be considered new work.

Process Models

A decades-long goal has been to find repeatable, predictable processes or methodologies that improve productivity and quality. Some try to systematize or formalize the seemingly unruly task of writing software. Others apply project management techniques to writing software. Without project management, software projects can easily be delivered late or over budget. With large numbers of software projects not meeting their expectations in terms of functionality, cost, or delivery schedule, effective project management is proving difficult.

Waterfall Processes

The best-known and oldest process is the waterfall model, where developers follow these steps in order. They state requirements, analyze them, design a solution approach, architect a software framework for that solution, develop code, test, deploy, and maintain. After each step is finished, the process proceeds to the next step.

Iterative Processes

Iterative development prescribes the construction of initially small but ever-larger portions of a software project to help all those involved to uncover important issues early before problems or faulty assumptions can lead to disaster. Commercial developers prefer iterative processes because it allows a potential of reaching the design goals of a customer who does not know how to define what he wants.

Agile software development processes are built on the foundation of iterative development. To that foundation they add a lighter, more people-centric viewpoint than traditional approaches. Agile processes use feedback, rather than planning, as their primary control mechanism. The feedback is driven by regular tests and releases of the evolving software.

Agile processes seem to be more efficient than older methodologies, using less programmer time to produce more functional, higher quality software, but have the drawback from a business perspective that they do not provide long-term planning capability. In essence, they say that they will provide the most bang for the buck, but won't say exactly when that bang will be.

Extreme Programming, XP, is the best-known agile process. In XP, the phases are carried out in extremely small (or "continuous") steps compared to the older, "batch" processes. The (intentionally incomplete) first pass through the steps might take a day or a week, rather than the months or years of each complete step in the Waterfall model. First, one writes automated tests, to provide concrete goals for development. Next is coding (by a pair of programmers), which is complete when all the tests pass, and the programmers can't think of any more tests that are needed. Design and architecture emerge out of refactoring, and come after coding. Design is done by the same people who do the coding. The incomplete but functional system is deployed or demonstrated for the users (at least one of which is on the development team). At this point, the practitioners start again on writing tests for the next most important part of the system.

While Iterative development approaches have their advantages, software architects are still faced with the challenge of creating a reliable foundation upon which to develop. Such a foundation often requires a fair amount of upfront analysis and prototyping to build a development model. The development model often relies upon specific design patterns and entity relationship diagrams (ERD). Without this upfront foundation, Iterative development can create long term challenges that are significant in terms of cost and quality.

Critics of iterative development approaches point out that these processes place what may be an unreasonable expectation upon the recipient of the software: that they must possess the skills and experience of a seasoned software developer. The approach can also be very kind of house you want, let me build you one and see if you like it. If you don't, we'll tear it all down and start over." A large pile of building-materials, which are now scrap, can be the final result of such a lack of upfront discipline. The problem with this criticism is that the whole point of iterative programming is that you don't have to build the whole house before you get feedback from the recipient. Indeed, in a sense conventional programming places more of this burden on the recipient, as the requirements and planning phases take place entirely before the development begins, and testing only occurs after development is officially over.

Software Release Life Cycle

Software release cycle is a process in software engineering which ensures the timely release of a software application from its coding to final release, in a well defined manner. The basic purpose of defining a software cycle is to assess the stability of a software product under development, at each level or stage of a lifecycle and accordingly developing the product for the next subsequent level, until it finally releases.

Generally, a software release lifecycle consists of five stages viz. pre-alpha, alpha, Beta, Release candidate, general availability. However, a project management or business team may visualize and define the software release lifecycle in their own way, depending upon their approach.

Let's go through each of these stages, to understand the concept of the software release life cycle.

Pre-alpha

All the activities done prior to the alpha release of a software product, falls in the phase of pre-alpha stage. These activities are nothing, but the development process of a software product, consisting of several milestones, where each milestone reflects the achievement of successful implementation and execution of the certain specific tasks.

Generally, the activities covered under pre-alpha phase comprises of requirement gathering & analysis, designing, development and unit testing.

Requirement Gathering and Analysis

This phase of pre-alpha stage consist of gathering of requirement and thereafter their analysis, feasibility study, etc. to consider and validate the implementation of these requirements in a software product. The Project Manager, Business Manager, developers and the client or the owner are accountable for the gathering & analysis of the requirements, so that they can make out a well define plan, to carry out the software development process.

Designing

Requirement gathering and analysis phase is followed by the designing phase, where the output of the former phase works as the resource for the latter. A design team is deployed, to work out and comes out with the structural view or may be called blueprint of a product, incorporating the specified requirements. This design helps the development team in visualizing and understanding an overview of a product, along with the need of certain hardware or software requirements, required in its development.

Development

Designing phase is followed by the implementation or the development phase. In development phase, a development team, equipped with all sort of resources such as SRS, software design, etc. and backed up by the design and other teams, carries out the task of development process and implementing specified requirements and specifications in the software product.

Unit Testing

Each unit developed by the developers, is evaluated by the developer itself, to assess the compliance of specified requirements and specifications by each individual unit, along with their stability, for going through the integration process and facing further testing techniques.

In pre-alpha stage, pre-alpha versions of a software product are being released such as milestone versions, where each milestone reflects the achievement in incorporating certain or specific functionalities or requirements in a product.

Alpha

It is one of first type of testing performed on a software product, after its initial development. Generally, alpha testing is an in-house testing process, performed within the organization by the testers or the developers.

During alpha testing, firstly white box testing techniques are performed by the developers, followed by the black box testing and gray box testing by the testing team.

The alpha released product, is generally of unstable nature, and may not be able to sustain further testing. Further, an alpha version of software does not ensure the compliance of all specified requirements but covers the majority of requirements.

Beta

The software product is deployed on the customer site, for getting tested by the intended users or the client in the real environment. It may be seen as the last testing phase, before the product is released in the market.

Basically, a software product is handed over to the targeted users, just before its release, so as to assess the usability and performance features of a software product.

Further, a beta phase may consist of two levels.

Open Beta: In open beta, a product is released and open to public, for testing the software application, in a real environment.

Closed Beta: In closed beta, product is being handed over to limited and specific users, to perform beta testing over a software product.

Release Candidate

It is considered as the beta version of a software product, and may be seen as the final product to be released, unless no serious issues or defects arise. At this moment of time, it is ensured that the product, which has gone through multiple beta cycles, does not needs any further improvement and no more changes, is required in the product. Thus, the version is potentially seen as the final product, to be ready for the market release.

General Availability

The final stable software product is released and is made available in the market for its selling and purchase, after completing all marketing formalities and commercialization activities, which may include security and compliance testing, along with the nationwide or the worldwide availability of the product.

Aspect-oriented Software Development

Aspect-oriented software development (AOSD) is a software design solution that helps address the modularity issues that are not properly resolved by other software approaches, like procedural, structured and object-oriented programming (OOP). AOSD complements, rather than replaces, these other types of software approaches.

AOSD is also known as aspect-oriented programming (AOP).

AOSD features are as follows:

- Considered a subset of post-object programming technologies.
- Better software design support through isolating application business logic from supporting and secondary functions.
- Provides complementary benefits and may be used with other agile processes and coding standards.
- Key focus - Identification, representation and specification of concerns, which also may be cross-cutting.

- Provides better modularization support of software designs, reducing software design, development and maintenance costs.

- Modularization principle based on involved functionalities and processes.

- Because concerns are encapsulated into different modules, localization of crosscutting concerns is better promoted and handled.

- Provides tools and software coding techniques to ensure modular content support at the source code level.

- Promotes reusability of code used for the modularization of cross-cutting concerns.

- Smaller code size, due to tackling cross cutting concerns.

- Reduced efficiency from increased overhead.

Iterative and Incremental Development

Iterative development was created as a response to inefficiencies and problems found in the waterfall model. Modified Waterfall, Rational Unified Process (RUP) and most, if not all, agile models are based on iterations.

General idea is to develop a system through iterations (repeated cycles) and incrementally (in small portions of time). Through them team members or stakeholders can learn from their mistakes and apply that knowledge on the next iteration.

Working through iterations means that the development of the application is split into smaller chunks. In each iteration features are defined, designed, developed and tested. Iteration cycles are repeated until fully functional software is ready to be delivered to production. The process does not try to start with the full set of requirements and design. Instead, team tries to prepare just what is needed for the successful delivery of the next iteration.

Some models have different names for iteration like sprint or time-boxed. Iterations can be limited in time; they end after the agreed period independently of the size of the scope that was done. Alternative way of doing iterations is to limit them in scope. They last until the agreed scope is fully finished (developed and tested).

It is a common practice that each iteration is finished with a demo to stakeholders. That demo is used as the learning process with the objective to correct the way next iteration is done or modify the scope. Since working model is available much earlier, it is much easier to spot problems before it is too late or too expensive to take corrective actions.

This way of developing is in stark contrast with the waterfall model where each phase of the software development life-cycle (SDLC) needs to be fully completed until the next one starts.

One of the main advantages of iterative development is that it allows more flexibility to adapt to changes. Unlike the waterfall model where unforeseen problems often surface late in the project and are very costly to fix, iterative approach, on the other hand, goes through short cycles that allow the team to learn, adapt and change the direction in the next iteration.

Not everyone can use iterative development effectively. Iterative development is much harder than the waterfall model. It requires higher level of technical excellence, more discipline and buyout from the whole team. It often requires that team members are capable of performing more than one type of tasks (for example develop and test or work on both front-end and back-end).

Changes need to be done across all roles when they come from the waterfall process. Two of those roles that are often most affected are integration engineers and testers.

Integration Engineers

Integration phase in iterative development is very short or, when done right, continuous. While in the waterfall model this phase can take even several weeks for bigger projects, iterations require it to be very short and done often. If, for example, testers need to test some functionality as soon as the code is done, integration and deployment needs to be almost instantaneous. There are many tools currently in use that facilitate the integration and deployment. Some of them are Puppet and Chef for configuration management and Jenkins, Hudson, Bamboo and Travis for Continuous Integration, Delivery and Deployment. Everything, or almost everything, should be scripted and run on certain events.

Testers

Testers (especially when used to only manual testing) are among those who have most difficulties adapting to the iterative process when they're coming from the waterfall, especially if they are used to test the application after it is done. Switch to iterations forces them to act in a different way and think in forms of specific functionalities that should be verified instead of a fully developed system.

They need to work in parallel with developers in order to meet iteration deadlines.

Often there is no time to perform manual testing after the code of some specific functionality is finished. High level of automation is required. While developers are writing the code, testers need to write scripts that will verify functionalities that code will create. Automation requires certain coding skills that testers might not posses. As a result, test automation might be left to developers while testers continue being focused on manual testing (both are required to certain extent). However, in those cases testers might feel that part of their work and security it brings is taken away from them.

Advantages

End products are often more aligned to client needs due to abilities to demo functionalities done in each iteration and adjust depending on the feedback. Higher level of automation required for successful iterations allows faster detection of problems and creation of reliable and repeatable processes. That same automation, after initial investment, leads to reduction in costs and time to market. Interdependency among team members increases the shared knowledge within the team leading to a better understanding.

Some of those changes can be applied to the waterfall model but in many cases they are not. The incentives for doing them are not big since they might not be perceived as necessities. For example, Continuous Integration has big potential savings in non-waterfall projects due to the need to perform installations, deployments, testing and other tasks often and fast. In the waterfall model intention is to do the integration once (after the development phase is finished) so the investment for scripts and jobs that will perform repeatable and scheduled processes does not look like it provides enough return.

In most situations, iterative and incremental process contains the complexity and mitigates risks within a defined time box. This allows the team to continually review and adapt the solution according to the realities of the ever-changing situation.

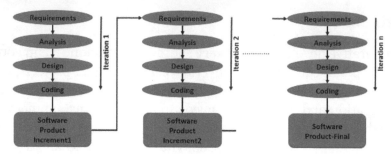

Iterative Incremental Model – Strengths

The advantages or strengths of Iterative Incremental model are –

- You can develop prioritized requirements first.

- Initial product delivery is faster.

- Customers gets important functionality early.

- Lowers initial delivery cost.

- Each release is a product increment, so that the customer will have a working product at hand all the time.

- Customer can provide feedback to each product increment, thus avoiding surprises at the end of development.

- Requirements changes can be easily accommodated.

Iterative Incremental Model – Weaknesses

The disadvantages of the Iterative Incremental model are –

- Requires effective planning of iterations.

- Requires efficient design to ensure inclusion of the required functionality and provision for changes later.

- Requires early definition of a complete and fully functional system to allow the definition of increments.

- Well-defined module interfaces are required, as some are developed long before others are developed.

- Total cost of the complete system is not lower.

Situations when Iterative Incremental Model can be used

Iterative Incremental model can be used when –

- Most of the requirements are known up-front but are expected to evolve over time.

- The requirements are prioritized.

- There is a need to get the basic functionality delivered fast.

- A project has lengthy development schedules.

- A project has new technology.

- The domain is new to the team.

Incremental Funding Methodology

In today's financially constrained IT industry, software development projects are unlikely to be funded unless they return clearly defined, low-risk value to the business. Demands for shorter investment periods, faster time-to-market, and increased operational agility require new and radical approaches to software development that draw upon the expertise of both software and financial stakeholders. Only by opening the traditional black box of software development to rigorous financial analysis, and by embracing software development as a value-creation activity, can organizations position themselves to maximize the returns on their software investments.

IFM is a financially informed approach to software development, designed to maximize returns through delivering functionality in 'chunks' of customer valued features, carefully sequenced so as to optimize Net Present Value (NPV). IFM applies a financially rigorous analysis to the delivery sequence in order to compare alternate options and when necessary to change the dynamics of a project in order to secure executive buy-in and funding.

The initial IFM concepts were drawn from several years of experience in winning competitive contracts for systems integration and application development projects. To succeed in this highly competitive environment, the bid has to meet the budget, the development costs have to be low enough to ensure a reasonable margin for the bidder, and the margin must be justified against the risks. Clearly these ideas are not new and are true for any competitive procurement. However, as the IT industry continues to tighten its belt, and margins become progressively tighter, competitive differentiation cannot always be achieved through technical or price innovation. A different approach is necessary.

The initial IFM concepts were drawn from several years of experience in winning competitive contracts for systems integration and application development projects. To succeed in this highly competitive environment, the bid has to meet the budget, the development costs have to be low enough to ensure a reasonable margin for the bidder, and the margin must be justified against the risks. Clearly these ideas are not new and are true for any competitive procurement. However, as the IT industry continues to tighten its belt, and margins become progressively tighter, competitive differentiation cannot always be achieved through technical or price innovation. A different approach is necessary.

By optimizing the time at which value is returned to the customer, instead of concentrating only on controlling risk and cost, it is possible to present a uniquely differentiated value proposition even in circumstances that preclude traditional differentiation. By categorizing customer requirements in terms of units of value, it is often possible to sequence their development and delivery in such a way as to reduce initial investment costs, generate early revenue, and in the right circumstances to even transition a project to early self-funding status. Furthermore, the overall project cost is amortized into more manageable portions, each part of which has accountability for its returns. This is the essence of IFM.

IFM can be applied in conjunction with any iterative software development process such as the Rational Unified Process (RUP) or eXtreme Programming (XP).

Rapid Application Development

The RAD (Rapid Application Development) model is based on prototyping and iterative development with no specific planning involved. The process of writing the software itself involves the planning required for developing the product.

Rapid Application Development focuses on gathering customer requirements through workshops or focus groups, early testing of the prototypes by the customer using iterative concept, reuse of the existing prototypes (components), continuous integration and rapid delivery.

Rapid application development is a software development methodology that uses minimal planning in favor of rapid prototyping. A prototype is a working model that is functionally equivalent to a component of the product.

In the RAD model, the functional modules are developed in parallel as prototypes and are integrated to make the complete product for faster product delivery. Since there is no detailed preplanning, it makes it easier to incorporate the changes within the development process.

RAD projects follow iterative and incremental model and have small teams comprising of developers, domain experts, customer representatives and other IT resources working progressively on their component or prototype.

The most important aspect for this model to be successful is to make sure that the prototypes developed are reusable.

RAD Model Design

RAD model distributes the analysis, design, build and test phases into a series of short, iterative development cycles.

Following are the various phases of the RAD Model –

Business Modeling

The business model for the product under development is designed in terms of flow of information and the distribution of information between various business channels. A complete business analysis is performed to find the vital information for business, how it can be obtained, how and when is the information processed and what are the factors driving successful flow of information.

Data Modeling

The information gathered in the Business Modeling phase is reviewed and analyzed to form sets of data objects vital for the business. The attributes of all data sets is identified and defined. The relation between these data objects are established and defined in detail in relevance to the business model.

Process Modeling

The data object sets defined in the Data Modeling phase are converted to establish the business information flow needed to achieve specific business objectives as per the business model. The process model for any changes or enhancements to the data object sets is defined in this phase. Process descriptions for adding, deleting, retrieving or modifying a data object are given.

Application Generation

The actual system is built and coding is done by using automation tools to convert process and data models into actual prototypes.

Testing and Turnover

The overall testing time is reduced in the RAD model as the prototypes are independently tested during every iteration. However, the data flow and the interfaces between all the components need to be thoroughly tested with complete test coverage. Since most of the programming components have already been tested, it reduces the risk of any major issues.

The following illustration describes the RAD Model in detail:

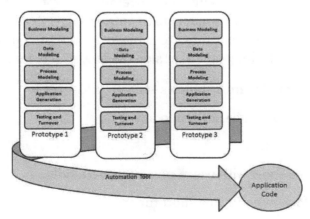

RAD Model Vs Traditional SDLC

The traditional SDLC follows a rigid process models with high emphasis on requirement analysis and gathering before the coding starts. It puts pressure on the customer to sign off the requirements before the project starts and the customer doesn't get the feel of the product as there is no working build available for a long time.

The customer may need some changes after he gets to see the software. However, the change process is quite rigid and it may not be feasible to incorporate major changes in the product in the traditional SDLC.

The RAD model focuses on iterative and incremental delivery of working models to the customer. This results in rapid delivery to the customer and customer involvement during the complete development cycle of product reducing the risk of non-conformance with the actual user requirements.

RAD Model - Application

RAD model can be applied successfully to the projects in which clear modularization is possible. If the project cannot be broken into modules, RAD may fail.

The following pointers describe the typical scenarios where RAD can be used –

- RAD should be used only when a system can be modularized to be delivered in an incremental manner.

- It should be used if there is a high availability of designers for modeling.

- It should be used only if the budget permits use of automated code generating tools.

- RAD SDLC model should be chosen only if domain experts are available with relevant business knowledge.

- Should be used where the requirements change during the project and working prototypes are to be presented to customer in small iterations of 2-3 months.

RAD Model - Pros and Cons

RAD model enables rapid delivery as it reduces the overall development time due to the reusability of the components and parallel development. RAD works well only if high skilled engineers are available and the customer is also committed to achieve the targeted prototype in the given time frame. If there is commitment lacking on either side the model may fail.

The advantages of the RAD Model are as follows –

- Changing requirements can be accommodated.

- Progress can be measured.

- Iteration time can be short with use of powerful RAD tools.

- Productivity with fewer people in a short time.

- Reduced development time.

- Increases reusability of components.

- Quick initial reviews occur.

- Encourages customer feedback.

- Integration from very beginning solves a lot of integration issues.

The disadvantages of the RAD Model are as follows –

- Dependency on technically strong team members for identifying business requirements.

- Only system that can be modularized can be built using RAD.

- Requires highly skilled developers/designers.

- High dependency on modeling skills.

- Inapplicable to cheaper projects as cost of modeling and automated code generation is very high.

- Management complexity is more.

- Suitable for systems that are component based and scalable.

- Requires user involvement throughout the life cycle.

- Suitable for project requiring shorter development times.

Spiral Model

Spiral model is one of the most important Software Development Life Cycle models, which provides support for Risk Handling. In its diagrammatic representation, it looks like a spiral with many loops. The exact number of loops of the spiral is unknown and can vary from project to project. Each loop of the spiral is called a Phase of the software development process. The exact number of phases needed to develop the product can be varied by the project manager depending upon the project risks. As the project manager dynamically determines the number of phases, so the project manager has an important role to develop a product using spiral model.

The Radius of the spiral at any point represents the expenses (cost) of the project so far, and the angular dimension represents the progress made so far in the current phase.

Each phase of Spiral Model is divided into four quadrants as shown in the above figure. The functions of these four quadrants are discussed below-

1. Objectives determination and identify alternative solutions: Requirements are gathered from the customers and the objectives are identified, elaborated and analyzed at the start of every phase. Then alternative solutions possible for the phase are proposed in this quadrant.

2. Identify and resolve Risks: During the second quadrant all the possible solutions are evaluated to select the best possible solution. Then the risks associated with that solution is identified and the risks are resolved using the best possible strategy. At the end of this quadrant, Prototype is built for the best possible solution.

3. Develop next version of the Product: During the third quadrant, the identified features are developed and verified through testing. At the end of the third quadrant, the next version of the software is available.

4. Review and plan for the next Phase: In the fourth quadrant, the Customers evaluate the so far developed version of the software. In the end, planning for the next phase is started.

A risk is any adverse situation that might affect the successful completion of a software project. The most important feature of the spiral model is handling these unknown risks after the project has started. Such risk resolutions are easier done by developing a prototype. The spiral model supports coping up with risks by providing the scope to build a prototype at every phase of the software development.

Below diagram shows the different phases of the Spiral Model:

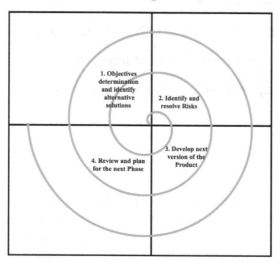

Prototyping Model also support risk handling, but the risks must be identified completely before the start of the development work of the project. But in real life project risk may occur after the development work starts, in that case, we cannot use Prototyping Model. In each phase of the Spiral Model, the features of the product dated and analyzed and the risks at that point of time are identified and are resolved through prototyping. Thus, this model is much more flexible compared to other SDLC models.

Reason why Spiral Model is called a Meta Model

The Spiral model is called as a Meta Model because it subsumes all the other SDLC models. For example, a single loop spiral actually represents the Iterative Waterfall Model. The spiral model incorporates the stepwise approach of the Classical Waterfall Model. The spiral model uses the approach of Prototyping Model by building a prototype at the start of each phase as a risk handling technique. Also, the spiral model can be considered as supporting the evolutionary model – the iterations along the spiral can be considered as evolutionary levels through which the complete system is built.

Advantages of Spiral Model

Below are some of the advantages of the Spiral Model:

- Risk Handling: The projects with many unknown risks that occur as the development proceeds, in that case, Spiral Model is the best development model to follow due to the risk analysis and risk handling at every phase.

- Good for large projects: It is recommended to use the Spiral Model in large and complex projects.

- Flexibility in Requirements: Change requests in the Requirements at later phase can be incorporated accurately by using this model.

- Customer Satisfaction: Customer can see the development of the product at the early phase of the software development and thus, they habituated with the system by using it before completion of the total product.

Disadvantages of Spiral Model

Below are some of the main disadvantages of the spiral model:

- Complex: The Spiral Model is much more complex than other SDLC models.

- Expensive: Spiral Model is not suitable for small projects as it is expensive.

- Too much dependable on Risk Analysis: The successful completion of the project is very much dependent on Risk Analysis. Without very highly experienced expertise, it is going to be a failure to develop a project using this model.

- Difficulty in time management: As the number of phases is unknown at the start of the project, so time estimation is very difficult.

Waterfall Model

Classical waterfall model is the basic software development life cycle model. It is very simple but idealistic. Earlier this model was very popular but nowadays it is not used. But it is very important because all the other software development life cycle models are based on the classical waterfall model.

Classical waterfall model divides the life cycle into a set of phases. This model considers that one phase can be started after completion of the previous phase. That is the output of one phase will be the input to the next phase. Thus the development process can be considered as a sequential flow in the waterfall. Here the phases do not overlap with each other. The different sequential phases of the classical waterfall model are shown in the below figure:

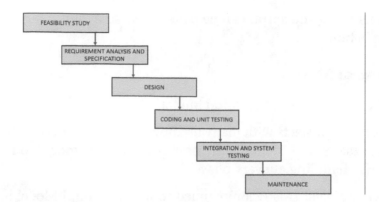

Let us now learn about each of these phases in brief details:

1. Feasibility Study: The main goal of this phase is to determine whether it would be financially and technically feasible to develop the software. The feasibility study involves understanding the problem and then determine the various possible strategies to solve the problem. These different identified solutions are analyzed based on their benefits and drawbacks, the best solution is chosen and all the other phases are carried out as per this solution strategy.

2. Requirements analysis and specification: The aim of the requirement analysis and specification phase is to understand the exact requirements of the customer and document them properly. This phase consists of two different activities.

   • Requirement gathering and analysis: Firstly all the requirements regarding the software are gathered from the customer and then the gathered requirements are analyzed. The goal of the analysis part is to remove incompleteness (an incomplete requirement is one in which some parts of the actual requirements have been omitted) and inconsistencies (inconsistent requirement is one in which some part of the requirement contradicts with some other part).

   • Requirement specification: These analyzed requirements are documented in a software requirement specification (SRS) document. SRS document serves as a contract between development team and customers. Any future dispute between the customers and the developers can be settled by examining the SRS document.

3. Design: The aim of the design phase is to transform the requirements specified in the SRS document into a structure that is suitable for implementation in some programming language.

4. Coding and Unit testing: In coding phase software design is translated into source code using any suitable programming language. Thus each designed module is coded. The aim of the unit-testing phase is to check whether each module is working properly or not.

5. Integration and System testing: Integration of different modules are undertaken soon after they have been coded and unit tested. Integration of various modules is carried out incrementally over a number of steps. During each integration step, previously planned modules are added to the partially integrated system and the resultant system is tested.

Finally, after all the modules have been successfully integrated and tested, the full working system is obtained and system testing is carried out on this.

System testing consists three different kinds of testing activities as described below :

- α-testing: α-testing is the system testing performed by the development team.

- β-testing: β-testing is the system testing performed by a friendly set of customers.

- Acceptance testing: After the software has been delivered, the customer performed the acceptance testing to determine whether to accept the delivered software or to reject it.

6. Maintenance: Maintenance is the most important phase of a software life cycle. The effort spent on maintenance is the 60% of the total effort spent to develop a full software. There are basically three types of maintenance:

Corrective Maintenance: This type of maintenance is carried out to correct errors that were not discovered during the product development phase.

Perfective Maintenance: This type of maintenance is carried out to enhance the functionalities of the system based on the customer's request.

Adaptive Maintenance: Adaptive maintenance is usually required for porting the software to work in a new environment such as work on a new computer platform or with a new operating system.

Advantages of Classical Waterfall Model

Classical waterfall model is an idealistic model for software development. It is very simple, so it can be considered as the basis for other software development life cycle models. Below are some of the major advantages of this SDLC model:

- This model is very simple and is easy to understand.

- Phases in this model are processed one at a time.

- Each stage in the model is clearly defined.

- This model has very clear and well understood milestones.

- Process, actions and results are very well documented.

- This model works well for smaller projects.

Drawbacks of Classical Waterfall Model

Classical waterfall model suffers from various shortcomings, basically we can't use it in real projects, but we use other software development lifecycle models which are based on the classical waterfall model. Below are some major drawbacks of this model:

No feedback path: In classical waterfall model evolution of a software from one phase to another phase is like a waterfall. It assumes that no error is ever committed by developers during any phases. Therefore, it does not incorporate any mechanism for error correction.

Difficult to accommodate change requests: This model assumes that all the customer requirements can be completely and correctly defined at the beginning of the project, but actually customers' requirements keep on changing with time. It is difficult to accommodate any change requests after the requirements specification phase is complete.

No overlapping of phases: This model recommends that new phase can start only after the completion of the previous phase. But in real projects, this can't be maintained. To increase the efficiency and reduce the cost, phases may overlap.

V-Model

The V-Model is a unique, linear development methodology used during a software development life cycle (SDLC). The V-Model focuses on a fairly typical waterfall-esque method that follows strict, step-by-step stages. While initial stages are broad design stages, progress proceeds down through more and more granular stages, leading into implementation and coding, and finally back through all testing stages prior to completion of the project.

The Process of the V-Model

Much like the traditional waterfall model, the V-Model specifies a series of linear stages that should occur across the life cycle, one at a time, until the project is complete. For this reason V-Model is not considered an agile development method, and due to the sheer volume of stages and their integration, understanding the model in detail can be challenging for everyone on the team, let alone clients or users.

The V-shape of the V-Model method represents the various stages that will be passed through during the software development life cycle. Beginning at the top-left stage and working, over time, toward the top-right tip, the stages represent a linear progression of development similar to the waterfall model.

The nine stages involved in the typical V-Model and how they all come together to generate a finished product are discussed below:

Requirements

During this initial phase, system requirements and analysis are performed to determine the feature set and needs of users. Just as with the same phase from the waterfall model or other similar methods, spending enough time and creating thorough user requirement documentation is critical during this phase, as it only occurs once.

Another component unique to the V-Model is that during each design stage, the corresponding tests are also designed to be implemented later during the testing stages. Thus, during the requirements phase, acceptance tests are designed.

System Design

Utilizing feedback and user requirement documents created during the requirements phase, this next stage is used to generate a specification document that will outline all technical components such as the data layers, business logic, and so on.

System Tests are also designed during this stage for later use.

Architecture Design

During this stage, specifications are drawn up that detail how the application will link up all its various components, either internally or via outside integrations. Often this is referred to as high-level design.

Integration tests are also developed during this time.

Module Design

This phase consists of all the low-level design for the system, including detailed specifications for how all functional, coded business logic will be implemented, such as models, components, interfaces, and so forth.

Unit tests should also be created during the module design phase.

Implementation/Coding

At this point, halfway through the stages along the process, the actual coding and implementation occur. This period should allot for as much time as is necessary to convert all previously generated design and specification docs into a coded, functional system. This stage should be fully complete once the testing phases begin.

Unit Testing

Now the process moves back up the far side of the V-Model with inverse testing, starting with the unit tests developed during the module design phase. Ideally, this phase should eliminate the vast majority of potential bugs and issues, and thus will be the lengthiest testing phase of the project.

That said, just as when performing unit testing with other development models, unit tests cannot (or should not) cover every possible issue that can occur in the system, so the less granular testing phases to follow should fill in these gaps.

Integration Testing

Testing devised during the architecture design phase are executed here, ensuring that the system functions across all components and third-party integrations.

System Testing

The tests created during system design are next executed, largely focusing on performance and regression testing.

Acceptance Testing

Lastly, acceptance testing is the process of implementing all tests created during the initial requirements phase and should ensure that the system is functional in a live environment with actual data, ready for deployment.

Advantages of the V-Model

- Suited for Restricted Projects: Due to the stringent nature of the V-Model and its linear design, implementation, and testing phases, it's perhaps no wonder that the V-Model has been heavily adopted by the medical device industry in recent years. In situations where the project length and scope are well-defined, the technology is stable, and the documentation & design specifications are clear, the V-Model can be a great method.

- Ideal for Time Management: Along the same vein, V-Model is also well-suited for projects that must maintain a strict deadline and meet key milestone dates throughout the process. With fairly clear and well understood stages that the whole team can easily comprehend and prepare for, it is relatively simple to create a time line for the entire development life cycle, while generating milestones for each stage along the way. Of course, the use of BM in no way ensures milestones will always be met, but the strict nature of the model itself enforces the need to keep to a fairly tight schedule.

Disadvantages of the V-Model

- Lacks Adaptability: Similar to the issues facing the traditional waterfall model on which the V-Model is based, the most problematic aspect to the V-Model is its inability to adapt to any necessary changes during the development life cycle. For example, an overlooked issue within some fundamental system design, that is then only discovered during the implementation phase, can present a severe setback in terms of lost man-hours as well as increased costs.

- Timeline Restrictions: While not an inherent problem with the V-Model itself, the focus on testing at the end of the life cycle means that it's all too easy to be pigeonholed at the end of the project into performing tests in a rushed manner to meet a particular deadline or milestone.

- Ill-Suited for Lengthy Life Cycles: Like the waterfall model, the V-Model is completely linear and thus projects cannot be easily altered once the development train has left the station. V-Model is therefore poorly suited to handle long-term projects that may require many versions or constant updates/patches.

- Encourages 'Design-by-Committee' Development: While V-Model is certainly not the only development model to fall under this criticism, it cannot be denied that the strict and methodical nature of the V-Model and its various linear stages tend to emphasize a development cycle befitting managers and users, rather than developers and designers. With a method like V-Model, it can be all too easy for project managers or others to overlook the vast complexities of software development in favor of trying to meet deadlines, or to simply feel overly confident in the process or current progress, based solely on what stage in the life cycle is actively being developed.

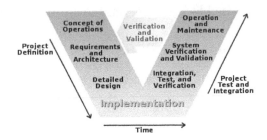

Extreme Programming

Agile Manifesto

A team of software developers published the Agile Manifesto in 2001, highlighting the importance of the development team, accommodating changing requirements and customer involvement.

The Agile Manifesto states that –

We are uncovering better ways of developing software by doing it and helping others do it. Through this work, we have come to value –

- Individuals and interactions over processes and tools.
- Working software over comprehensive documentation.
- Customer collaboration over contract negotiation.
- Responding to change over following a plan.

That is, while there is value in the items on the right, we value the items on the left more.

Characteristics of Agility

Following are the characteristics of Agility –

- Agility in Agile Software Development focuses on the culture of the whole team with multi-discipline, cross-functional teams that are empowered and self-organizing.
- It fosters shared responsibility and accountability.
- Facilitates effective communication and continuous collaboration.
- The whole-team approach avoids delays and wait times.
- Frequent and continuous deliveries ensure quick feedback that in in turn enable the team align to the requirements.
- Collaboration facilitates combining different perspectives timely in implementation, defect fixes and accommodating changes.

- Progress is constant, sustainable, and predictable emphasizing transparency.

Software Engineering Trends

The following trends are observed in software engineering –

- Gather requirements before development starts. However, if the requirements are to be changed later, then following is usually noticed –

  o Resistance to the changes at a later stage of development.

  o There is a requirement of a rigorous change process that involves a change control board that may even push the changes to later releases.

  o The delivery of a product with obsolete requirements, not meeting the customer's expectations.

  o Inability to accommodate the inevitable domain changes and technology changes within the budget.

- Find and eliminate defects early in the development life cycle in order to cut the defect-fix costs.

  o Testing starts only after coding is complete and testing is considered as a tester's responsibility though the tester is not involved in development.

  o Measure and track the process itself. This becomes expensive because of

  o Monitoring and tracking at the task level and at the resource level.

  o Defining measurements to guide the development and measuring every activity in the development.

  o Management intervention.

- Elaborate, analyze, and verify the models before development.

  o A model is supposed to be used as a framework. However, focus on the model and not on the development that is crucial will not yield the expected results.

- Coding, which is the heart of development is not given enough emphasis. The reasons being –

  o Developers, who are responsible for the production, are usually not in constant communication with the customers.

  o Coding is viewed as a translation of design and the effective implementation in code is hardly ever looped back into the design.

- Testing is considered to be the gateway to check for defects before delivery.

  o Schedule overruns of the earlier stages of development are compensated by overlooking the test requirements to ensure timely deliveries.

  o This results in cost overruns fixing defects after delivery.

- o Testers are made responsible and accountable for the product quality though they were not involved during the entire course of development.

- Limiting resources (mainly team) to accommodate budget leads to –

  - o Resource over allocation.

  - o Team burnout.

  - o Loss in effective utilization of team competencies.

  - o Attrition.

Extreme programming: A way to handle the specific needs of software development

Software Engineering involves –

- Creativity

- Learning and improving through trials and errors

- Iterations

Extreme Programming builds on these activities and coding. It is the detailed (not the only) design activity with multiple tight feedback loops through effective implementation, testing and refactoring continuously.

Extreme Programming is based on the following values –

- Communication

- Simplicity

- Feedback

- Courage

- Respect

XP is a lightweight, efficient, low-risk, flexible, predictable, scientific, and fun way to develop a software.

eXtreme Programming (XP) was conceived and developed to address the specific needs of software development by small teams in the face of vague and changing requirements.

Extreme Programming is one of the Agile software development methodologies. It provides values and principles to guide the team behavior. The team is expected to self-organize. Extreme Programming provides specific core practices where –

- Each practice is simple and self-complete.

- Combination of practices produces more complex and emergent behavior.

Embrace Change

A key assumption of Extreme Programming is that the cost of changing a program can be held mostly constant over time.

This can be achieved with –

- Emphasis on continuous feedback from the customer
- Short iterations
- Design and redesign
- Coding and testing frequently
- Eliminating defects early, thus reducing costs
- Keeping the customer involved throughout the development
- Delivering working product to the customer

Extreme Programming in a Nutshell

Extreme Programming involves –

- Writing unit tests before programming and keeping all of the tests running at all times. The unit tests are automated and eliminates defects early, thus reducing the costs.
- Starting with a simple design just enough to code the features at hand and redesigning when required.
- Programming in pairs (called pair programming), with two programmers at one screen, taking turns to use the keyboard. While one of them is at the keyboard, the other constantly reviews and provides inputs.
- Integrating and testing the whole system several times a day.
- Putting a minimal working system into the production quickly and upgrading it whenever required.
- Keeping the customer involved all the time and obtaining constant feedback.

Iterating facilitates the accommodating changes as the software evolves with the changing requirements.

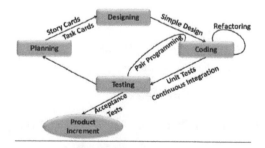

Why is it Called "Extreme?"

Extreme Programming takes the effective principles and practices to extreme levels:

- Code reviews are effective as the code is reviewed all the time.
- Testing is effective as there is continuous regression and testing.
- Design is effective as everybody needs to do refactoring daily.
- Integration testing is important as integrate and test several times a day.
- Short iterations are effective as the planning game for release planning and iteration planning.

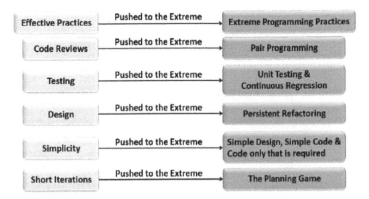

Kent Beck, Ward Cunningham and Ron Jeffries formulated extreme Programming in 1999. The other contributors are Robert Martin and Martin Fowler.

In Mid-80s, Kent Beck and Ward Cunningham initiated Pair Programming at Tektronix. In the 80s and 90s, Smalltalk Culture produced Refactoring, Continuous Integration, constant testing, and close customer involvement. This culture was later generalized to the other environments.

In the Early 90s, Core Values were developed within the Patterns Community, Hillside Group. In 1995, Kent summarized these in Smalltalk Best Practices, and in 1996, Ward summarized it in episodes.

In 1996, Kent added unit testing and metaphor at Hewitt. In 1996, Kent had taken the Chrysler C3 project, to which Ron Jeffries was added as a coach. The practices were refined on C3.

Scrum practices were incorporated and adapted as the planning game. In 1999, Kent published his book, 'Extreme Programming Explained'. In the same year, Fowler published his book, Refactoring.

Extreme Programming has been evolving since then, and the evolution continues through today.

Success in Industry

The success of projects, which follow Extreme Programming practices, is due to –

- Rapid development.

- Immediate responsiveness to the customer's changing requirements.

- Focus on low defect rates.

- System returning constant and consistent value to the customer.

- High customer satisfaction.

- Reduced costs.

- Team cohesion and employee satisfaction.

Extreme Programming Advantages

Extreme Programming solves the following problems often faced in the software development projects:

- Slipped schedules: and achievable development cycles ensure timely deliveries.

- Cancelled projects: Focus on continuous customer involvement ensures transparency with the customer and immediate resolution of any issues.

- Costs incurred in changes: Extensive and ongoing testing makes sure the changes do not break the existing functionality. A running working system always ensures sufficient time for accommodating changes such that the current operations are not affected.

- Production and post-delivery defects: Emphasis is on: the unit tests to detect and fix the defects early.

- Misunderstanding the business and domain: Making the customer a part of the team ensures constant communication and clarifications.

- Business changes: Changes are considered to be inevitable and are accommodated at any point of time.

- Staff turnover: Intensive team collaboration ensures enthusiasm and good will. Cohesion of multi-disciplines fosters the team spirit.

Lean Software Development

Lean development is the application of Lean principles to software development. Lean got its start in manufacturing, as a way to optimize the production line to minimize waste and maximize value to the customer. These two goals are also relevant to software development, which also follows a repeatable process, requires particular quality standards, and relies on the collaboration of a group of specialized workers in order to get done.

Of course, there are some major differences between manufacturing and software development, as well - namely, that manufacturing deals with the production of physical goods, while the value being created in software development is created within the mind of the developer.

Applying Lean principles to knowledge work requires a shift in mindset however, in terms of how value, waste, and other key Lean concepts are defined.

Lean Development Principles

The seven principles of Lean development are: Eliminate Waste, Build Quality In, Create Knowledge, Defer Commitment, Deliver Fast, Respect People, and Optimize the Whole. In their book, Lean Software Development: An Agile Toolkit, Mary and Tom Poppendieck outlined how these Lean principles can be applied to software development. Here is a brief summary of each of these principles, as well as practical tips on how to apply them in software development.

Eliminate Waste

One of the key elements of practicing Lean is to eliminate anything that does not add value to the customer. There are seven wastes (or *muda)* defined in the Toyota school of Lean manufacturing. They are:

- Over-production: Manufacturing an item before it is required.

- Unnecessary transportation: Moving inventory from place to place, which puts it at risk for damage without adding any value.

- Inventory: Holding inventory adds cost without adding any value to the customer; excess inventory takes up valuable space, increases lead times, and delays innovation.

- Motion: Literally refers to unnecessary movement of workers on the shop floor.

- Defects: Quality issues result in rework or scrap and can add tremendous additional costs to organizations who don't habitually find ways to eliminate sources of defects.

- Over-processing: Using advanced, expensive tools to do what could be done with simpler tools

- Waiting: When inventory waits between value-adding steps.

Tom and Mary Poppendieck translated those wastes to software development. Each of these wastes should be systematically eliminated in order to maximize customer value:

- Unnecessary code or functionality: Delays time to customer, slows down feedback loops.

- Starting more than can be completed: Adds unnecessary complexity to the system, results in context-switching, handoff delays, and other impediments to flow.

- Delay in the software development process: Delays time to customer, slows down feedback loops.

- Unclear or constantly changing requirements: Results in rework, frustration, quality issues, lack of focus.

- Bureaucracy: Delays speed.

- Slow or ineffective communication: Results in delays, frustrations, and poor communication to stakeholders which can impact IT's reputation in the organization.

- Partially done work: Does not add value to the customer or allow team to learn from work.

- Defects and quality issues: Results in rework, abandoned work, and poor customer satisfaction.

- Task switching: Results in poor work quality, delays, communication breakdowns, and low team morale.

Build Quality In

It might seem self-evident - every team wants to build quality into their work. But unless this is part of a disciplined practice, it's far easier said than done. In trying to ensure quality, many teams actually create waste - through excessive testing, for example, or an excessive logging of defects.

In recent decades, many Lean development teams have found success by applying the following Lean development tools to build quality into their work. In Lean development, quality is everyone's job - not just QA's.

These are some of the most popular Lean development tools for building quality in:

- Pair programming: Avoid quality issues by combining the skills and experience of two developers instead of one.

- Test-driven development: Writing criteria for code before writing the code to ensure it meets business requirements.

- Incremental development and constant feedback.

- Minimize wait states: Reduce context switching, knowledge gaps, and lack of focus.

- Automation: Automate any tedious, manual process or any process prone to human error.

Create Knowledge

The Lean development principle of Create Knowledge is another one that seems simple, but requires discipline and focus to implement. This principle encourages Lean teams to provide the infrastructure to properly document and retain valuable learning. This can be done by using any combination of the following tools:

- Pair Programming
- Code reviews
- Documentation
- Wiki – to let the knowledge base build up incrementally
- Thoroughly commented code
- Knowledge sharing sessions

- Training

- Use tools to manage requirements or user stories

Defer Commitment

This Lean development principle is easily misused. Defer Commitment does not mean that teams should be flaky or irresponsible about their decision-making. Rather, the opposite: This Lean principle encourages team to demonstrate responsibility by keeping their options open and continuously collecting information, rather than making decisions without the necessary data.

To defer commitment means to not plan (in excessive detail) for months in advance, to not commit to ideas or projects without a full understanding of the business requirements, and to constantly be collecting and analyzing information regarding any important decisions.

Deliver Fast

Every team wants to deliver fast, to put value into the hands of the customer as quickly as possible. The question isn't why teams want to deliver fast, but rather, what slows them down. Here are a few common culprits:

- Thinking too far in advance about future requirements

- Blockers that aren't responded to with urgency

- Over-engineering solutions and business requirements

The Lean way of delivering quickly isn't working longer hours and weekends, or working recklessly for the sake of speed. Lean development is based on this concept: Build a simple solution, put it in front of customers, enhance incrementally based on customer feedback. This is important, especially in software, because speed to market is an incredible competitive advantage.

Respect People

The Lean principle of Respect for People is often one of the most neglected, especially in the fast-paced, burnout-ridden world of software development. It applies to every aspect of the way Lean teams operate, from how they communicate, handle conflict, hire and onboard new team members, deal with process improvement, and more. Lean development teams can encourage respect for people by communicating proactively and effectively, encouraging healthy conflict, surfacing any work-related issues as a team, and empowering each other to do their best work.

Optimize the Whole

Sub optimization is a serious issue in software development, and is often a self-fulfilling prophecy. In their book, Mary and Tom Poppendieck describe two vicious cycles that Lean development teams often fall into.

The first is releasing sloppy code for the sake of speed. When developers feel pressured to deliver at all costs, they release code that may or may not meet quality requirements. This increases the complexity of the code base, resulting in more defects. With more defects, there is more work to do, putting more pressure on developers to deliver quickly so the cycle continues.

The second is an issue with testing. When testers are overloaded, it creates a long cycle time between when developers write code and when testers are able to give feedback on it. This means that developers continue writing code that may or may not be defective, resulting in more defects and therefore requiring more testing.

As the antidote to sub optimization, optimizing the whole is a Lean development principle that encourages Lean organizations to eliminate these sorts of vicious cycles by operating with a better understanding of capacity and the downstream impact of work.

It's based on the idea that every business represents a value stream — the sequence of activities required to design, produce, and deliver a product or service to customers. If our goal is to deliver as much value to our customers as quickly as possible, then we have to optimize our value streams to be able to do just that. To understand how to optimize our value streams, first we have to properly identify them.

After identifying how value flows through their teams, many organizations decide to organize their software development teams to be complete, multi-disciplined, co-located product teams, which enables them to have everything they need to deliver a request from start to finish, without reference to other teams. This is an approach popularized by Spotify, that has been adopted by many Lean organizations as a way to optimize the whole and increase the speed of value delivery.

Test-driven Development

TDD can be defined as a programming practice that instructs developers to write new code only if an automated test has failed. This avoids duplication of code. TDD means "Test Driven Development". The primary goal of TDD is to make the code clearer, simple and bug-free.

Test-Driven Development starts with designing and developing tests for every small functionality of an application. In TDD approach, first, the test is developed which specifies and validates what the code will do.

In the normal Testing process, we first generate the code and then test. Tests might fail since tests are developed even before the development. In order to pass the test, the development team has to develop and refactors the code. Refactoring a code means changing some code without affecting its behavior.

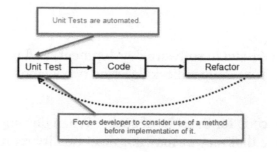

The simple concept of TDD is to write and correct the failed tests before writing new code (before development). This helps to avoid duplication of code as we write a small amount of code at a time in order to pass tests. (Tests are nothing but requirement conditions that we need to test to fulfill them).

Test-Driven development is a process of developing and running automated test before actual development of the application. Hence, TDD sometimes also called as Test First Development.

Ways to Perform TDD Test

Following steps define how to perform TDD test,

1. Add a test.

2. Run all tests and see if any new test fails.

3. Write some code.

4. Run tests and Refactor code.

5. Repeat.

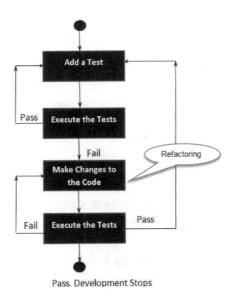

TDD Cycle Defines

1. Write a test.

2. Make it run.

3. Change the code to make it right i.e. Refactor.

4. Repeat process.

Some Clarifications About TDD

- TDD is neither about "Testing" nor about "Design".

- TDD does not mean "write some of the tests, then build a system that passes the tests.
- TDD does not mean "do lots of Testing."

TDD Vs. Traditional Testing

TDD approach is primarily a specification technique. It ensures that your source code is thoroughly tested at confirmatory level:

- With traditional testing, a successful test finds one or more defects. It is same as TDD. When a test fails, you have made progress because you know that you need to resolve the problem.
- TDD ensures that your system actually meets requirements defined for it. It helps to build your confidence about your system.
- In TDD more focus is on production code that verifies whether testing will work properly. In traditional testing, more focus is on test case design. Whether the test will show the proper/improper execution of the application in order to fulfill requirements.
- In TDD, you achieve 100% coverage test. Every single line of code is tested, unlike traditional testing.
- The combination of both traditional testing and TDD leads to the importance of testing the system rather than perfection of the system.
- In Agile Modeling (AM), you should "test with a purpose". You should know why you are testing something and what level its need to be tested.

Acceptance TDD and Developer TDD

There are two levels of TDD

Acceptance TDD (ATDD): With ATDD you write a single acceptance test. This test fulfills the requirement of the specification or satisfies the behavior of the system. After that write just enough production/functionality code to fulfill that acceptance test. Acceptance test focuses on the overall behavior of the system. ATDD also was known as Behavioral Driven Development (BDD).

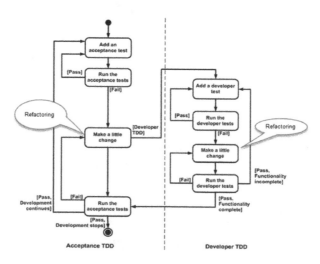

Developer TDD: With Developer TDD you write single developer test i.e. unit test and then just enough production code to fulfill that test. The unit test focuses on every small functionality of the system. Developer TDD is simply called as TDD.

The main goal of ATDD and TDD is to specify detailed, executable requirements for your solution on a just in time (JIT) basis. JIT means taking only those requirements in consideration that are needed in the system. So increase efficiency.

Scaling TDD via Agile Model Driven Development (AMDD)

TDD is very good at detailed specification and validation. It fails at thinking through bigger issues such as overall design, use of the system, or UI. AMDD addresses the Agile scaling issues that TDD does not.

Thus AMDD used for bigger issues.

The lifecycle of AMDD

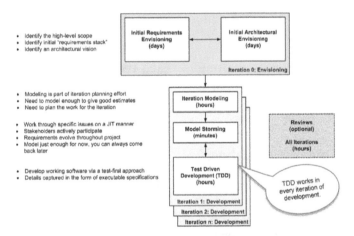

In Model-driven Development (MDD), extensive models are created before the source code is written. Which in turn have.

In above figure, each box represents a development activity.

Envisioning is one of the TDD process of predicting/imagining tests which will be performed during the first week of the project. The main goal of envisioning is to identify the scope of the system and architecture of the system. High-level requirements and architecture modeling is done for successful envisioning.

It is the process where not a detailed specification of software/system is done but exploring the requirements of software/system which defines the overall strategy of the project.

Iteration 0: Envisioning

There are two main sub-activates:

*   Initial requirements envisioning.

It may take several days to identify high-level requirements and scope of the system. The main focus is to explore usage model, Initial domain model, and user interface model (UI).

- Initial Architectural envisioning.

It also takes several days to identify architecture of the system. It allows setting technical directions for the project. The main focus is to explore technology diagrams, User Interface (UI) flow, domain models, and Change cases.

Iteration Modeling

Here team must plan the work that will be done for each iteration:

- Agile process is used for each iteration, i.e. during each iteration, new work item will be added with priority.

- First higher prioritized work will be taken into consideration. Work items added may be reprioritized or removed from items stack any time.

- The team discusses how they are going to implement each requirement. Modeling is used for this purpose.

- Modeling analysis and design is done for each requirement which is going to implement for that iteration.

Model Storming

This is also known as Just in time Modeling:

- Here modeling session involves a team of 2/3 members who discuss issues on paper or whiteboard.

- One team member will ask another to model with them. This modeling session will take approximately 5 to 10 minutes. Where team members gather together to share whiteboard/paper.

- They explore issues until they don't find the main cause of the problem. Just in time, if one team member identifies the issue which he/she wants to resolve then he/she will take quick help of other team members.

- Other group members then explore the issue and then everyone continues on as before. It is also called as stand-up modeling or customer QA sessions.

Test Driven Development (TDD).

- It promotes confirmatory testing of your application code and detailed specification.

- Both acceptance test (detailed requirements) and developer tests (unit test) are inputs for TDD.

- TDD makes the code simpler and clear. It allows the developer to maintain less documentation.

Reviews

- This is optional. It includes code inspections and model reviews.

- This can be done for each iteration or for the whole project.

- This is a good option to give feedback for the project.

Test Driven Development (TDD) Vs. Agile Model Driven Development (AMDD)

TDD	AMDD
TDD shortens the programming feedback loop	AMDD shortens modeling feedback loop.
TDD is detailed specification	AMDD works for bigger issues
TDD promotes the development of high-quality code	AMDD promotes high-quality communication with stakeholders and developers.
TDD speaks to programmers	AMDD talks to business analyst, stakeholders, and data professionals.
TDD non-visually oriented	AMDD visually oriented
TDD has limited scope to software works	AMDD has a broad scope including stakeholders. It involves working towards a common understanding
Both support evolutionary development	----------------------

Example of TDD

Here in this example, we will define a class password. For this class, we will try to satisfy following conditions.

A condition for Password acceptance:

- The password should be between 5 to 10 characters.

First, we write the code that fulfills all the above requirements.

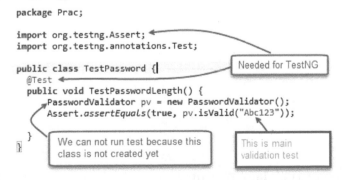

Scenario 1: To run the test, we create class PasswordValidator ();

```
package Prac;

public class PasswordValidator {
  public boolean isValid(String Password)
  {
      if (Password.length()>=5 && Password.length()<=10)
      {
          return true;
      }
      else
          return false;
  }
}
```

This is main condition checking length of password. If meets return true otherwise false.

We will run above class TestPassword ();

Output is PASSED as shown below;

Output

```
<terminated> TestPassword [TestNG] C:\Program Files\Java\jre1.8.0_77\bin\javaw.exe (Jul 25, 2016, 2:10:22 PM)
[TestNG] Running:
  C:\Users\kanchan\AppData\Local\Temp\testng-eclipse--571370159\testng-customsuite.xml

PASSED: TestPasswordLength

===============================================
    Default test
    Tests run: 1, Failures: 0, Skips: 0
===============================================


===============================================
Default suite
Total tests run: 1, Failures: 0, Skips: 0
===============================================

[TestNG] Time taken by org.testng.reporters.EmailableReporter2@1b40d5f0: 202 ms
[TestNG] Time taken by org.testng.reporters.XMLReporter@28f67ac7: 63 ms
[TestNG] Time taken by org.testng.reporters.jq.Main@546a03af: 78 ms
[TestNG] Time taken by org.testng.reporters.JUnitReportReporter@5a01ccaa: 2 ms
[TestNG] Time taken by [FailedReporter passed=0 failed=0 skipped=0]: 1 ms
[TestNG] Time taken by org.testng.reporters.SuiteHTMLReporter@2b80d80f: 10 ms
```

Result of test as Passed

Scenario 2: Here we can see in method TestPasswordLength() there is no need of creating an instance of class PasswordValidator. Instance means creating an object of class to refer the members (variables/methods) of that class.

```
package Prac;

import org.testng.Assert;

public class TestPassword {
  @Test
  public void TestPasswordLength() {

      PasswordValidator pv = new PasswordValidator();

      Assert.assertEquals(true, pv.isValid("Abc123"));
  }
}
```

We will remove it.

We will remove class PasswordValidator pv = new PasswordValidator () from the code. We can call the isValid () method directly by PasswordValidator. IsValid ("Abc123").

So we Refactor (change code) as below:

```
package Prac;

import org.testng.Assert;
import org.testng.annotations.Test;

public class TestPassword {
  @Test
  public void TestPasswordLength() {

     Assert.assertEquals(true, PasswordValidator.isValid("Abc123"));

  }
}
```

Re factor code as there is no need of creating instance of class PasswordValidator().

Scenario 3: After refactoring the output shows failed status this is because we have removed the instance. So there is no reference to non –static method isValid ().

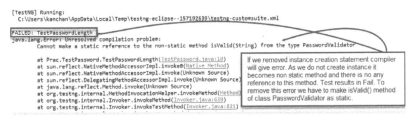

```
[TestNG] Running:
  C:\Users\kanchan\AppData\Local\Temp\testng-eclipse--157192639\testng-customsuite.xml
FAILED: TestPasswordLength
java.lang.Error: Unresolved compilation problem:
     Cannot make a static reference to the non-static method isValid(String) from the type PasswordValidator

     at Prac.TestPassword.TestPasswordLength(TestPassword.java:10)
     at sun.reflect.NativeMethodAccessorImpl.invoke0(Native Method)
     at sun.reflect.NativeMethodAccessorImpl.invoke(Unknown Source)
     at sun.reflect.DelegatingMethodAccessorImpl.invoke(Unknown Source)
     at java.lang.reflect.Method.invoke(Unknown Source)
     at org.testng.internal.MethodInvocationHelper.invokeMethod(MethodI
     at org.testng.internal.Invoker.invokeMethod(Invoker.java:639)
     at org.testng.internal.Invoker.invokeTestMethod(Invoker.java:821)
```

If we removed instance creation statement compiler will give error. As we do not create instance it becomes non static method and there is no any reference to this method. Test results in Fail. To remove this error we have to make isValid() method of class PasswordValidator as static.

So we need to change this method by adding "static" word before Boolean as public static boolean isValid (String password). Refactoring Class PasswordValidator () to remove above error to pass the test.

```
package Prac;

public class PasswordValidator {
  public static boolean isValid(String Password)
  {
      if (Password.length()>=5 && Password.length()<=10)
      {
          return true;
      }
      else
          return false;
  }
}
```

Re factor : Added static word to pass test.

Output

After making changes to class PassValidator () if we run the test then the output will be PASSED as shown below.

```
<terminated> TestPassword [TestNG] C:\Program Files\Java\jre1.8.0_77\bin\javaw.exe (Jul 25, 2016, 3:02:16 PM)
[TestNG] Running:
  C:\Users\kanchan\AppData\Local\Temp\testng-eclipse--1385484104\testng-customsuite.xml

PASSED: TestPasswordLength

===========================================
    Default test
    Tests run: 1, Failures: 0, Skips: 0
===========================================


===========================================
Default suite
Total tests run: 1, Failures: 0, Skips: 0
===========================================

[TestNG] Time taken by org.testng.reporters.EmailableReporter2@1b40d5f0: 19 ms
[TestNG] Time taken by org.testng.reporters.XMLReporter@28f67ac7: 10 ms
[TestNG] Time taken by org.testng.reporters.jq.Main@546a03af: 34 ms
```

Test results passed as we changed code in class PasswordValidator().

Benefits of TDD

- Early bug notification.

  Developers test their code but in the database world, this often consists of manual tests or one-off scripts. Using TDD you build up, over time, a suite of automated tests that you and any other developer can rerun at will.

- Better Designed, cleaner and more extensible code.

  o It helps to understand how the code will be used and how it interacts with other modules.

  o It results in better design decision and more maintainable code.

  o TDD allows writing smaller code having single responsibility rather than monolithic procedures with multiple responsibilities. This makes the code simpler to understand.

  o TDD also forces to write only production code to pass tests based on user requirements.

- Confidence to Refactor.

  o If you refactor code, there can be possibilities of breaks in the code. So having a set of automated tests you can fix those breaks before release. Proper warning will be given if breaks found when automated tests are used.

    o Using TDD, should results in faster, more extensible code with fewer bugs that can be updated with minimal risks.

- Good for teamwork.

  In the absence of any team member, other team members can easily pick up and work on the code. It also aids knowledge sharing, thereby making the team more effective overall.

- Good for Developers.

  Though developers have to spend more time in writing TDD test cases, it takes a lot less time for debugging and developing new features. You will write cleaner, less complicated code.

Agile Software Development

Agile SDLC model is a combination of iterative and incremental process models with focus on process adaptability and customer satisfaction by rapid delivery of working software product. Agile Methods break the product into small incremental builds. These builds are provided in iterations. Each iteration typically lasts from about one to three weeks. Every iteration involves cross-functional teams working simultaneously on various areas like –

- Planning

- Requirements Analysis

- Design

- Coding

- Unit Testing and

- Acceptance Testing.

At the end of the iteration, a working product is displayed to the customer and important stakeholders.

Agile model believes that every project needs to be handled differently and the existing methods need to be tailored to best suit the project requirements. In Agile, the tasks are divided to time boxes small time frames to deliver specific features for a release.

Iterative approach is taken and working software build is delivered after each iteration. Each build is incremental in terms of features; the final build holds all the features required by the customer.

The Agile thought process had started early in the software development and started becoming popular with time due to its flexibility and adaptability.

The most popular Agile methods include Rational Unified Process, Scrum, Crystal Clear, Extreme Programming, Adaptive Software Development, Feature Driven Development, and Dynamic Systems Development Method (DSDM). These are now collectively referred to as Agile Methodologies, after the Agile Manifesto was published in 2001.

Here is a graphical illustration of the Agile Model –

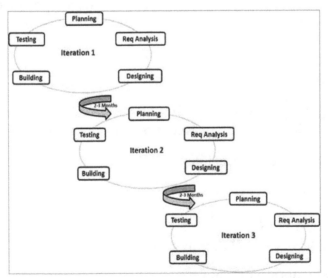

Following are the Agile Manifesto principles:

- Individuals and interactions: In Agile development, self-organization and motivation are important, as are interactions like co-location and pair programming.

- Working software: Demo working software is considered the best means of communication with the customers to understand their requirements, instead of just depending on documentation.

- Customer collaboration: As the requirements cannot be gathered completely in the beginning of the project due to various factors, continuous customer interaction is very important to get proper product requirements.

- Responding to change: Agile Development is focused on quick responses to change and continuous development.

Agile Vs Traditional SDLC Models

Agile is based on the adaptive software development methods, whereas the traditional SDLC models like the waterfall model is based on a predictive approach. Predictive teams in the traditional SDLC models usually work with detailed planning and have a complete forecast of the exact tasks and features to be delivered in the next few months or during the product life cycle.

Predictive methods entirely depend on the requirement analysis and planning done in the beginning of cycle. Any changes to be incorporated go through a strict change control management and prioritization.

Agile uses an adaptive approach where there is no detailed planning and there is clarity on future tasks only in respect of what features need to be developed. There is feature driven development and the team adapts to the changing product requirements dynamically. The product is tested very frequently, through the release iterations, minimizing the risk of any major failures in future.

Customer Interaction is the backbone of this Agile methodology, and open communication with minimum documentation are the typical features of Agile development environment. The agile teams work in close collaboration with each other and are most often located in the same geographical location.

Agile Model - Pros and Cons

Agile methods are being widely accepted in the software world recently. However, this method may not always be suitable for all products. Here are some pros and cons of the Agile model.

The advantages of the Agile Model are as follows:

- Is a very realistic approach to software development.

- Promotes teamwork and cross training.

- Functionality can be developed rapidly and demonstrated.

- Resource requirements are minimum.

- Suitable for fixed or changing requirements

- Delivers early partial working solutions.

- Good model for environments that change steadily.

- Minimal rules, documentation easily employed.

- Enables concurrent development and delivery within an overall planned context.

- Little or no planning required.

- Easy to manage.

- Gives flexibility to developers.

The disadvantages of the Agile Model are as follows –

- Not suitable for handling complex dependencies.

- More risk of sustainability, maintainability and extensibility.

- An overall plan, an agile leader and agile PM practice is a must without which it will not work.

- Strict delivery management dictates the scope, functionality to be delivered, and adjustments to meet the deadlines.

- Depends heavily on customer interaction, so if customer is not clear, team can be driven in the wrong direction.

- There is a very high individual dependency, since there is minimum documentation generated.

- Transfer of technology to new team members may be quite challenging due to lack of documentation.

Pair Programming

As the name implies, pair programming is where two developers work using only one machine. Each one has a keyboard and a mouse. One programmer acts as the driver who codes while the other will serve as the observer who will check the code being written, proofread and spell check it, while also figuring out where to go next. These roles can be switched at any time: the driver will then become the observer and vice versa.

It's also commonly called "pairing," "programming in pairs," and "paired programming."

Pair Programming Advantages

There are several compelling reasons you should consider this strategy:

- Two heads are better than one: If the driver encounters a hitch with the code, there will be two of them who'll solve the problem.

- More efficient: Common thinking is that it slows down the project completion time because you are effectively putting two programmers to develop a single program, instead of having them work independently on two different programs. But studies have shown that two programmers working on the same program are only 15% slower than when these programmers work independently, rather than the presupposed 50% slow down.

- Fewer coding mistakes: Because there is another programmer looking over your work, it results in better code. In fact, an earlier study shows that it results in 15% fewer bugs than code written by solo programmers. Plus, it allows the driver to remain focus on the code being written while the other attends to external matters or interruption.

- An effective way to share knowledge: Code Fellows talks about how it could help programmers learn from their peers in this blog post. It would allow programmers to get instant face-to-face instruction, which is much better than online tutorials and faster than looking for resources on the Internet. Plus, you can learn things better from your partner, especially in areas that may be unfamiliar to you. Developers can also pick up best practices and better techniques from more advanced programmers. It can also facilitate mentoring relationships between two programmers.

- Develops your staff's interpersonal skills: Collaborating on a single project helps your team to appreciate the value of communication and teamwork.

- Fewer mistakes are introduced into your code because a lot of errors are caught as they are being typed. This level of continuous code reviews gives rise to fewer bugs in your code.

- You have shorter and tighter code.

- Two people can solve the problems that crop up along the way faster and quicker.

- Your developers learn more about things that are specific to the applications that they are working on as well as software development in general, best practices, and other areas.

- You have more people who know how the new program works. This means that if one of the pair leaves the company, it will not kill the project.

- Your team develops better interpersonal and social skills. Team members can learn to communicate with each other, work together, and share information.

- Your team members are more satisfied.

Programming is better than code Reviews in Terms of Pair

Code reviews are a process wherein another programmer takes a look at your code to find something that needs improvement or find defects in it. It combines testing with quality control to ensure that everything in your code is good. This helps you ensure that your code is improved.

However, it is challenging to find somebody to review your code because people may not want to look at another's code and understand their reasoning just for the sake of checking its quality. Most of the time, code reviews happen when somebody else tries to add some functionality to your code, or fixes bugs. But by then, you, as the original programmer, might not even be around to appreciate the code review.

With pairing, it is like having somebody review your code instantly and regularly. It is a higher form of code reviews. Two people have to be there and understand the program being written. And if one sees problems with the other's code, then it can be instantly corrected. You also have fewer chances of having bugs written into your code. Code reviews are not as proactive as you have to wait until the code is completed — bugs and all — before somebody could take a look at and correct it.

Challenges of Pairing

The common problems observed when it comes to pair programming include the following:

- The pair should be equally engaged and be participative for the duration of the task. Otherwise, there would be no benefits.

- People who have not tried it may think that it will double the cost because you are putting two programmers on one project. However, this is a misconception that needs to be clarified. On top of the fact that pairing, done right, will only result in 15% slowdowns in terms of the individual output, it actually speeds up the coding process and ensures better quality code, which lessens the chances that the program would have to be redone.

- Pair programming should also be a programming out loud process, where the pair is verbally detailing what it is doing.

- It's not something that you can force your team to do. It's highly social and interactive, so you should be able to detect pairs that may have problems with each other, such as clashing personalities or even problems with personal hygiene.

Ways to Effectively Pair your Programmers

The best way to approach pairing is to partner two programmers and have them share a computer. Make them work together to architect, code and then test their codes in a genuine sense of a partnership. While the ideal setup would include two programmers who are equally skilled (expert – expert or novice – novice), you can also use pair programming for training and educational purposes (expert – novice).

The pair should be able to decide how to split the work, and it is advisable that they should switch roles often.

References

- Software-development: techtarget.com, Retrieved 30 June 2018

- What-is-a-software-development-process, analysis-and-design: selectbs.com, Retrieved 22 March 2018

- 6-stages-of-software-development-process-141: synapseindia.com, Retrieved 14 July 2018

- Software-release-life-cycle: professionalqa.com, Retrieved 24 June 2018

- Aspect-oriented-software-development-aosd-205: techopedia.com, Retrieved 10 April 2018

- Software-development-models-iterative-and-incremental-development: technologyconversations.com, Retrieved 14 July 2018

- Pair-programming-advantages: stackify.com, Retrieved 31 March 2018

Software Development Tools

A variety of tools and techniques are used in software development for creating high-quality software products. The topics elaborated in this chapter will help in developing a better perspective about the different software development tools such as graphical user interface builder and integrated development environment, etc.

A computer program that is used by the software developers for creating, editing, maintaining, supporting and debugging other applications, frameworks and programs is termed as a Software Development Tool or a Software Programming Tool.

Development tools can be of many forms like linkers, compilers, code editors, GUI designer, assemblers, debugger, performance analysis tools etc. There are certain factors to be considered while selecting the corresponding development tool, based on the type of the project.

Few of such factors include:

- Company standards
- Tool usefulness
- Tool integration with another tool
- Selecting appropriate environment
- Learning curve

Selecting the right development tool has its own effect on the project's success and efficiency.

Uses of Software Development Tools

- Software development tools are used to accomplish and investigate the business processes, document the development process of the software and optimize all the processes.
- By using these tools in the software development process, the outcome of the projects will be more productive.
- Using the software development tools, a developer can easily maintain the workflow of the project.

Top Software Development Tools

Atom

Atom is an open source and free desktop editor cum source code editor that is up-to-date, friendly and hackable to the core.

Key Features:

- Atom supports cross-platform editing and works for various operating systems like Windows, Linux and OS X.

- Atom is a customizable tool with which one can effectively edit the look & feel of the User Interface, add few important features etc., without editing the configuration file.

- Important features of Atom which made it a remarkable tool are its built-in package manager, smart autocomplete, multiple panes, file system browser, find & replace feature etc.

- Atom is used to build cross-platform applications with web technologies using a framework called 'Electron'.

Cloud 9

AWS Cloud9

Initially in 2010 Cloud 9 was an open source, cloud-based IDE (Integrated Development Environment) that supports various programming languages like C, Perl, Python, JavaScript, PHP etc. Later in 2016, AWS (Amazon Web Service) acquired it for further improvement and made it chargeable as per the usage.

Key Features:

- Cloud 9 IDE is a web-based platform that is used for scripting, running and debugging the code in the cloud.

- Using Cloud 9, the users can work with serverless applications which help to switch between remote and local testing and debugging activities.

- The features like code completion suggestions, debugging, file dragging etc., makes Cloud 9 a powerful tool.

- Cloud 9 is an IDE for web and mobile developers that help to collaborate together.

- Developers using AWS Cloud 9 can share the environment with the workmates for projects.

- Cloud 9 IDE lets to replica the entire development environment.

GitHub

GitHub is a powerful collaboration tool and development platform for code review and code management. With this GitHub, the users can build applications and software, manage the projects, host the code, review the code etc.

Key Features:

- With GitHub, developers can easily document their code and can host the same from the repositories.

- GitHub's project management tools help its users to stay aligned, co-ordinate easily and get their task done accordingly.

- Few features of GitHub that make it a useful tool are its code security, access control among the team members, integration with other tools etc.

- Few developers use GitHub for experimenting new programming languages in their personal projects.

- GitHub can be hosted on servers and on a cloud platform. It runs on Windows and Mac OS.

- GitHub is free for open source projects and public use. For developers it is charged @ $7/month, for teams @ $9/month and for organizations it is $21/month.

NetBeans

NetBeans is an open source and a free software development tool written in Java that develops world-class web, mobile, and desktop applications easily and quickly. It uses C / C++, PHP, JavaScript, Java etc.

Key Features:

- NetBeans supports cross-platform and works on any operating system like Linux, Mac OS, Solaris, Windows etc.

- NetBeans offers features like Smart Code Editing, writing bug-free code, easy management process, and quick user interface development.

- Java applications can be easily updated to its newer editions using the code analyzers, editors and converters offered by NetBeans 8 IDE.

- Features of NetBeans IDE that made it the best tool are debugging, profiling, dedicated support from the community, powerful GUI builder, out of box working, support for Java platforms etc.

- The well-organized code in NetBeans allows its new developers to understand the structure of the application.

Bootstrap

Bootstrap is an open source and free framework for developing responsive websites and mobile-first projects using CSS, HTML, and JS. Bootstrap is widely used to design faster and simpler websites.

Key Features:

- As Bootstrap is an open source toolkit, one can customize it according to their project's requirement.

- Bootstrap is provided with built-in components which are used in accumulating responsive websites by a smart drag and drop facility.

- Powerful features of Bootstrap like a responsive grid system, plug-ins, pre-built components, sass variables & mixins allow its users to build their applications.

- Bootstrap is a front-end web framework that is used for quick modeling of the ideas and building of the web applications.

- This tool guarantees consistency among all the developers or users working on the project.

Node.js

Node.js is an open source, cross-platform and JavaScript run-time environment that is built to design a variety of web applications and to create web servers and networking tools.

Key Features:

- Node.js applications run on Windows, Linux, Mac OS, Unix etc.

- Node.js is efficient and lightweight as it uses non-blocking and event-driven I/O model.

- Node.js is used by developers to write server-side applications in JavaScript.

- Node.js modules are used to provide rapid and well-organized solutions for developing back-end structure and integrating with the front-end platforms.

- The largest ecosystem of open source libraries is available with node.js package.

- Various IT Companies, software developers, small & large business organizations use node.js for developing web and network server applications in their projects.

Bitbucket

Bitbucket is a distributed, web-based version control system that is used for collaboration between software development teams (code and code review). It is used as a repository for source code and development projects.

Key Features:

- Useful features of Bitbucket that makes it a powerful tool are its flexible deployment models, unlimited private repositories, code collaboration on steroids etc.

- Bitbucket supports few services like code search, issue tracking, Git large file storage, bitbucket pipelines, integrations, smart mirroring etc.

- Using Bitbucket, one can organize the repositories into the projects with which they can focus easily on their goal, process or product.

- To rationalize the development process of any software it can integrate into the prevailing workflow.

- Bitbucket offers a free plan for 5 users with unlimited private repositories, standard plan @ $2/user/month for growing teams and premium plan @ $5/user/month for large teams.

CodeCharge Studio

CodeCharge Studio is the most creative and leading IDE and RAD (Rapid Application Development) that is used to create data-driven web applications or enterprise internet and intranet systems with minimal coding.

Key Features:

- CodeCharge Studio supports various platforms like Windows, Mac, Linux etc.

- Using CodeCharge Studio, one can analyze and modify the code generated to study the web technologies which are used to work with programming projects in any environment.

- It supports various Databases like MySQL, Postgre SQL, Oracle, MS Access, MS SQL etc.

- Few important features of CodeCharge Studio are Visual IDE & Code Generator, web reports, online calendar, gallery builder, flash charts, AJAX, menu builder, database-to-web converter etc.

- By using CodeCharge Studio, one can minimize the errors, reduce the development time, reduce the learning curve etc.

- CodeCharge Studio can be used for a 20-day free trial and then it can be purchased at $139.95.

CodeLobster

CodeLobster is a free as well as a convenient PHP IDE that is used to develop fully featured web applications. It supports HTML, JavaScript, Smarty, Twig, and CSS.

Key Features:

- CodeLobster PHP Edition rationalizes & makes things easier in the development process and also supports CMS like Joomla, Magneto, Drupal, WordPress etc.

- Few important and advanced features of CodeLobster PHP IDE are PHP Debugger, PHP Advanced autocomplete; CSS code inspector, DOM elements, auto-completing of keywords etc.

- PHP Debugger facilitates the users in debugging the programs at the time of coding and before executing the code.

- CodeLobster offers its users to enjoy the file explorer facilities and browser previews.

- CodeLobster is available in 3 versions namely free version, lite version @ $39.95 and professional version @ $99.95.

Codenvy

Codenvy is a cloud development environment used for coding and debugging the applications. It can support sharing projects in real-time and can collaborate with others.

Key Features:

- As Codenvy is a cloud-based IDE there is no need for any installation and configuration of this software development tool.

- Codenvy can be integrated with Jira, Jenkins, Eclipse Che extensions and to any private toolchain.

- Codenvy can be customized in many ways using IDE extensions, Eclipse Che, commands, stacks, editors, assemblies, RESTful APIs, and server-side extension plug-ins.

- Codenvy can run on any operating system like Windows, Mac OS, and Linux. It can also run in the public or private cloud.

- Command-line installers generated by Codenvy are used for deploying in any environment.

- It is available at a free of cost up to 3 developers and for more users, it costs at $20/user/month.

Graphical User Interface Builder

While most engineers concern themselves only with the behavior of materials, machines, and the environment as they are affected by physical laws, user interface engineers also must consider the behavior of humans as they interact with materials, machines, and the environment. The human-machine interaction is becoming an increasingly important aspect of the industrial field, as technology permeates every avenue of life. Thus, user interface engineers are responsible for making sure people can interact with technology-driven products in an effective manner.

Hundreds of companies are producing tools, products, software, and applications to make user interface engineers' jobs more manageable. The technology, however, must work for the engineer in order to be effective, and we have searched for the top UI tools that do just that. User interface engineers cannot afford to get bogged down with the technology or the processes involved in building cost-effective products that meet users' needs and expectations.

Top 25 UI tools for user interface engineers are listed here, in no particular order.

Atmel Qtouch

Altium Limited, a software company providing PC-based electronics design software for engineers, offers Atmel Qtouch. With Atmel QTouch, UI engineers use the Altium Designer's platform-based data model to link all aspects of electronics product design into one process and in a single application.

Key Features:

- Easily add touch buttons, sliders and wheels to schematics and PCB layout

- The fastest touch development solution on the market

- Select and place from a range of configurable component types

- Configure your touch component and change the type as required

- Customize parameters

- Initiate and control the ECO process

- Reconfigure at any time and sync between SCH and PCB

Altia Design

ALTIA DESIGN   Altia Design: The GUI Software for Embedded Systems

Altia Design, "the centerpiece of Altia's tool-chain," is a detailed, completely functional, fully integrated interface that engineers turn into deployable code. With Altia Design, UI engineers also completely control custom objects and then connect to application code or simulations.

Key Features:

- Describe animation, stimulus and behavior without programming

- Easily implement and verify product specifications and changes

- Can start with PhotoProto output, static images, pre-built Altia library components, or build from scratch

- Altia Design output has several uses, including a fully functional, interactive stand-alone virtual prototype, front-end to a simulation model, software GUI connected to application code, and more

Nucleus Add-on for the Qt Framework

Products   Nucleus Add-on for the Qt Framework

For UI engineers looking for an open source solution for creating rich UIs based on the open source Qt Project, Nucleus Add-on for the Qt application framework is a smart choice. According to Mentor Graphics, "the Nucleus port of the Qt framework provides access to widely deployed technology, cross-platform support, and access to a large development community of more than 450,000 developers in over 70 countries."

Key Features:

- An integrated UI development tool

- Support for key Qt library modules

- Host based UI development and simulations

- A footprint management tool

- System Level Trace and Analysis Visualization

GrabCAD

GrabCAD Workbench

The fast, easy way to manage and share CAD files without PDM cost and hassle.

Workbench allows teams on any CAD system to work smoothly together by syncing local CAD files to cloud projects, tracking versions and locking files to prevent conflicts.

GrabCAD is known for its role as a leader in the Open Engineering movement, and it aims to help engineers speed up the process of getting products to the market by enabling collaborative product development. Specifically, GrabCAD Workbench allows teams on any CAD system to sync local CAD files to cloud projects, track versions, and lock files to prevent conflicts. For UI engineers working in teams, GrabCAD Workbench is a must-have collaboration tool.

Key Features:

- Full set of file management and collaboration tools

- User-controlled desktop sync

- Download as neutral format

- Works inside your CAD system

- Revision management

- Markup and communication tools

- Data security

- Mobile application

Autodesk Inventor

Autodesk Inventor, 3D CAD software, provides easy-to-use tools for 3D design, documentation, and product simulation. UI engineers can design and validate products with Inventor's Digital Prototyping to deliver better products, reduce development costs, and get to market more quickly.

Features:

- Freeform modeling shape creation

- Large assembly design

- Sketch constraint control

- Layout and system design

- Flexible sketching tools

- BIM compatibility

- Manufacturing and design documentation

- Data management

- Inventor 2015: Contact for a quote

- Inventor Professional 2015: Perpetual license – $8,390

- Factory Design Suite Ultimate 2015: Contact for a quote

- Product Design Suite Ultimate 2015: Contact for a quote

CATIA

Based on the 3DEXPERIENCE platform, CATIA offers "a unique Digital Product Experience" for users. CATIA 3D Master is 3D CAD design software that allows UI engineers to focus on sustainable development.

Key Features:

- Industrial design, Class-A, advanced surface modeling

- Reduces the time to perform 3D modeling changes

- A unified, integrated approach to systems engineering

- Design, collaborate, simulate, and validate model-based embedded stems applications across multi-disciplinary teams

SketchUp

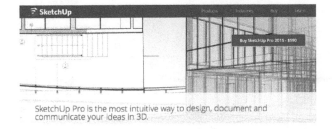

SketchUp Pro is the most intuitive way to design, document and communicate your ideas in 3D.

SketchUp Pro is the choice of hundreds of thousands of professionals who need an all-purpose solution to complicated, expensive CAD software. UI engineers appreciate SketchUp Pro's range of tools that span the simplest to most complex of tasks.

Key Features:

- Accurate measurements
- Copying and arrays
- Edges and faces
- Innovative, do-everything Follow Me tool
- Inferencing
- Push/pull
- Solid tools
- SketchUp Pro 2015: $590 – non-expiring license for SketchUp Pro and LayOut
- Corporate purchasing: contact for a quote suitable for enterprise or network license purchases

Kompas-3D

UI engineers choose Kompas-3D when looking for a flexible 3D modeling system to create models using several methods, including bottom-up modeling using finished components, top-down modeling by designing components to match specific designs, modeling based on layout drawings, or a combination of these modeling methods. The result is an editable associative model.

Key Features:

- Supports all capabilities of 3D solids and surface modeling
- Associative settings for element parameters
- Advanced surface and shape modeling
- Component modeling with assemblies, with relative positioning of parts in assemblies

Rhino 3D

After a five-year development period geared toward removing workflow bottlenecks and working to make Rhino faster and capable of handling much larger models and project teams, Rhino 5 is available as "the most stable version ever." With more than 3,500 enhancements and 40,000 pre-release users, Rhino 5 is a popular choice among UI engineers.

Key Features:

- New tools for editing and object creation

- Hundreds of new and enhanced editing commands

- Dozens of refinements to existing modeling tools with new commands and new lightweight extrusion objects

- Enhanced support for large point clouds and plug-ins such as RhinoTerrain

- Rhino/Flamingo/Penguin/Bongo Bundle: $1695

- Rhino/Flamingo Bundle: $1295

- Rhino/Brazil Bundle: $1495

- Full Rhino 5 for Windows: $995

- Upgrade from any version Rhino 5 for Windows: $495

IronCAD

IronCAD, "the leading provider of Innovative Design Collaboration Solutions," strives to provide productivity and design freedom for all of its users, including UI engineers. IronCAD is a popular choice for engineers facing tight deadlines and expecting high levels of unanticipated changes because "it provides a revolutionary replacement to today's history-based parametric-only systems."

Key Features:

- Seamlessly integrated design tools that are intuitive and user friendly

- Innovative and structured design

- Model data exchange

- Customer communication tools include photorealistic rendering, 3D/2D PDF, web publishing of models, and a standalone 3D viewer

- Design validation

TurboCAD

TurboCAD offers a wide selection of CAD solutions perfect for UI engineers, including TurboCAD Windows products and TurboCAD Macintosh products. TurboCAD Pro Platinum is the premium, professional CAD package. TurboCAD Pro Platinum includes all of the technology for drafting, detailing, modeling, rendering, and extensive file sharing, plus advanced tools for design, making it a top choice for enterprises that promote collaboration among its engineering team members.

Key Features:

- More than 30 new features and major improvements to every area of the program

- Extract custom data from property sets or custom properties and export to the newly supported IFC format

- Faster drafting and detailing with new Auto-Shapes, Arrow Tools, and more

- 3D modeling with ACIS R24 3D solid modeling engine

- More ways to share work with the latest AutoCAD DXF/DWG file filters, new SketchUP 2013 SKP filters, and new IFC export

Patran

Patran

Patran is "the world's most widely used pre/post-processing software for Finite Element Analysis (FEA), providing solid modeling, meshing, analysis setup and post-processing for multiple solvers including MSC Nastran, Marc, Abaqus, LS-DYNA, ANSYS, and Pam-Crash." Patran's complete FEA modeling solution ensures that UI engineers' virtual prototypes provide fast results for evaluating product performance against requirements and optimizing designs.

Key Features:

- Direct access of CAD geometry

- Advanced geometry creation, editing and feature recognition

- Support for multiple FEA solvers

- Post-processing and reporting tools for easy results evaluation

- Patran command language

MapleSim

MapleSim is an advanced system-level modeling solution that "applies modern techniques to reduce development time, provide greater insight into system behavior, and produce fast, high-fidelity simulations." With MapleSim, UI engineers are able to build even the most sophisticated of systems while still minimizing development time and costs.

Key Features

- Powerful symbolic and numeric math engine

- Multidomain modeling with built-in components

- Drag-and-drop physical modeling environment

- Equation-based custom components

- Integration with your toolchain

- Units management

- Automated knowledge capture

KeyCreator

KeyCreator Direct CAD is a popular choice among UI engineers who want a flexible way to quickly create, change, analyze, or communicate a mechanical part or design. Comprehensive Direct CAD software, KeyCreator allows users to "master your geometry."

Key Features:

- Modify nearly any geometry

- Never experience rebuilding errors; create geometry in real time

- Compare CAD models to identify and organize design changes and communicate findings via automated PDF reporting

- Export CAD files in multiple formats
- Import CAD models from other software packages and make edits directly to the geometry

SolidFace

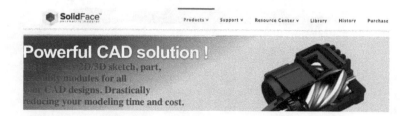

SolidFace Professional, a 2D/3D parametric historic constructive CAD modeler, also allows UI engineers and other users to complete project creation entirely in 2D. Because SolidFace is the result of Parasolid Siemens 3D modeler core and 15 years of UniCAD 2D/3D development, it has powerful detailing, solid modeling, assembly, and parameterization capabilities.

Key Features:

- Part module: Automatically creates parametric reference for modeling features that can be edited simply and interactively
- Assembly module: Build assemblies using modeled parts and subassemblies
- Drawing module: Insert parts and assemblies into the drawing module to generate automatic orthographic, sections and details views
- 3D direct modeling
- 2D/3D movement simulation

Space Claim

SpaceClaim, "the world's fastest and most innovative 3D direct modeler," aims to make technology work for UI engineers. With SpaceClaim, working with 3D models is less complicated because users can create, edit, or repair geometry without spending time on the underlying technology.

Key Features:

- Edit, repair, and create any geometry
- Increase productivity by removing the CAD bottleneck in the workflow

- Manipulate geometry faster, easier, and more intuitively and dedicate more time to primary job functions like analysis and concept modeling

Scheme-it

UI engineers choose Scheme-It as a solution for drawing circuit diagrams. The online schematic and diagramming tool allows users to build and share electronic circuit diagrams and includes a comprehensive electronic symbol library and integrated Digi-Key component catalog allowing for a wide range of circuit diagrams.

Key Features:

- Diagram at the block, icon, system, or schematic level

- Library of more than 700 generic symbols, plus allows for custom symbol creation

- Access to over 4 million components via Digi-Key Catalog integration

- Keep designs private, make them public, share them via links, or embed them in web pages, blogs, or emails

- Rapid design evolution via Bill of Material import capability

- Export into PDF or PNG files

- FREE to use as a guest

- FREE registration – Registered users are able to share and save designs

Fritzing

A free software tool, Fritzing supports designers and UI engineers who work creatively with interactive electronics. As part of the open-source hardware initiative, Fritzing offers a software tool, community website, and services that allow users to document prototypes, share them with others, teach electronics in a classroom, and layout and manufacture professional PCBs. UI engineers often use Fritzing Fab to easily and inexpensively turn their circuits into a custom-made PCB.

Key Features:

- Upgraded to Qt5.2.1

- ADI analog parts

- Intel Galileo

- Arduino Yún

- Linino One

- ChipKIT WF32, MX4 and shields

- Spark Core

- Atlas Scientific sensors

- Raspberry Pi versions (A, B, B rev2)

- Teensy 3.0/3.1

MicroEJ Embedded UI

MicroEJ products   MicroEJ embedded UI

IS2T is known for providing innovative software solutions for embedded systems, and MicroEJ Embedded UI is a popular extension choice among UI engineers. IS2T's embedded UI is a "set of libraries that extends the functionalities of MicroEJ Java platform with a flexible User Interface development solution for embedded systems."

Key Features:

- Quickly and easily design cross-platform Human-Machine Interfaces (HMI) independently from operating system and hardware configurations

- Includes user-friendly tools for improving your application's user experience

- Full-featured IDE supports visualization screens, any size and type of display, 1 to 32-bits color management, dynamic look and feel changes, and more

Storyboard Suite

Crank Software's tools and services enable UI engineers to develop embedded user interfaces more quickly, efficiently, and successfully. Crank Software's Storyboard Suite provides UI engineers with an even better way to "do embedded UI development, from start to finish."

Key Features:

- Easily prototype the look and fell of a product

- Move the UI prototype directly to the embedded target for deployment

- Photoshop import

- Animation timeline

- Desktop simulation

- Team collaboration

- Contact for a quote

Renesas Embedded GUI Solution Kit

Renesas Electronics is the result of the 2010 merger between NEC Electronics and Renesas Technology and strives to respond to customer needs with the company's creative power and technology innovations. Thee Renesas Embedded GUI Solution Kit stays true to Renesas' mission because it offers a quick and easy way for UI engineers to add cost-efficient LCD touch screens to any embedded designs.

Key Features:

- Hardware based on RX Dircct Drive LCD (DDLCD) technology

- Provides the performance required to handle the GUI and other functions at the same time

- Multiple GUI software development options are available for starting development efforts

easyGUI

Available from IBIS Solutions, easyGUI allows for more creative development with less difficult programming. easyGUI includes a complete graphical library in plain C code, plus all necessary graphical routines, making it easier for UI engineers to complete their jobs more efficiently.

Key Features:

- Supports virtually all monochrome, grayscale, and color display controllers

- Independent of kernel/OS

- Supports ANSI C compiler systems

- Multi-language applications

- Rapid prototyping through easySIM PC simulator

Disko Framework

An LGPL-licensed user interface framework, Disko allows UI engineers to build flexible applications quickly and easily. Specifically, Disko Framework is an embedded Linux UI Framework.

Key Features:

- Flexible GUI development

- Event-based communication

- Multilingual

- Media rich UIs and effects

PEG Pro

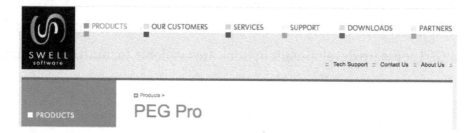

PEG Pro is a software solution for UI engineers who want to create complex, high-color depth embedded graphic applications. PEG Pro is intended for use "in the development of GUI applications in automotive, consumer electronics, infotainment and medical devices" and runs on a variety of real-time operating systems and microprocessors.

Key Features:

- Supports the key features and advanced applications demanded by interactive devices

- Accelerates product delivery by providing comprehensive functionality such as drag-and-drop visual development tools and the ability to start development on Windows or Linux platforms

- Provides run-time selection of themes to allow end-users to tailor their experience

- Written with the embedded market in mind, so the value of every feature is weighed against code size and performance requirements for that feature

Kanzi UI

The Kanzi UI Solution from Rightware, "the leader in interactive 2D and 3D UI software," is an advanced design and deployment solution for automotive, mobile, and consumer devices. Kanzi is a comprehensive solution that includes UI design tools, runtime and complimentary libraries that separates the designer and engineering tasks across the workflow, making it a great solution for UI development teams.

Key Features:

- Provides a real-time WYSIWYG editor for UI designers and embedded engineers
- Work through mock-ups with 3D content placeholders to interactive experiences refined in look and performance
- Create UI projects with multiple profiles for different targets
- Import 2D and 3D assets from DCC tools using COLLADA, png, jpeg, and psd
- Create interactivity with UI components and messages using interaction events and actions

Integrated Development Environment

An Integrated Development Environment (IDE) is a software application that provides a programming environment to streamline developing and debugging software. Rather than performing all the steps required to make an executable program as unrelated individual tasks, it brings all the tools needed into one application and workspace. Each of the tools has an awareness of the environment, and they work together to present a seamless development set for the developer.

Even a simple search for IDEs will turn up quite a few choices. IDEs are available from Open Source communities, vendors, and software companies. They range from free to pricing dependent upon the number of licenses required. There isn't a standard for IDEs and each has its own capabilities, along with strengths and weaknesses. Generally, an IDE provides an easy-to-use interface, automates development steps, and allows developers to run and debug programs all from one screen. It can also provide the link from a development operating system to an application target platform, like a desktop environment, smartphone or microprocessor.

Benefits of IDEs

The overall goal and main benefit of an integrated development environment is improved developer productivity. IDEs boost productivity by reducing setup time, increasing the speed of development tasks, keeping developers up to date and standardizing the development process.

- Faster setup: Without an IDE interface, developers would need to spend time configuring multiple development tools. With the application integration of an IDE, developers have the same set of capabilities in one place, without the need for constantly switching tools.

- Faster development tasks: Tighter integration of all development tasks improves developer productivity. For example, code can be parsed and syntax checked while being edited, providing instant feedback when syntax errors are introduced. Developers don't need to switch between applications to complete tasks. In addition, the IDE's tools and features helps developers organize resources, prevent mistakes and take shortcuts.

Further, IDEs streamline development by encouraging holistic thinking. They force developers to think of their actions in terms of the entire development lifecycle, rather than as a series of discrete tasks.

- Continual learning: Staying up to date and educated is another benefit. For instance, the IDE's help topics are constantly being updated, as well as new samples, project templates, etc. Programmers who are continually learning and current with best practices are more likely to contribute value to the team and the enterprise, and to boost productivity.

- Standardization: The IDE interface standardizes the development process, which helps developers work together more smoothly and helps new hires get up to speed more quickly.

Languages Supported by IDEs

Some IDEs are dedicated to a specific programming language or set of languages, creating a feature set that aligns with the particulars of that language. For instance, Xcode for the Objective-C and Swift languages, Cocoa and Cocoa Touch APIs.

However, there are many multiple-language IDEs, such as Eclipse (C, C++, Python, Perl, PHP, Java, Ruby and more), Komodo (Perl, Python, Tcl, PHP, Ruby, Javascript and more) and NetBeans (Java, JavaScript, PHP, Python, Ruby, C, C++ and more).

Support for alternative languages is often provided by plugins. For example, Flycheck is a syntax checking extension for GNU Emacs 24 with support for 39 languages.

Different Types of IDEs

There are a variety of different IDEs, catering to the many different ways developers work and the different types of code they produce. There are IDEs that are designed to work with one specific language, cloud-based IDEs, IDEs customized for the development of mobile applications or for HTML, and IDEs meant specifically for Apple development or Microsoft development.

Multi-language IDEs

Multi-language IDEs, such as Eclipse, NetBeans, Komodo, Aptana and Geany, support multiple programming languages.

- Eclipse: Supports C, C++, Python, Perl, PHP, Java, Ruby and more. This free and open source editor is the model for many development frameworks. Eclipse began as a Java development environment and has expanded through plugins. Eclipse is managed and directed by the Eclipse.org Consortium.

- NetBeans: Supports Java, JavaScript, PHP, Python, Ruby, C, C++ and more. This option is also free and open source. All the functions of the IDE are provided by modules that each provide a well-defined function. Support for other programming languages can be added by installing additional modules.

- Komodo IDE: Supports Perl, Python, Tcl, PHP, Ruby, Javascript and more. This enterprise-level tool has a higher price point.

- Aptana: Supports HTML, CSS, JavaScript, AJAX and others via plugins. This is a popular choice for web app development.

- Geany: Supports C, Java, PHP, HTML, Python, Perl, Pascal and many more. This is a highly customizable environment with a large set of plugins.

IDEs for Mobile Development

There are IDEs specifically for mobile development, including PhoneGap and Appcelerator's Titanium Mobile.

Many IDEs, especially those that are multi-language, have mobile-development plugins. For instance, Eclipse has this functionality.

HTML IDEs

Some of the most popular IDEs are those for developing HTML applications. For example, IDEs such as HomeSite, DreamWeaver or FrontPage automate many tasks involved in web site development.

Cloud-based IDEs

Cloud-based IDEs are starting to become mainstream. The capabilities of these web-based IDEs are increasing rapidly, and most major vendors will likely need to offer one to be competitive. Cloud IDEs give developers access to their code from anywhere. For example, Nitrous is a cloud-based development environment platform that supports Ruby, Python, Node.js and more. Cloud9 IDE supports more than 40 languages, including PHP, Ruby, Python, JavaScript with Node.js, and Go. Heroku is a cloud-based development platform as a service (PaaS), supporting several programming languages.

IDEs Specific to Microsoft or Apple

These IDEs cater to those working in Microsoft or Apple environments:

- Visual Studio: Supports Visual C++, VB.NET, C#, F# and others. Visual Studio is Microsoft's IDE and is designed to create applications for the Microsoft platform.

- MonoDevelop: Supports C/C++, Visual Basic, C# and other .NET languages.

- Xcode: Supports the Objective-C and Swift languages, and Cocoa and Cocoa Touch APIs. This IDE is just for creating iOS and Mac applications and includes an iPhone/iPad simulator and GUI builder.

- Espresso: Supports HTML, CSS, XML, JavaScript and PHP. This is a tool for Mac web developers.

- Coda: Supports PHP, JavaScript, CSS, HTML, AppleScript and Cocoa API. Coda bills itself as "one-window development" for the Mac user.

IDEs for Specific Languages

Some IDEs cater to developers working in a single language. These include CodeLite and C-Free for C/C++, Jikes and Jcreator for Java, Idle for Python, and RubyMine for Ruby/Rails.

Software Development Steps

In any environment, to develop executable software you need to create source file(s), compile the source files to produce machine code (object files), and link the object files with each other and any libraries or other resources required to produce an executable file.

Source files contain the code statements to do the tasks your program is being created for. They contain program statements specific to the language you are using. If programming in c, the source files contain c code statements; java source files contain java statements. Usually source files names have extensions indicating the code they contain. A c source file may be named "myfile.c". Compilers translate the source files to appropriate machine level code for the target environment. Linkers take all the object files required for a program and link them together, assigning memory and registers to variables, setting up data. They also link in library files to support operating system tasks and any other files the program needs. Linkers output executable files.

Life without IDEs

When not using an IDE, developers use an editor, compiler, and linker installed on their development machine to create code files, compile, and link them.

Using the editor to create a source file, the code blocks, comments, and program statements are entered and the file saved. There are no "corrective actions," taken as the editor doesn't know this is supposed to be a "source file" as opposed to notes for class. If working in a position-dependent language like Python, the developer would have to be very careful about indenting. The file has to be saved with the correct file extension and in a directory where the compiler can find it.

Each source file has to be compiled separately; if the program has a few source files, they all have to be named separately in the compiler. When invoking the compiler, it has to be directed to look in the correct directory for the source files and where the output files should be stored. If there is an error in the source file, the compiler will output messages and fail to complete. For any errors, the developer goes back and edits the source file, working from line numbers and compiler messages to fix the problems and these steps continue until all the source files compile without errors.

When linking, each object file is specified as being part of the build. Again, the locations for the object files and executable are given. There may be errors at this point because it isn't until the entire program is linked that some errors can be detected. Assuming the linker finds all the variables and functions, it produces a file that can be run.

If the program is run and it works, all's well! If it seems to do nothing that means it's debugging time! Since there is no insight to what the program is doing, the developer may go back and put in some brute force methods, like print statements to print messages out at certain points in the program or blink some LEDs at strategic places, which means back to the editor, and the cycle continues.

Using IDEs

Bringing up an IDE presents a workspace:

With an IDE, a Project provides a workspace where all the files for a program can be collected.

Select the language and the type of program to create. This IDE supports c and c++ and various application types.

If set for a Windows Application in C, it brings up a template:

A console C program brings up a different template:

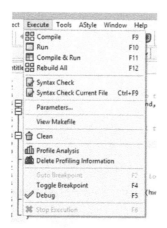

Depending on the IDE, it may set up code blocks automatically, indent as required, track variable names in colors, show comments.   To compile just click the compile selection on the dropdown menu (or press F9).

Compiler results will show in one of the windows and in the log. Compiler options and directories are set up using the Options menus.

As source files are created, they are added to the project. The Rebuild selection rebuilds all the files, first checking for the latest versions, then compiles and links to produce an executable result.

Errors on the compile or link? The offending code will be shown in the code window. The statement containing the error or the lines around it is known, since the compiler, linker, and editor are seamlessly connected. You can run the executable from the IDE by selecting Run:

The results show in a separate window.

Problems when running your new program? Usually IDEs provide an option to create a debug version.

With a debug version, the IDE controls the execution of the program, allowing insight to data variables and memory locations. Some IDEs show both the high level source statements as well as the machine code. The debugger may include options to "watch" local variables and track the contents of memory locations, offer line by line execution, provide the ability to set break points to run to a certain point in the program, and the ability to step into or over function calls.

Some IDEs include emulators, allowing debugging in the IDE environment without having to export the code to the target device.

IDE vs. Tool Chains

The term "tool chain" usually applies to a related set of development tools: a builder, compiler, linker and debugger. The builder tells the compiler the files and options to use, and the linker and debugger are connected. An IDE includes these as well as an editor and other tools.

Choosing an IDE

When selecting an IDE you'll find there are a lot to choose from and the price can vary from no cost to pricing options dependent on the environment and number of users. The license type is important as well if you intend to produce commercial code. Some things to check:

Does it provide support for your:

> Development platform? (Some only run on specific operating systems.)

> Programming language(s)? (Some only support a specific language.)

> Target environment(s)? (IDEs targeting desktops may not support Android environments.)

Capabilities: What is included? Does it have watch points for debugging? Can it single-step through code? Do you need to see the low-level language used or is source code debugging good enough?

Pricing and Licensing: Are you looking for a supported environment and willing to pay for it? Does your company need several licenses? Are there royalties required? Are there fees per use?

Just as the IDE in these examples brought up template code blocks for certain applications, there are IDEs that support specific microcontrollers. These specialized IDEs automatically set up some code for the microcontroller.

An IDE makes software development and debugging easier by providing a single development workspace containing all the tools needed for development; it tracks files automatically and saves time. Choosing one suited to your programming needs makes developing and debugging software much easier

References

- Software-development-tools: softwaretestinghelp.com, Retrieved 11 April 2018

- Top-ui-tools-for-user-interface-engineers: pannam.com, Retrieved 24 May 2018

- What-are-integrated-development-environments: allaboutcircuits.com, Retrieved 16 March 2018

- Integrated-development-environments: veracode.com, Retrieved 15 July 2018

5

Software Design and Architecture

Software designing primarily involves problem solving and planning software solutions. The complex structures of a software system are referred to as software architecture. This chapter closely examines the key concepts of software design and architecture, through an analysis of software architectural model, software architectural style, software architecture description and software architecture analysis method, besides many others.

Software Architecture

In simple words, software architecture is the process of converting software characteristics such as flexibility, scalability, feasibility, reusability, and security into a structured solution that meets the technical and the business expectations. This definition leads us to ask about the characteristics of software that can affect a software architecture design. There is a long list of characteristics which mainly represent the business or the operational requirements, in addition to the technical requirements.

The Characteristics of Software Architecture

As explained, software characteristics describe the requirements and the expectations of software in operational and technical levels. Thus, when a product owner says they are competing in a rapidly changing markets, and they should adapt their business model quickly. The software should be "extendable, modular and maintainable" if a business deals with urgent requests that need to be completed successfully in the matter of time. As a software architect, you should note that the performance and low fault tolerance, scalability and reliability are your key characteristics. Now, after defining the previous characteristics the business owner tells you that they have a limited budget for that project, another characteristic comes up here which is "the feasibility."

Software Architecture Patterns

Most people have probably heard of the term "MicroServices" before. MicroServices is one of many other software architecture patterns such as Layered Pattern, Event-Driven Pattern, Serverless Pattern and many more. The Microservices pattern received its reputation after being adopted by Amazon and Netflix and showing its great impact. Now, let's dig deeper into the architecture patterns.

Serverless Architecture

This element refers to the application solution that depends on third-party services to manage the complexity of the servers and backend management. Serverless Architecture is divided into two main categories. The first is "Backend as a service (BaaS)" and the second is "Functions as a Service

(FaaS)." The serverless architecture will help you save a lot of time taking care and fixing bugs of deployment and servers regular tasks.

The most famous provider for serverless API is Amazon AWS "Lambda."

Event-driven Architecture

This architecture depends on Event Producers and Event Consumers. The main idea is to decouple your system's parts and each part will be triggered when an interesting event from another part has got triggered. Is it complicated? Let's simplify it. Assume you design an online store system and it has two parts. A purchase module and a vendor module. If a customer makes a purchase, the purchase module would generate an event of "orderPending" Since the vendor module is interesting in the "orderPending" event, it will be listening, in case one is triggered. Once the vendor module gets this event, it will execute some tasks or maybe fire another event for order more of the product from a certain vendor.

Just remember the event-producer does not know which event-consumer listening to which event. Also, other consumers do not know which of them listens to which events. Therefore, the main idea is decoupling the parts of the system.

Microservices Architecture

Microservices architecture has become the most popular architecture in the last few years. It depends on developing small, independent modular services where each service solves a specific problem or performs a unique task and these modules communicate with each other through well-defined API to serve the business goal.

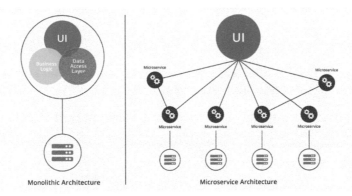

Goals of Architecture

The primary goal of the architecture is to identify requirements that affect the structure of the application. A well-laid architecture reduces the business risks associated with building a technical solution and builds a bridge between business and technical requirements.

Some of the other goals are as follows:

- Expose the structure of the system, but hide its implementation details.
- Realize all the use-cases and scenarios.

- Try to address the requirements of various stakeholders.
- Handle both functional and quality requirements.
- Reduce the goal of ownership and improve the organization's market position.
- Improve quality and functionality offered by the system.
- Improve external confidence in either the organization or system.

Limitations

Software architecture is still an emerging discipline within software engineering. It has the following limitations:

- Lack of tools and standardized ways to represent architecture.
- Lack of analysis methods to predict whether architecture will result in an implementation that meets the requirements.
- Lack of awareness of the importance of architectural design to software development.
- Lack of understanding of the role of software architect and poor communication among stakeholders.
- Lack of understanding of the design process, design experience and evaluation of design.

Role of Software Architect

A Software Architect provides a solution that the technical team can create and design for the entire application. A software architect should have expertise in the following areas:

Design Expertise

- Expert in software design, including diverse methods and approaches such as object-oriented design, event-driven design, etc.
- Lead the development team and coordinate the development efforts for the integrity of the design.
- Should be able to review design proposals and tradeoff among themselves.

Domain Expertise

- Expert on the system being developed and plan for software evolution.
- Assist in the requirement investigation process, assuring completeness and consistency.
- Coordinate the definition of domain model for the system being developed.

Technology Expertise

- Expert on available technologies that helps in the implementation of the system.
- Coordinate the selection of programming language, framework, platforms, databases, etc.

Methodological Expertise

- Expert on software development methodologies that may be adopted during SDLC (Software Development Life Cycle).

- Choose the appropriate approaches for development that helps the entire team.

Deliverables of the Architect

An architect is expected to deliver clear, complete, consistent, and achievable set of functional goals to the organization. Besides, he is also responsible to provide:

- A simplified concept of the system.

- A design in the form of the system, with at least two layers of decomposition.

- A functional description of the system, with at least two layers of decomposition.

- A notion of the timing, operator attributes, and the implementation and operation plans.

- A document or process which ensures functional decomposition is followed, and the form of interfaces is controlled.

Hidden Role of Software Architect

Besides, facilitating the technical work among team members, it has also some subtle roles such as reinforce the trust relationship among team members and protect team members from the external forces that could distract them and bring less value to the project.

Space-based Architecture

The space-based pattern (also sometimes referred to as the cloud architecture pattern) minimizes the factors that limit application scaling. This pattern gets its name from the concept of *tuple space,* the idea of distributed shared memory. High scalability is achieved by removing the central database constraint and using replicated in-memory data grids instead. Application data is kept in-memory and replicated among all the active processing units. Processing units can be dynamically started up and shut down as user load increases and decreases, thereby addressing variable scalability. Because there is no central database, the database bottleneck is removed, providing near-infinite scalability within the application.

Most applications that fit into this pattern are standard websites that receive a request from a browser and perform some sort of action. A bidding auction site is a good example of this. The site continually receives bids from internet users through a browser request. The application would receive a bid for a particular item, record that bid with a timestamp, and update the latest bid information for the item, and send the information back to the browser.

There are two primary components within this architecture pattern: a *processing unit* and *virtualized middleware*. Figure below illustrates the basic space-based architecture pattern and its primary architecture components.

The processing-unit component contains the application components (or portions of the application components). This includes web-based components as well as backend business logic. The contents of the processing unit varies based on the type of application—smaller web-based applications would likely be deployed into a single processing unit, whereas larger applications may split the application functionality into multiple processing units based on the functional areas of the application. The processing unit typically contains the application modules, along with an in-memory data grid and an optional asynchronous persistent store for failover. It also contains a replication engine that is used by the virtualized middleware to replicate data changes made by one processing unit to other active processing units.

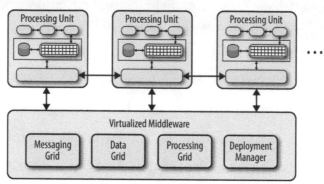

Figure: Space-based architecture pattern

The virtualized-middleware component handles housekeeping and communications. It contains components that control various aspects of data synchronization and request handling. Included in the virtualized middleware are the messaging grid, data grid, processing grid, and deployment manager. These components can be custom written or purchased as third-party products.

Pattern Dynamics

The magic of the space-based architecture pattern lies in the virtualized middleware components and the in-memory data grid contained within each processing unit. Figure below shows the typical processing unit architecture containing the application modules, in-memory data grid, optional asynchronous persistence store for failover, and the data-replication engine.

The virtualized middleware is essentially the controller for the architecture and manages requests, sessions, data replication, distributed request processing, and process-unit deployment. There are four main architecture components in the virtualized middleware: the messaging grid, the data grid, the processing grid, and the deployment manager.

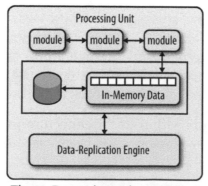

Figure: Processing-unit component

Messaging Grid

The messaging grid, manages input request and session information. When a request comes into the virtualized-middleware component, the messaging-grid component determines which active processing components are available to receive the request and forwards the request to one of those processing units. The complexity of the messaging grid can range from a simple round-robin algorithm to a more complex next-available algorithm that keeps track of which request is being processed by which processing unit.

Data Grid

The data grid component is perhaps the most important and crucial component in this pattern. The data grid interacts with the data-replication engine in each processing unit to manage the data replication between processing units when data updates occur. Since the messaging grid can forward a request to any of the processing units available, it is essential that each processing unit contains *exactly* the same data in its in-memory data grid. Although Figure below shows a synchronous data replication between processing units, in reality this is done in parallel asynchronously and *very quickly*, sometimes completing the data synchronization in a matter of microseconds (one millionth of a second).

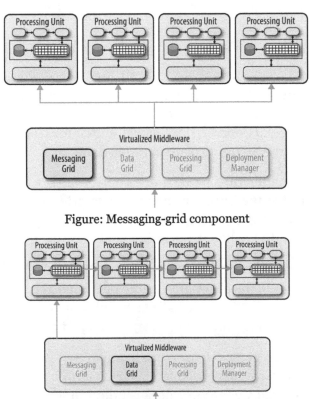

Figure: Messaging-grid component

Figure: Data-grid component

Processing Grid

The processing grid, is an optional component within the virtualized middleware that manages distributed request processing when there are multiple processing units, each handling a portion of the application. If a request comes in that requires coordination between processing unit types (e.g., an order processing unit and a customer processing unit), it is the processing grid that mediates and orchestrates the request between those two processing units.

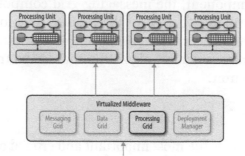

Figure: Processing-grid component

Deployment Manager

The deployment-manager component manages the dynamic startup and shutdown of processing units based on load conditions. This component continually monitors response times and user loads, and starts up new processing units when load increases, and shuts down processing units when the load decreases. It is a critical component to achieving variable scalability needs within an application.

Considerations

The space-based architecture pattern is a complex and expensive pattern to implement. It is a good architecture choice for smaller web-based applications with variable load (e.g., social media sites, bidding and auction sites). However, it is not well suited for traditional large-scale relational database applications with large amounts of operational data.

Although the space-based architecture pattern does not require a centralized datastore, one is commonly included to perform the initial in-memory data grid load and asynchronously persist data updates made by the processing units. It is also a common practice to create separate partitions that isolate volatile and widely used transactional data from non-active data, in order to reduce the memory footprint of the in-memory data grid within each processing unit.

It is important to note that while the alternative name of this pattern is the cloud-based architecture, the processing units (as well as the virtualized middleware) do not have to reside on cloud-based hosted services or PaaS (platform as a service). It can just as easily reside on local servers.

From a product implementation perspective, you can implement many of the architecture components in this pattern through third-party products such as GemFire, JavaSpaces, GigaSpaces, IBM Object Grid, nCache, and Oracle Coherence. Because the implementation of this pattern varies greatly in terms of cost and capabilities (particularly data replication times), as an architect, you should first establish what your specific goals and needs are before.

Web-oriented Architecture

Web-oriented architecture (WOA) is a type of software architecture that is designed to be used for website and Web applications. It builds on service-oriented architecture (SOA) by adding support for Web-based software application and services. The key difference between SOA and WOA is the use of REST APIs by WOA instead of SOAP by SOA.

WOA is primarily a sub-style of SOA with Web capabilities. It integrates and connects systems and users through the global set of hypermedia (Internet) technologies and works on user interfaces and API. It is commonly used as service architecture in social media websites and cloud-based services.

WOA has five fundamental interface constraints:

- Identification of the resource, such as uniform resource identifier

- Manipulation of resources through Web-based representations such as HTTP

- Self-descriptive messages like MIME

- Hypermedia for the engine of application state

- Application neutrality, meaning the application/service created on WOA can be deployed/used on any platform

Nick Gall, a Gartner analyst who coined the term WOA, also provided a simple formula to describe WOA:

WOA = SOA + WWW + REST

Open Architecture

An Open system architecture or OSA is any system (or software) architecture that exhibits the following three beneficial characteristics:

1. It is modular, being decomposed into architectural components that are cohesive, loosely coupled with other components (and external systems), and encapsulate (hide) their implementations behind visible interfaces.

2. Its key interfaces between architectural components conform to open interface standards (that is, consensus based, widely used, and easily available to potential users).

3. Its key interfaces have been verified to conform to the associated open interface standards.

By mandating contractors to engineer OSA (e.g., via Better Buying Power 3.0), government acquisition organizations hope to achieve several benefits, two of the most important of which are to increase competition among developers of the architectural components and to avoid vendor lock when it comes to acquiring and updating these components. Given these benefits, government program offices may get the impression at first glance that all system architectures should be *completely* open. This impression is especially true when one considers the DoD policies (such as DoDI 5000.02) that require program offices to ensure defense contractors produce open system architectures.

One critical word in the definition of open system architectures, however, reveals this initial impression to be false. The definition does not state that *all* interfaces must conform to open interface standards, but rather only key interfaces must be open. Moreover, if one examines actual system architectures, one quickly learns that openness is not black and white but rather a matter of degree. Some interfaces are highly open (e.g., they conform to widely used international standards), some interfaces are relatively open (i.e., they conform to less-widely used, more application-domain-specific standards or widely used *de* facto standards), some interfaces are slightly open (e.g., they conform to product-line-specific conventions), and some interfaces are essentially closed (i.e., they are system-unique or conform to contractor-proprietary "standards").

Steps to Producing an OSA

Several steps required to produce an OSA are described below.

- Step 1: Decide how to modularize the system. The main OSA modularization approach typically decomposes the system into separately procurable architectural components to support competition, minimize vendor lock, and enable technology refresh. This approach is used to identify the key architectural components of the system that should be open, while the other parts potentially may be closed or partially open. The interfaces of these key components are then defined as the key interfaces that should conform to open interface standards.

- Step 2: Determine the associated open interface standards to use for key interfaces. When should an interface be identified as a key interface and, therefore, when should that interface be open? The answer is really a matter of cost-benefit analysis. While there are clearly benefits to being open, there are also associated costs and challenges. Mandating the use of an open interface standard may necessitate the replacement of an existing closed (e.g., proprietary) interface, training the developers to use the new interface standard, and lowered developer productivity until the new interface standard is mastered.

- Step 3: Verify conformance to the open interface standards. As mentioned earlier, an open interface must be verified (via testing or static analysis) to conform, both syntactically and semantically, to the associated open interface standard. It is also important to document and verify any implementation-defined portions of the standard.

In theory and if all things were equal, it would be good if all architectural components were modular and open. In practice, however, all things are not equal and other quality attributes (such as dependability, performance, robustness, safety, and security) may be more important than openness alone for some architectural components. Perfectly good reasons may therefore exist for why these components should not be open or at most partially open. For example, conforming to a specific open interface standard may decrease system performance or have negative security ramifications. In other words, when engineering a system architecture, the architects must weigh competing requirements (especially the non-functional quality attributes) against each other, and openness is only one such requirement to consider when making engineering and business trade-offs.

In summary, architects of OSA-based solutions should forego openness in those parts of the system and software architecture where the following conditions hold:

1. There are no strong reasons to make the architectural component separately procurable. For example, there is currently only a single vendor qualified, or the costs of transition-

ing away from a sole-source contract would be excessive or unaffordable given current or foreseen funding levels. Note that program managers and architects need to realize that short-term and long-term affordability may be quite different, and that an over-emphasis on short-term affordability may be a case of "penny wise and pound foolish."

2. There are overriding reasons to violate modularity or to modularize in a way that minimizes competition. For example, the existing poorly modularized architecture would cost too much or take too long to re-architect.

3. There are overriding reasons to use relatively closed interface standards, to use proprietary standards, or to use no standard at all. For example, no open interface standard exists, the open interface standards result in inadequate quality (e.g., performance, robustness, safety, or security), the open interfaces standards are too immature or not sufficiently specified, or the cost of replacing an existing proprietary interface exceeds the anticipated cost savings from making the interface more open.

When decisions are made to use closed or relatively unopened architectures, it is important to document the associated rationales and justifications. This documentation is invaluable when trade-offs and choices regarding openness must be revisited (e.g., due to rapid changes in technologies and the emphasis on obtaining needed capabilities by integrating independent systems into systems-of-systems).

Note that nothing in the above justifies ignoring openness, and it should not be misused as an excuse to engineer closed system architecture. Program offices should ensure that integrators provide adequate justification for the relatively or completely closed parts of the system architecture and that they are not avoiding openness to avoid competition and ensure vendor lock.

Multitier Architecture

N-tier architecture is also called multi-tier architecture because the software is engineered to have the processing, data management, and presentation functions physically and logically separated. That means that these different functions are hosted on several machines or clusters, ensuring that services are provided without resources being shared and, as such, these services are delivered at top capacity. The "N" in the name n-tier architecture refers to any number from 1.

Not only does your software gain from being able to get services at the best possible rate, but it's also easier to manage. This is because when you work on one section, the changes you make will not affect the other functions. And if there is a problem, you can easily pinpoint where it originates.

A More In-Depth Look at N-Tier Architecture N-tier architecture would involve dividing an application into three different tiers. These would be:

1. The logic tier,

2. The presentation tier, and

3. The data tier.

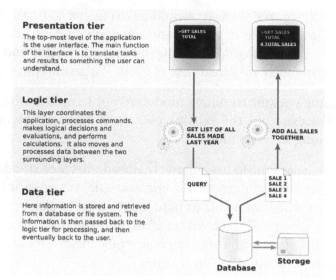

The separate physical location of these tiers is what differentiates n-tier architecture from the model-view-controller framework that only separates presentation, logic, and data tiers in concept. N-tier architecture also differs from MVC framework in that the former has a middle layer or a logic tier, which facilitates all communications between the different tiers. When you use the MVC framework, the interaction that happens is triangular; instead of going through the logic tier, it is the control layer that accesses the model and view layers, while the model layer accesses the view layer. Additionally, the control layer makes a model using the requirements and then pushes that model into the view layer.

This is not to say that you can only use either the MVC framework or the n-tier architecture. There are a lot of software that brings together these two frameworks. For instance, you can use the n-tier architecture as the overall architecture, or use the MVC framework in the presentation tier.

Benefits of N-tier Architecture

There are several benefits to using n-tier architecture for your software. These are scalability, ease of management, flexibility, and security:

- Secure: You can secure each of the three tiers separately using different methods.

- Easy to manage: You can manage each tier separately, adding or modifying each tier without affecting the other tiers.

- Scalable: If you need to add more resources, you can do it per tier, without affecting the other tiers.

- Flexible: Apart from isolated scalability, you can also expand each tier in any manner that your requirements dictate.

In short, with n-tier architecture, you can adopt new technologies and add more components without having to rewrite the entire application or redesigning your whole software, thus making it easier to scale or maintain. Meanwhile, in terms of security, you can store sensitive or confidential information in the logic tier, keeping it away from the presentation tier, thus making it more secure.

Other benefits include:

- More efficient development: N-tier architecture is very friendly for development, as different teams may work on each tier. This way, you can be sure the design and presentation professionals work on the presentation tier and the database experts work on the data tier.

- Easy to add new features: If you want to introduce a new feature, you can add it to the appropriate tier without affecting the other tiers.

- Easy to reuse: Because the application is divided into independent tiers, you can easily reuse each tier for other software projects. For instance, if you want to use the same program, but for a different data set, you can just replicate the logic and presentation tiers and then create a new data tier.

Working and Examples of N-tier Architecture

When it comes to n-tier architecture, a three-tier architecture is fairly common. In this setup, you have the presentation or GUI tier, the data layer, and the application logic tier.

The application logic tier: The application logic tier is where all the "thinking" happens, and it knows what is allowed by your application and what is possible, and it makes other decisions. This logic tier is also the one that writes and reads data into the data tier.

The data tier: The data tier is where all the data used in your application are stored. You can securely store data on this tier, do transaction, and even search through volumes and volumes of data in a matter of seconds.

The presentation tier: The presentation tier is the user interface. This is what the software user sees and interacts with. This is where they enter the needed information. This tier also acts as a go-between for the data tier and the user, passing on the user's different actions to the logic tier.

Just imagine surfing on your favorite website. The presentation tier is the Web application that you see. It is shown on a Web browser you access from your computer, and it has the CSS, JavaScript, and HTML codes that allow you to make sense of the Web application. If you need to log in, the presentation tier will show you boxes for username, password, and the submit button. After filling out and then submitting the form, all that will be passed on to the logic tier. The logic tier will have the JSP, Java Servlets, Ruby, PHP and other programs. The logic tier would be run on a Web server. And in this example, the data tier would be some sort of database, such as a MySQL, NoSQL, or PostgreSQL database. All of these are run on a separate database server. Rich Internet applications and mobile apps also follow the same three-tier architecture.

And there are n-tier architecture models that have more than three tiers. Examples are applications that have these tiers:

- Services – such as print, directory, or database services

- Business domain – the tier that would host Java, DCOM, CORBA, and other application server object.

- Presentation tier

- Client tier – or the thin clients

One good instance is when you have an enterprise service-oriented architecture. The enterprise service bus or ESB would be there as a separate tier to facilitate the communication of the basic service tier and the business domain tier.

Model-driven Architecture

The Model-Driven Architecture (MDA) is a software design approach that was officially launched in 2001 by its sponsor, the Object Management Group (OMG).

MDA is intended to support model-driven engineering of software systems. The MDA is a specification that provides a set of guidelines for structuring specifications expressed as models. Using the MDA methodology, system functionality may first be defined as a platform-independent model (PIM) through an appropriate Domain Specific Language. Given a Platform Definition Model (PDM) corresponding to CORBA, .Net, the Web, etc., the PIM may then be translated to one or more platform-specific models (PSMs) for the actual implementation, using different Domain Specific Languages, or a General Purpose Language like Java, C#, Python, etc. The translations between the PIM and PSMs are normally performed using automated tools, like model transformation tools, for example tools compliant to the new OMG standard named QVT. The overall process is documented in a document produced and regularly maintained by the OMG and called the MDA Guide. The principles of MDA can also be applied to other areas like business process modeling where the architecture and technology neutral PIM is mapped onto either system or manual processes.

The MDA model is related to multiple standards, such as the Unified Modeling Language (UML). Note that the term "architecture" in Model-driven architecture does not refer to the architecture of the system being modeled, but rather to the architecture of the various standards and model forms that serve as the technology basis for MDA.

The Object Management Group holds trademarks on MDA, as well as several similar terms including Model Driven Development (MDD).

Model Driven Architecture Approach

One of the main aims of the MDA is to separate design from architecture and realization technologies facilitating that design and architecture can alter independently. The design addresses the functional (use case) requirements while architecture provides the infrastructure through which non-functional requirements like scalability, reliability and performance are realized. MDA envisages that the platform independent model (PIM), which represents a conceptual design realizing the functional requirements, will survive changes in realization technologies and software architectures.

Of particular importance to model-driven architecture is the notion of model transformation. A specific standard for model transformation has been defined called QVT. One example of a QVT language for model transformation is ATL.

MDA Tools

An MDA tool is a tool used to develop, interpret, compare, align, measure, verify, transform, etc. models or metamodels. In the following part "model" is interpreted as meaning any kind of model (e.g. a UML model) or metamodel. In any MDA approach we have essentially two kinds of models: initial models are created manually by human agents while derived models are created automatically by programs. For example an analyst may create a UML initial model from its observation of some loose business situation while a Java model may be automatically derived from this UML model by a Model transformation operation. An MDA tool may be one or more of the following types:

- Creation

- Analysis

- Transformation

- Composition

- Test

- Simulation

- Metadata Management

- Reverse Engineering

Some tools perform more than one of the functions listed above. For example, the Select Solution for MDA covers all of the above except Metadata Management.

Usually MDA tools focus on rudimentary architecture specification, although in some cases the tools are architecture-independent (or platform independent).

Functional Software Architecture

Functional Architecture (FA) is an architectural model which represents at a high level the software product's major functions from a usage perspective, and specifies the interactions of functions, internally between each other and externally with other products.

The Functional Architecture Model (FAM) includes all the necessary modules and structures for the visualization of the functional architecture of a software product and its relevant applications in the business domain. Consequently, it constitutes a standard arrangement of all the requirements positioned in modules that correspond to the product's functionalities. The Functional Architecture should be designed together with product managers, architects, partners and customers, and should be expressed in easy to understand diagrams. Referring back to the definition of viewpoints, we clarify that Functional Architecture addresses mainly the concerns of stakeholders like customers, marketing and sales employees, end-users, i.e. stakeholders with no technical expertise.

The Functional Architecture Model, can be used by software product manages to show the product roadmap to their customers and can constitute a reference base for the architecture design phase in the software product lifecycle. As a consequence, it can also be used as reference for managing the product vision for subsequent releases, registering incoming requirements and dividing work amongst development teams.

Many organizations already tend to design intuitively the functional architecture of their software systems. A practical example is the effort to model the functional architecture of Baan ERP, the main product of Baan, a vendor of enterprise resource planning software that is currently owned by Infor Global Solutions.

IBM Insurance Application Architecture is reference architecture for the insurance domain, which covers all related business functions. Another example is the Supply Chain Operations Reference, which is a process reference model in the area of supply chain management. The use of reference architecture in software engineering helps indicate the complete functional coverage of a product, define the technical quality of its modules, and identify market growth options and functionalities to put in the product roadmap.

Functional Architecture Modeling: Design Principles and Structures

On our way of modeling the functional architecture of a software product, we get to notice that architecture is a premier key to the success of the product. The elegancy of a product is reflected in the elegancy of its architecture. A look at well known software products that have met huge commercial success over the years, such as the Google search engine, SAP R3 or Linux OS, gives us an insight that a robust and well designed architecture constitutes a significant factor for the development, maintenance, usability and performance of a software product. A good functional architecture enables the usability of a software system, and should be able to survive many releases, so that new functionalities can easily be incorporated without making fundamental changes. These observations lead us to the search of structures that will enable the design of a high-quality functional architecture. Bass et al. suggest that there is no scientific evidence to decide whether an architecture design is good or bad, but there are several rules that should be applied in the architecture design. In table below, we mention their recommendations adjusted for the construction of a functional architecture.

Table: Font sizes of headings. Table captions should always be positioned above the tables.

Principles for the FA design process	Principles for the structure of a FA
One single architect or else a group of a few architects with an appointed leader to design the architecture	Featuring of unambiguous modules following the principles of hiding information and separating concerns, with well-defined interfaces
Existence of a list of requirements and prioritized qualities	Modules should be developed as much independently from one another as possible
Documentation with notation understandable by all stakeholders	Architecture independent of technical changes
Involvement of all stakeholders in the review of FA	Architecture independent of particular commercial products
Early inspection for quantitative measures and qualitative properties that should be followed	Separation of modules that "produce data" from modules that "consume data"
Forming of a "skeletal system'" that will be used for the incremental growth and expansion of the software product	Small number of simple interaction patterns, in order to increase performance and enhance reliability and modifiability

The design of a functional architecture is influenced by four main factors: First of all the requirements set by the stakeholders, functional and non-functional, determine what kind of functionalities are going to be incorporated, as also technical restrictions that have to be taken under consideration. Secondly, the developing organization affects the architecture, with regard to earlier versions of the product, or available design patterns to be used, or already known data such as an existing database, etc. But also the customer organization has a strong opinion in the division of functionalities, since they might also be affected by the architectural decisions later on. Furthermore, the technical environment, which includes software engineering techniques or industry standards available, available design tools and development platform, can influence the architectural decisions. Finally, the background and expertise of the architect influence the selection of architectural techniques to be followed.

Based on the aforementioned principles and the influences on architecture, we distinct three design structures for the functional architecture:

- Modularity: According to Anderson, modular design is "a design technique in which functions are designed in modules that can be combined in subsequent designs". Modularity is related to the decomposition of the software products in several components, their positioning in the system and their connectivity. Modularity in functional architecture has to be given a robust structure, so that each module incorporates a well-defined functionality and can be developed independent of other modules. Flexibility is also an important aspect of modularity, in the sense that the structure should not change often in subsequent releases of the product, but should easily direct new requirements to its current modules or a new functionality in a new module.

- Variability deals with the fact that the product might need to run in different organizational settings and cooperate with multiple products. Consequently, variability is related to the extent to which the various components can differ. Functional variability includes the product's modules that need to interact with different functional components; for example an ERP system used in multiple customer organizations might interact with different products in each organization. We also recognize technical variability, in the sense that technical features may need to differ on different platforms.

Modeling the Functional Architecture of Software Products

As we mentioned earlier, the Functional Architecture reflects a software product's architecture from a usage perspective. Evidently, such a model should resemble the functions performed in the individual user context, or –when we have to do with a corporate customer– the enterprise functions of the customer organization that are supported by the software product.

In figure below we can see an example of the functional architecture of Baan ERP Product. Following the principle of modularity, each module in the FA represents a function in the customer domain (e.g. Requirement Planning, Production, etc). The flows represent interactions between functions or with external products. The principle of variability is also reflected in the functional architecture of the ERP Product, as it should easily run in different operating systems and platforms (technical variability) and in different customer organizations (functional variability). Finally, the interactions with other products or with the user indicate the interfaces that need to be built so that the product can interoperate with external factors.

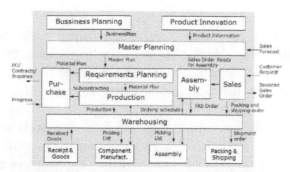

Figure: Functional Architecture of an ERP product

We define the Functional Architecture Model (FAM) as the representation of the primary functionality of a software product, consisting of its main functions and supportive operations. The purpose of designing the FAM is to identify the main functionalities performed by the software product; show the interactions of these functions between each other and with external products; and create a clear overview of how the product should operate in order to satisfy the user's requirements.

In order to model the FA of a software product we borrow the notation and rules of Enterprise Function Diagrams, which are used in the domain of Enterprise Architecture to model the primary process of an enterprise, its physical and administrative functions. Consequently, a Functional Architecture Diagram (FAD) will contain modules that resemble the functions of a software product. A function is defined as a collection of coherent processes, continuously performed within a software system and supporting its use. Functions are implemented in a software product by modules. The interactions between modules are represented in the function diagrams by flows.

In figure below, we can see the FAD of a collaborative authoring tool. This diagram visualizes the product's usage context, and could be useful for the phase of product road mapping as it indicates which modules need to be developed for each functionality of the product, thus the management can plan the development of the product releases. Furthermore, such a diagram could be useful for modeling domain components of the software product in the context of core assets development in the software product line.

Figure: Usage Context for a Collaborative Authoring Tool

For instance, supposing that the functions of Publishing Strategy, Market Intelligence, Reference Management, Reviewing and Image Handling are left out of the first release, we can see the product usage scope of the collaborative authoring tool in figure below. The boxes (Authoring, Version Management, Templates Management, Publishing, etc) are called modules, and correspond to the software product parts that implement the respective functions. In the diagram, we can also see how the modules interact with each other through information flows, by sending and receiving requests, documents etc. An interface needs to be implemented in a module, for each information flow with other modules or external products.

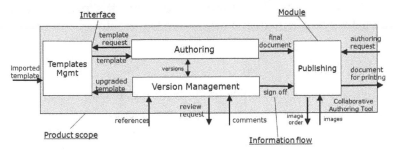

Figure: Product scope

Modular Decomposition

The Functional Architecture of a software product is not limited in the product scope level. Instead, it can be modeled in more layers, supporting the functional decomposition of the product. A module of the software product represents a set of sub-modules which correspond to lower level functions that interoperate to implement the corresponding functionality. On a second FA layer, we could consequently model the functional architecture on the module level. In figure 4 we can see the FAD that visualizes the module scope for the function Authoring. We strongly encourage preserving the consistency between FADs on different levels. For example, in figure 4 we can notice the same external interactions for the module Authoring, as the internal flows between this module and other modules in the FAD of the product scope in figure below.

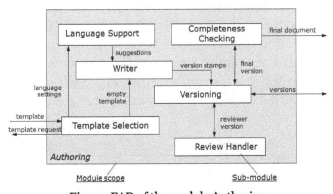

Figure: FAD of the module Authoring

From our experience, we have noticed that the functional architecture is usually modeled in two to three layers. The FADs are designed following the same notation and rules. On the lowest level, each module is supported by features, which represent the processes that constitute the respective function that the module implements. We remind here that functions were defined as collections of processes. A process is defined as an activity, the start and end of which are clearly defined and its execution can be described in terms of needed and delivered data. The features indicate what the software system does and not how it realizes it. They include lower level of details than the module.

The names of features usually start with a verb, to indicate the process they correspond to. Examples are: "open template", "send template to", "select rules", etc. Processes are modeled by Feature

Models, which constitute a modeling tool for the process support functionality in a software product. Riebisch has elaborated on defining feature models for supporting processes in software product lines. The feature models are considered as a criterion for ending the modular decomposition of the functional architecture, as we know that by reaching the process level we have created a sufficient number of views of the functional architecture model.

Reference Architecture

A reference architecture is in essence, a predefined architectural pattern, or set of patterns, possibly partially or completely instantiated, designed, and proven for use in particular business and technical contexts, together with supporting artifacts to enable their use. Often, these artifacts are harvested from previous projects.

In both the Inception and Elaboration phases, the Rational Unified Process or RUP goes on to say, the team should consult its reference architecture as part of the Architectural Analysis activity for the new project. However, RUP further states that "creation of reference architectures is an organizational issue and currently outside the scope of the RUP." This is not an oversight on the part of the RUP far from it. The structure, content, and management of reference architecture should be based on the organization's unique structure and needs. Small organizations, for example, often do a good job of communicating about past projects via low ceremony, face-to-face consultations between team members in the project's development "bullpen," and they might not need a lot of formal documentation. Larger organizations might maintain a repository on the corporate Intranet that team members can consult throughout the project lifecycle. Unfortunately, many large organizations do not take the time to do this well.

As figure below depicts, the RUP consists of four phases and nine disciplines. Iteration is a distinct sequence of activities with a baseline plan and valuation criteria resulting in an internal or external release. It slices through the nine disciplines, drawing from the available activities in each one. The resulting set of tasks comprises what is known as the iteration plan. A given phase may have multiple iterations, and the number is usually a factor of the technical complexity and size of the project. Sample iteration plans for each of the four phases are provided in the RUP.

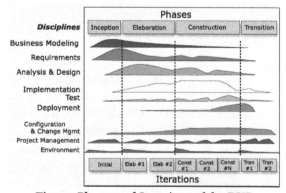

Figure: Phases and Iterations of the RUP

The end of each phase is marked by the completion of a milestone. The milestones for the four phases of the RUP are: Lifecycle Objective, Lifecycle Architecture, Initial Operational Capability, and Product Release.

Unlike waterfall-based process models, the RUP's iterative model acknowledges that activities from the broad spectrum of disciplines (requirements, analysis and design, and so forth) actually take place concurrently throughout the lifecycle of the project.

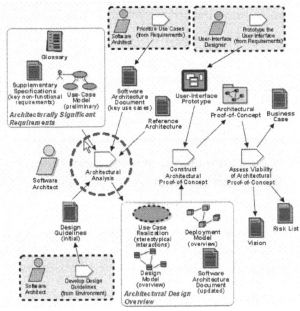

Figure: Architecture Analysis Activity in the Perform Architectural Synthesis Discipline

Reference Architecture Design

The RUP suggests that a reference architecture should be defined along different levels of abstraction, or "views," thereby providing more flexibility in how it can be used. Ideally, these views map to the 4+1 Views of software architecture outlined in the RUP and embodied in the RUP's Software Architecture Document.

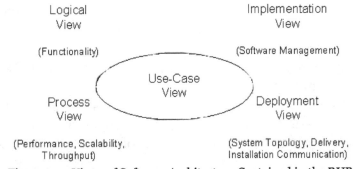

Figure: 4+1 Views of Software Architecture Contained in the RUP

Note that according to the RUP, only the Use Case and Logical Views are required on all projects. The other views should be used if the particular system to be constructed requires them (e.g., the Process View is necessary when there are multiple threads of control; the Deployment View is necessary when the system is to be distributed across more than one node). Although there are certainly many ways to portray reference architecture diagrammatically, I prefer a familiar set of functional layers tied to the Logical View of the 4+1 framework. I also like to expand upon the RUP's definition of reference architecture to include technology compatibility and tool selection for projects as well.

User Interface	Standards and tools to support the user interface and or presentation services (e.g., html, rich, client, dumb terminal)
Business	Standards and tools to support the Business logic (e.g., language, component standards)
Middleware	Standards and tools to support transaction management and interprocess communication (e.g., container services, ipc APIs)
System Software	Standards and tools to support systems management (e.g.,operating systems, database management system)

In addition to the layers shown in figure above, in some cases there might be layers within layers. For example, the System Software layer contains architectural information on both database management systems (DBMS) as well as operating systems.

Deciding how to present the information for the different layers can be a challenge. In general, the presentation must be to-the-point and concise. At a minimum, the organization needs to publish simple matrices/tables that facilitate a quick look up and easy communication of the material.

We also like to include in these matrices real project artifacts from prior efforts. These might be in the form of both paper documentation and actual running code (components) that may be reused.

And finally, we like to add references to both external and internal resources to the matrices. These might be sections of books or Web sites that describe best practices and design strategies. These resources might also reference internal company whitepapers that discuss or review, at length, different architectural choices.

Creating a Reference Architecture

The creation of reference architecture is typically spearheaded by an architecture group. Usually, we are not a fan of formal, permanently appointed architecture groups; many times the individuals in these groups become very savvy about technology but lose sight of the business' needs and how people need to *use* technology. A more effective approach is to set up an informal architecture group that includes representatives from various IT organizational departments (e.g., development, support, operations). Business representatives should also be part of this group. With an informal group, the challenge is to ensure that there is adequate management support and follow-through, and it might be effective to appoint a group member to remind people of their commitments and responsibilities.

Using the layered reference architecture presented in figure above, the group could simply fill in the slots shown in each Table above, drawing upon both their knowledge of the organization's technology and a heavy dose of the best practices they would like to see furthered across all projects.

In summary, getting a reference architecture off the ground requires an effort that combines the effective tools, technology, and approaches currently in place within the organization (i.e., harvesting of existing assets) with an infusion of best practices, suggested patterns, and approaches that the organization thinks will make applications even better and projects more successful.

Using a Reference Architecture

Early in the creation of the project's Vision, it is necessary to assess the impact of the business case on other solutions already in production as well as the benefits the existing reference architecture can bring to the project.

In the RUP, this is the desired outcome of the Architectural Analysis activity, which truly leverages the reference architecture to its fullest. The organization might discover that it needs to adjust its reference architecture in response to this early assessment. For example, requirements might dictate a new middleware service not yet articulated in the existing reference architecture.

For example, suppose an organization's business case calls for implementing a Web Services application that integrates two disparate legacy applications. Web Services requires the exchange of eXtensible Markup Language (XML)-based messages as well as decisions on protocols (i.e., Simple Object Access Protocol (SOAP) vs. XML-Remote Procedure Call (RPC)). If the reference architecture doesn't currently address any of these technologies, then questions will arise as to which standards to follow (e.g., Microsoft Web Services, Java support for Web Services, etc.). If the reference architecture does indicate a preferred development language - perhaps Java - then there will be fewer decisions, but additions to the reference architecture will still be required (e.g., now we have a preferred SOAP implementation standard that requires placement in the reference architecture).

In addition, these new reference items might cascade and affect established architectural standards. Again, using the previous example, because security issues are not as clear-cut for Web Services as they are for more traditional applications, the organization would have to review and possibly adjust its standard security policies.

Quite often, the first project that bumps up against an architectural issue not addressed in the reference architecture will, by default, set new architectural standards for future projects. However, it is still vitally important that the reference architecture be able to absorb the addition without *destroying* all previous standards. It is important to watch for a ripple effect and carefully monitor any decisions to alter standards.

Keeping the Reference Architecture Up to Date

A development history, along with benchmarks, for each project is the key to keeping reference architecture from becoming stale and obsolete. In the RUP, the Activity Prepare for Project Close-Out, found in the Transition Phase, calls for an update of the reference architecture.

Another valuable addition to reference architecture is a description of experiences in supporting applications following implementation. The project team should assess the architectural soundness of applications that turned out to be troublesome in a production environment. Although the team might have made correct decisions, the system's combination of technologies might be just too difficult to support. Note that adding this wisdom is different than harvesting assets for the reference architecture at the end of a project lifecycle.

For example, suppose you have implemented several client-centric applications. Perhaps the architectures are effective and the applications work according to specifications, but support issues, such as software distribution and synchronization of releases, are problematic. The reference architecture might respond to these issues by mandating that, in future applications, the application architecture should follow a thin-client model unless there is demonstrable evidence it won't work. In such a case, direct support issues would have a far-reaching impact on the reference architecture. Yet there wouldn't be a great deal of data on them until well into the application's support cycle.

Making it Work

Ultimately, responsibility for maintaining and continually updating the reference architecture rests in the hands of front-line project management and the architecture group. Project managers must take quite seriously both the *Architecture Analysis* activity (asset consumption) that the RUP suggests during the Inception and Elaboration phases as well as the Prepare for Project Close-Out activity it recommends during the Transition phase. As the RUP states, it is in closing out the project that architectural fruits are harvested. However, as we have discussed, to be of real use, the reference architecture must be continually updated and refined, not only with information in prior project artifacts, but also with data gathered from managing applications in a production environment.

Senior management must look beyond the short-term tactical costs of constructing and maintaining a reference infrastructure and see the strategic importance and payback of having such an architecture in place. Although the creation, care, and feeding of a reference architecture requires resources - to assist with project compliance and for potential common component enhancements - these resources may simply matrix over from existing projects when services are needed.

Ultimately, organizations don't want project teams to agonize over what programming language to use or what logging API to follow. They don't want their teams trying to figure out what pattern is best to use when there is a need to separate externalized information from its internal state. Nor do they want them pondering over whether to use Model 1 or Model 2 architecture when building J2EE applications. All of these decisions should already be made for every project, waiting to be extracted from the reference architecture. And if choices *do* need to be made, then the options should be few and clearly articulated via the reference architecture.

A reference architecture isn't meant to stifle creativity, but rather to enforce commonality across projects. Ultimately, the supreme goal is to reduce total cost of ownership (TCO) for technology usage in the organization. Organizations report today that vertical reuse on projects is common. Horizontal reuse across applications is much more rare, especially in medium- to large-scale organizations. Here there is low-hanging fruit ripe for the picking.

For an organization, introducing a technology is akin to administering a drug. It's important to monitor reactions closely and anticipate side-effects. Establishing a reference architecture infrastructure that will continually evolve and grow is one way to ensure that the side-effects will be much more manageable.

Resource-oriented Architecture

Resource Oriented Architectures (ROA) are based upon the concept of resource; each resource is a directly accessible distributed component that is handled through a standard, common interface making possible resources handling. RESTFul platforms based on REST development technology enable the creation of ROA.

The main ROA concepts are the following

- Resource
  - o Anything that's important enough to be referenced as a thing itself
- Resource name
  - o Unique identification of the resource
- Resource representation
  - o Useful information about the current state of a resource
- Resource link
  - o Link to another representation of the same or another resource
- Resource interface
  - o Uniform interface for accessing the resource and manipulating its state

The resource interface semantics is based on the one of HTTP operations. The following table summarizes the resource methods and how they could be implemented[1] using the HTTP protocol:

Resource method	Description	HTTP operation
createResource	Create a new resource (and the corresponding unique identifier)	PUT
getResourceRepresentation	Retrieve the Representation of the resource	GET
deleteResource	Delete the resource (optionally including linked resources)	DELETE (referred resource only), POST (can be used if the delete is including linked resources)
modifyResource	Modify the resource	POST
getMetaInformation	Obtain meta information about the resource	HEAD

In terms of platform implementation specification, each resource must be associated to a unique identifier that usually consists of the URL exhibiting the resource interface.

Designing Resource Oriented Architectures

One of the most important decisions that have to be taken in the design of a Resource Oriented Architecture is what must be considered a resource (by definition, each component deserving to be directly represented and accessed).

This is one of the main differences between ROA and SOA where in the latter one the single, directly accessible distributed component, represents one or more business functionalities that often process different potential resources. Such resources are credited candidates for being considered resources in a ROA, thus deserving to be represented as distributed components (e.g. features offered by WFS, registers or items of registries/catalogues, WFS and Registry/Catalogue services functionalities).

Once having defined the granularity of the resources composing the ROA it is necessary to define, for each resource type, the content of the messages for invoking the methods as well as the corresponding responses. More in detail, beside the definition of resource types (and sub types), an addressing schema for accessing instances of those resource types, a response schema (response is not binary) and a mapping of logical functions to the HTTP operations. All resources in a ROA are accessed via the same common interface which is plain HTTP. It is worth noting that the usage of a common interface does not necessarily mean that all the necessary information enabling interoperability and collaboration among resources are available. The necessity of integrating a standard common interface description with some specific service instance aspects has been already addressed in other existing solutions such as, for instance, for the OGC WPS execute operation where the specific processing detailed information are offered through the describeProcess operation. In a ROA, this information completes the description of the resources and their interface thus enabling: i) system integration and interoperability through tools for the creation of resource clients, ii) message validation processes, and iii) model driven development (top-down approach) for which a typed description of the interface and its operation is necessary. In the REST technology such a description is based on WADL documents that play the same role of WSDL in the W3C Web Services platform; both languages use XML schema for expressing the structure of exchanged messages.

Implementing Resource Oriented Architectures

Here we reason on costs and benefits of implementing a ROA starting from an already available SOA. Where necessary we will focus on OGC services and INSPIRE network services architecture that are both based on such distributed architecture model. The debate on ROA (and REST) is spanning on different abstraction levels and in particular most of the discussion is focusing on REST rather than ROA design patterns. We present and reason on three different scenarios, two of them (REST) platform dependent and the other one aiming at reasoning at the abstract architecture level where ROA is conceived.

The cases we consider are the following:

- Weakly REST compliant architecture: it is based on distributed components offering their functionalities through the HTTP operations.

- RESTFul compliant architecture: it is based on distributed components faithfully implementing the concept of common resource interface and of binding.

- Resource Oriented Architecture: it is composed by distributed components representing all the resource types deserving to be defined and exposed in the architecture.

It is clear that the first and the second category are principally related with REST and in particular with distributed component binding and interface aspects. These two views are in accordance with who is claiming that REST is a SOA development platform. The third one instead is more centring the architectural issue abstracting away from specific development platforms; this is the pure ROA where all the resources have an URI.

Event-driven Architecture

An event-driven architecture consists of event producers that generate a stream of events, and event consumers that listen for the events.

Events are delivered in near real time, so consumers can respond immediately to events as they occur. Producers are decoupled from consumers — a producer doesn't know which consumers are listening. Consumers are also decoupled from each other, and every consumer sees all of the events. This differs from a Competing Consumers pattern, where consumers pull messages from a queue and a message is processed just once (assuming no errors). In some systems, such as IoT, events must be ingested at very high volumes.

An event driven architecture can use a pub/sub model or an event stream model:

- Pub/sub: The messaging infrastructure keeps track of subscriptions. When an event is published, it sends the event to each subscriber. After an event is received, it cannot be replayed, and new subscribers do not see the event.

- Event streaming: Events are written to a log. Events are strictly ordered (within a partition) and durable. Clients don't subscribe to the stream, instead a client can read from any part of the stream. The client is responsible for advancing its position in the stream. That means a client can join at any time, and can replay events.

On the consumer side, there are some common variations:

- Simple event processing: An event immediately triggers an action in the consumer. For example, you could use Azure Functions with a Service Bus trigger, so that a function executes whenever a message is published to a Service Bus topic.

- Complex event processing: A consumer processes a series of events, looking for patterns in the event data, using a technology such as Azure Stream Analytics or Apache Storm. For example, you could aggregate readings from an embedded device over a time window, and generate a notification if the moving average crosses a certain threshold.

- Event stream processing: Use a data streaming platform, such as Azure IoT Hub or Apache Kafka, as a pipeline to ingest events and feed them to stream processors. The stream processors act to process or transform the stream. There may be multiple stream processors for different subsystems of the application. This approach is a good fit for IoT workloads.

The source of the events may be external to the system, such as physical devices in an IoT solution. In that case, the system must be able to ingest the data at the volume and throughput that is required by the data source.

In the logical diagram above, each type of consumer is shown as a single box. In practice, it's common to have multiple instances of a consumer, to avoid having the consumer become a single point of failure in system. Multiple instances might also be necessary to handle the volume and frequency of events. Also, a single consumer might process events on multiple threads. This can create challenges if events must be processed in order, or require exactly-once semantics.

Use of event-driven Architecture

- Multiple subsystems must process the same events.

- Real-time processing with minimum time lag.

- Complex event processing, such as pattern matching or aggregation over time windows.

- High volume and high velocity of data, such as IoT.

Benefits

- Producers and consumers are decoupled.

- No point-to point-integrations. It's easy to add new consumers to the system.

- Consumers can respond to events immediately as they arrive.

- Highly scalable and distributed.

- Subsystems have independent views of the event stream.

Challenges

- Guaranteed delivery. In some systems, especially in IoT scenarios, it's crucial to guarantee that events are delivered.

- Processing events in order or exactly once. Each consumer type typically runs in multiple instances, for resiliency and scalability. This can create a challenge if the events must be processed in order (within a consumer type), or if the processing logic is not idempotent.

Software Architectural Model

Software architecture involves the high level structure of software system abstraction, by using decomposition and composition, with architectural style and quality attributes. A software architecture design must conform to the major functionality and performance requirements of the system, as well as satisfy the non-functional requirements such as reliability, scalability, portability, and availability.

Software architecture must describe its group of components, their connections, interactions among them and deployment configuration of all components.

Software architecture can be defined in many ways –

- UML (Unified Modeling Language) : UML is one of object-oriented solutions used in software modeling and design.

- Architecture View Model (4+1 view model) : Architecture view model represents the functional and non-functional requirements of software application.

- ADL (Architecture Description Language) : ADL defines the software architecture formally and semantically.

UML

UML stands for Unified Modeling Language. It is a pictorial language used to make software blueprints. UML was created by Object Management Group (OMG). The UML 1.0 specification draft was proposed to the OMG in January 1997. It serves as a standard for software requirement analysis and design documents which are the basis for developing a software.

UML can be described as a general purpose visual modeling language to visualize, specify, construct, and document a software system. Although UML is generally used to model software system, it is not limited within this boundary. It is also used to model non software systems such as process flows in a manufacturing unit.

The elements are like components which can be associated in different ways to make a complete UML picture, which is known as a diagram. So, it is very important to understand the different diagrams to implement the knowledge in real-life systems. We have two broad categories of diagrams and they are further divided into sub-categories i.e. Structural Diagrams and Behavioral Diagrams.

Structural Diagrams

Structural diagrams represent the static aspects of a system. These static aspects represent those parts of a diagram which forms the main structure and is therefore stable. These static parts are represented by classes, interfaces, objects, components and nodes.

The structural diagrams are sub-divided as (shown in the following image) :

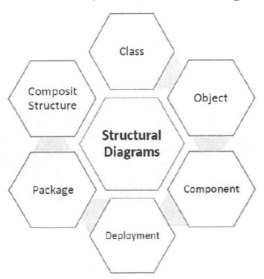

The following table provides a brief description of these diagrams:

Diagram	Description
Class	Represents the object orientation of a system. Shows how classes are statically related.
Object	Represents a set of objects and their relationships at runtime and also represent the static view of the system.
Component	Describes all the components, their interrelationship, interactions and interface of the system.
Composite structure	Describes inner structure of component including all classes, interfaces of the component, etc.
Package	Describes the package structure and organization. Covers classes in the package and packages within another package.
Deployment	Deployment diagrams are a set of nodes and their relationships. These nodes are physical entities where the components are deployed.

Behavioral Diagrams

Behavioral diagrams basically capture the dynamic aspect of a system. Dynamic aspects are basically the changing/moving parts of a system. UML has the following types of behavioral diagrams (shown in the image given below) –

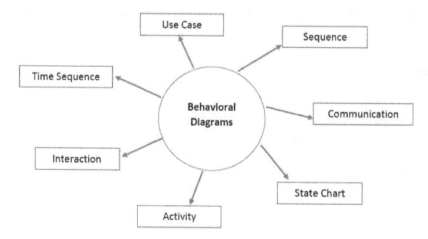

The following table provides a brief description of these diagram:

Diagram	Description
Use case	Describes the relationships among the functionalities and their internal/external controllers. These controllers are known as actors.
Activity	Describes the flow of control in a system. It consists of activities and links. The flow can be sequential, concurrent, or branched.
State Machine/state chart	Represents the event driven state change of a system. It basically describes the state change of a class, interface, etc. Used to visualize the reaction of a system by internal/external factors.
Sequence	Visualizes the sequence of calls in a system to perform a specific functionality.

Interaction Overview	Combines activity and sequence diagrams to provide a control flow overview of system and business process.
Communication	Same as sequence diagram, except that it focuses on the object's role. Each communication is associated with a sequence order, number plus the past messages.
Time Sequenced	Describes the changes by messages in state, condition and events.

Architecture View Model

A model is a complete, basic, and simplified description of software architecture which is composed of multiple views from a particular perspective or viewpoint.

A view is a representation of an entire system from the perspective of a related set of concerns. It is used to describe the system from the viewpoint of different stakeholders such as end-users, developers, project managers, and testers.

4+1 View Model

The 4+1 View Model was designed by Philippe Kruchten to describe the architecture of a software–intensive system based on the use of multiple and concurrent views. It is a multiple view model that addresses different features and concerns of the system. It standardizes the software design documents and makes the design easy to understand by all stakeholders.

It is an architecture verification method for studying and documenting software architecture design and covers all the aspects of software architecture for all stakeholders. It provides four essential views:

- The logical view or conceptual view: It describes the object model of the design.

- The process view: It describes the activities of the system, captures the concurrency and synchronization aspects of the design.

- The physical view: It describes the mapping of software onto hardware and reflects its distributed aspect.

- The development view: It describes the static organization or structure of the software in its development of environment.

This view model can be extended by adding one more view called scenario view or use case view for end-users or customers of software systems. It is coherent with other four views and are utilized to illustrate the architecture serving as "plus one" view, (4+1) view model. The following figure describes the software architecture using five concurrent views (4+1) model.

Reason for Calling it 4+1 Instead of 5

The use case view has a special significance as it details the high level requirement of a system while other views details — how those requirements are realized. When all other four views are completed, it's effectively redundant. However, all other views would not be possible without it. The following image and table shows the 4+1 view in detail:

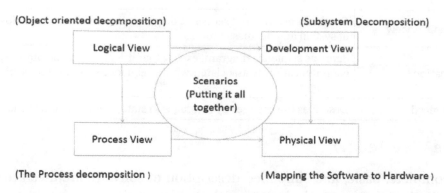

	Logical	Process	Development	Physical	Scenario
Description	Shows the component (Object) of system as well as their interaction	Shows the processes and Workflow rules of system and how those processes communicate, focuses on dynamic view of system	Gives building block views of system and describe static organization of the system modules	Shows the installation, configuration and deployment of software application	Shows the design is complete by performing validation and illustration
Viewer or Stake holder	End-User, Analysts and Designer	Integrators & developers	Programmer and software project managers	System engineer, operators, system administrators and system installers	All the views of their views and evaluators
Consider	Functional requirements	Non Functional Requirements	Software Module organization (Software management reuse, constraint of tools)	Nonfunctional requirement regarding to underlying hardware	System Consistency and validity
UML – Diagram	Class, State, Object, sequence, Communication Diagram	Activity Diagram	Component, Package diagram	Deployment diagram	Use case diagram

Architecture Description Languages (ADLs)

An ADL is a language that provides syntax and semantics for defining a software architecture. It is a notation specification which provides features for modeling a software system's conceptual architecture, distinguished from the system's implementation.

ADLs must support the architecture components, their connections, interfaces, and configurations which are the building block of architecture description. It is a form of expression for use in architecture descriptions and provides the ability to decompose components, combine the components, and define the interfaces of components.

An architecture description language is a formal specification language, which describes the software features such as processes, threads, data, and sub-programs as well as hardware component such as processors, devices, buses, and memory.

It is hard to classify or differentiate an ADL and a programming language or a modeling language. However, there are following requirements for a language to be classified as an ADL –

- It should be appropriate for communicating the architecture to all concerned parties.

- It should be suitable for tasks of architecture creation, refinement, and validation.

- It should provide a basis for further implementation, so it must be able to add information to the ADL specification to enable the final system specification to be derived from the ADL.

- It should have the ability to represent most of the common architectural styles.

- It should support analytical capabilities or provide quick generating prototype implementations.

Software Architectural Style

The architectural styles that are used while designing the software as follows:

Data-centered Architecture

- The data store in the file or database is occupying at the center of the architecture.

- Store data is access continuously by the other components like an update, delete, add, modify from the data store.

- Data-centered architecture helps integrity.

- Pass data between clients using the blackboard mechanism.

- The processes are independently executed by the client components.

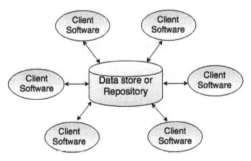

Data centered architecture

Data-flow Architecture

- This architecture is applied when the input data is converted into a series of manipulative components into output data.

- A pipe and filter pattern is a set of components called as filters.

- Filters are connected through pipes and transfer data from one component to the next component.

- The flow of data degenerates into a single line of transform then it is known as batch sequential.

Call and Return Architectures

This architecture style allows achieving a program structure which is easy to modify.

Following are the sub styles exist in this category:

Main Program or Subprogram Architecture

- The program is divided into smaller pieces hierarchically.
- The main program invokes many of program components in the hierarchy that program components are divided into subprogram.

Remote Procedure Call Architecture

- The main program or subprogram components are distributed in network of multiple computers.
- The main aim is to increase the performance.

Object-oriented Architectures

- This architecture is the latest version of call-and-return architecture.
- It consists of the bundling of data and methods.

Layered Architectures

- The different layers are defined in the architecture. It consists of outer and inner layer.
- The components of outer layer manage the user interface operations.
- Components execute the operating system interfacing at the inner layer.
- The inner layers are application layer, utility layer and the core layer.
- In many cases, It is possible that more than one pattern is suitable and the alternate architectural style can be designed and evaluated.

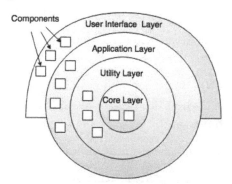

Layered Architecture

Software Architecture Description

The ability to clearly and concisely describe (and document) the architecture for a solution is a key skill for architects, since the Architecture Description forms the "common language" by which the technical team gains a consistent understanding of the system to be delivered; additionally the Architecture Description is the starting point for other views and perspectives which may need to be created to communicate to other (non-technical) stakeholders. Another important role of the AD is to quickly and consistently bring new members of the technical team up-to-speed with the architecture of the system; as such the AD must be maintained during the SDLC to ensure it reflects the current state of the architecture for the system.

The AD provides detailed architecture communication and acts as a repository of architecture decisions for current and new team members, and for future maintainers of the solution – "If it's not documented it doesn't exist". Architects should not underestimate the level of writing and communication skills necessary to be able to clearly and concisely communicate complex in a clear and understandable manner, since much of a typical AD is made up of narrative text.

Architects must be capable of delivering Architecture Descriptions in the preferred ADL of an organization, and to guide the selection of an appropriate ADL if necessary. The Architect must be able to apply judgment with regard to the level of rigor required for a particular project and the level of detail that the AD must deliver to support the needs of the solution through the entire SDLC. The process of Architecting is contingent on the application of experience and knowledge, not simply following a prescribed set of deliverables – all elements of the AD must add value and contribute to the success of the solution during the relevant phases of the SDLC. As such, the architect must be aware of the purpose and value of each component of the architecture description and be able to recognize (and justify) when to utilize (or not) each component of the AD.

Architecture description is the end-product of an architecture development process that begins with exploring and understanding the context within which a technology solution will be deployed (e.g., business architecture, business drivers, stakeholder concerns), constraints and risks, vision for and purpose of the system, its goal(s), and relevant usage scenarios. The Architecture Description will not contain only models, but also textual and other artifacts which provide context and background to the models, in addition to providing an overall "design narrative" for the architecture.

The AD should support the necessary views and perspectives needed to satisfy the requirements to both model the solution, and communicate the architecture to the key stakeholders (not just technologists). For example, a successful AD should:

- Be suitable for communicating architecture to all interested parties.

- Support the tasks of architecture creation, refinement, and validation.

- Provide a basis for further implementation – so it must be able to add information to the AD to enable the final system specification to be derived from the AD.

- Provide the ability to represent most of the common architectural styles.

- Support analytical capabilities or provide quick generating prototype implementations.

- Provide Architecture vision and views:

  o Conceptual Descriptions and Notations: Standard notations for representing architectural concepts that help promote mutual communication and understanding of high-level ideas, sketches and solution concepts.

  o Logical Descriptions and Notations: Notations and descriptions that promote the embodiment of early design decisions, and creation of a transferable abstraction of a system, comprised of components and connections among them.

  o Implementation Descriptions and Notations: Specific, concrete and implementation-ready descriptions of envisioned system that allow analysis, feasibility testing and implementation of architectural design decisions.

- Summarize major competitive products.

- Provide an analysis of pros/cons in features and in technical implementations.

- Document patterns used.

- Document principles.

- Explicitly state known constraints and risks.

- Describe value to the business.

- State existing standards and strategies which will guide the development of the architecture.

Software Architecture Analysis Method

Software Architecture Analysis Method (SAAM) shows how the software architecture meets certain properties through a method that explains and analyzes software architecture. These properties are functionality, structure, and allocation. SAAM quickly assess many quality attributes such as modifiability, portability, extensibility and integrability. It can also assess quality aspects of software architectures such as performance or reliability.

The main objective of SAAM is architectural suitability and risk analysis. The direct and indirect scenarios are identified as shown in fig. The impact analysis counts the affected components. The objects are analyzed in the logical views of Architectural documentation.

The steps involved in the SAAM are:

1. Scenarios development.

2. Architecture description.

3. Scenarios classification and prioritization.

4. Indirect scenarios evaluation individually.

5. Scenario Interaction assessment.

6. Overall evaluation of the interaction.

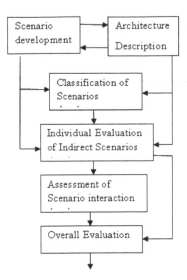

Figure: SAAM steps

Software Architecture Recovery

The software architecture of a program or computing system is the structure or structures of the system, which comprise software elements, the externally visible properties of those elements, and the relationships among them. Software architecture design is concerned with gross organization and global control structure of a system. Architecture bridges the gap between the requirements and implementation of the system. Software architecture is very important concern due to understanding, analysis, reusability, evolution and management of legacy systems.

Architecture recovery is a process of identifying and extracting higher level of abstractions from existing software systems. Architecture recovery and reengineering to handle legacy code is critical for large and complex systems. Architecture recovery deals with the issues of recovering the past design decisions that has been taken by the experts during the development of a system. These are decisions that has been lost due to some reasons; not documented, document revisions or developer have left or unknown (i.e. assumptions not initially taken in account). In architecture recovery the research is continue on issues of interoperability: techniques for detecting component mismatch and bridging them. The recovery process can be assisted by different tools available in the market like Dali, PBS, Imagix4D and Bauhaus. No one tool can perform all the tasks required for architecture recovery. So we used our custom built tool DRT having excellent features.

Architecture Representation/Properties

Architecture has different stakeholders with different concerns. Architectural representations enable software developers to explicitly describe, access and manage the architecture of software systems. Architecture representation consist of structural and non-structural information about software architecture. Structural information are components and connectors describing the configuration of a system and non structural information are architectural properties. Architectural properties are for example, safety patterns, communications patterns, behavioral patterns, structural patterns and creational patterns. The recognition of different type of similar patterns is very important knowledge for understanding the existing legacy systems and architecture recovery. The user understands the conceptual and concrete architecture of the system through architectural documents, design patterns, source code and architectural properties. The architecture properties can not be ignored during the recovery of different architecture artifacts.

Architectural Descriptions

The language for specifying an architecture should ideally be expressive, well-defined, abstract, concise and compact For example ADL for specifying an architecture recovery results is used that permits formal reasoning and supported by tools. Most ADL are formally defined but their actual use in industry is very limited. It is still interesting to evaluate whether formality is of importance to architecture extraction. A lexical based regular extraction technique is used as a specification language to extract different artifacts from source code of different programming languages. It allows the user to use the specifications according to the requirements based on action and analysis in the regular expressions for task at hand.

Related Approaches

There are different approaches for reverse engineering, which can be attempted at different level of abstractions. These approaches are related to our work. The structural recovery techniques are mostly used for components recovery. The Murphy's Reflection model allow the user to test the high level conceptual model of the system against the existing high level relations between the components of the system. The recovery approaches are classified as follows according to type of information they provide:

- Data Flow based approaches
- Knowledge based approaches
- Design patter based approaches
- Program slicing based approaches
- Formal method based approaches
- Program comprehension based approaches
- Domain based approaches
- Clustering based approaches
- Concept analysis approaches
- Machine Learning approaches
- Metrics Based approaches
- Structural Based approaches

We used the unification of best approaches for extraction of different artifacts from the source code and documents. The best features of domain based, program comprehension based, design pattern based and clustering based recovery approaches are used to recover the architecture of software systems under study. Regular expressions are used to write different pattern specifications to extract desired artifact at different levels of abstractions.

Framework for Architecture Recovery

The Proposed Framework integrates the existing architecture recovery tools to support architecture recovery process. In many cases, architectural information is available as block-line diagrams. However, most architecture information is inherent and hidden in different styles and views of source code and design documentation. The extraction of architectural information is required using different techniques and tools.

Figure below sketches an overview of the proposed framework for an architecture recovery. The input of the recovery process is the source code, design documentation, domain knowledge, artifacts recovered from pattern based, clustering techniques and expert knowledge if any experts or rational exists. Finally results are represented in different formats and styles.

The recovery of design documentation and domain knowledge delivers additional information into already existing abstractions such as data flow diagrams and support the generation of additional software views, for example state transition diagrams, component diagrams and architecture descriptions.

Source code and required artifacts can be extracted with the help of reverse engineering tools. Reverse engineering tools perform static analysis on the code and extract information like call graphs, cross-reference tables, data flow diagrams, quality metrics, hierarchies in classes, relationship and other useful information.

Reverse engineering tools provide a higher level of abstraction since information that is not of interest for the specific view is excluded. The results of reverse engineering tools are analyzed and verified with some of the available source of information (documents, source code and comments available in the source code). User knowledge is incorporated in the tool to write different lexical specifications. RE tool generate different views which can be used to recover the architecture of the system. Similarly we can use the bottom up approach and can take artifacts as an input and can generate different software views.

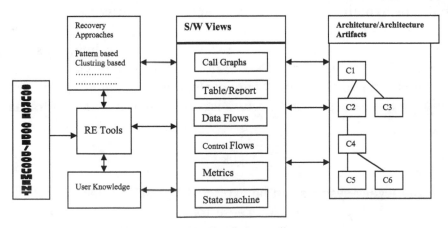

Figure: Framework for architecture recovery

Based on our experience and knowledge we determined the following strategy for architecture recovery:

1. Study the different architecture recovery approaches (such as Domain based, Design patter based, clustering based etc).

2. Develop architecture conceptual model and formed architecture hypothesis regarding the system and its structure.

3. Analyze, verify and refine the architecture hypothesis against the software system under study.

4. Generate different software views and architecture styles of the examined system.

5. Iterative Use of architecture recovery Process.

6. Use the reverse engineering tools.

7. Conducted a case study on the code of five different programming languages software.

8. Used existing documents for understanding of system structure and its components.

Recovery Process

The selection of architecture recovery process is the key concern for extracting the artifacts from the legacy system architecture. Different research groups define the process according to the nature of the system. Recovery Process adopted in our study consists of following Phases.

1) Architecture concepts

2) Legacy architecture analysis

3) Extraction

4) Abstraction

5) Evaluation

6) Presentation.

In first step we built the hypothesis about the architecture of the existing system. In second phase we analyze the hypothesis developed in the first phase with the help of tools. The next phase extracts the different artifacts from the system using extraction techniques and Reverse Engineering tools. Abstraction process produces architecture styles and views at different level of abstractions. In evaluation stage, the results are evaluated and compared with existing sources of information. Finally the recovered architecture is represented in different formats, styles, and UML notations.

Tool Support

The artifacts from the legacy systems can be extracted by using different tools available in the market like Imagix 4D, Rigi and Refine/C. These tools have certain limitations like language dependency and compiled code. Due to these reasons we used custom built DRT which supports the limitations mentioned above. The results of extracted artifacts from different programming languages source code are shown in Table given below. Our custom-oriented tool supports the following features:

1) It is language independent and used in a study of source code and documents of five different programming languages to extract different required artifacts.

2) It takes source code as input which may be incomplete, uncompilied or have errors.

3) User can write specification of similar types to extract artifacts from code and documents of different programming languages software's.

4) Artifacts can be presented in different formats and styles.

5) Internal/External knowledge can be included in the tool to extract the desired artifacts.

6) The matched patterns may be further analyzed to extract further relationships between the patterns and may be represented in different formats.

7) The vocabulary of the tool can be extended according to nature of maintenance task at hand and requirement of the source code.

8) The hierarchal and abstract pattern specifications may be used to extract the required artifacts.

9) It can filter out the false matches by action pattern specifications.

Table: Extracted artifacts

Software	Size on	Lines of	Files		Include	Functions	Blank lines	Lines of Comments
	disk	Source code in KLOC	Total Files	Code files	files			
Alligance Game/C++	823MB	450	7629	1341	3463	612	71964	74679
Elm/C++	8.05MB	35	479	455	905	422	6566	7686
Tac_Plus/C	592KB	20	50	50	153	310	3181	2600
Mining/Java	150KB	6	6	6	11	126	684	1088
Monica/VB	2.50MB	18	50	33	-	621	5	50
Drawing Editor/Pascal	1.53MB	8	45	10	-	252	847	524
Client Messaging/Cobol	1.40 MB	20	47	23	-	-	194	7000

In addition to above artifacts extracted in the Table above, the specifications can be used to extract further artifacts required for architecture recovery. The technique has been used to extract classes, inheritance, Cobol files, Record formats, functions, function calls and the relations between different entities. For example the following specification is used to extract different procedure names from a Source code of Pascal program as shown in table.

Pattern: (\procedure|Procedure)((\s+\w+\d+)|(.*))

Similarly we can write different specification to extract our required artifacts from source code of different programming language. Expressions allow us to attach actions and analysis when expression match with desired pattern. The few constraints can also be placed on the condition of system artifacts. Different pattern specification can be written even to extract artifacts from text file having associations in different data attributes. The nested specifications can also be used to extract the required artifacts.

The regular expression patterns designed by the other programmers become difficult by the novice users to understand. So we can use comments in the regular expression syntax to explain the specification of patterns as shown in the following pattern specification.

Pattern: (?#comments)\{(.*)\}

Table: Extracted from pascal code

.+commandhandling.pas		20	procedure
HandleNewCommand;			
**	22	procedure	InstallAppCommands;
**	28	procedure	andleAbout(theWindow
: WindowRef);			
**	34	procedure	HandleNewCommand;
**	130	procedure	InstallAppCommand

In our case study our concentrated on Cobol legacy code because still industry is converting the legacy systems of Cobol into new software applications. The following pattern specification is used to extract the Cobol file name from Source code of (Human Resource Program) developed in Cobol.

Pattern: FD\s+\w+

We can also extract the complete file and record structuresfrom the source code of COBOL by different patternspecifications. These specifications further may be used forrecovering the ERD model of COBOL applications.

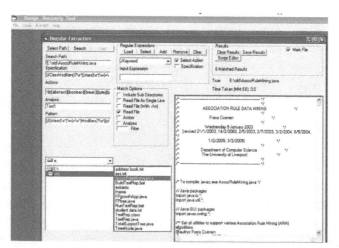

We use the regular expression specifications at different abstraction levels to extract the desired artifacts. For example the following pattern specifications are used to extract Java classes from the source code of Java applications.

Pattern: ((class)\s*(\w)+\s*\{})

Pattern will extract only classes without extends and implements functions of Java classes. We use the above pattern specification to further extract the derived classes with extends and implements arguments in pattern 2.

Pattern:

(JClasModifiers)?\s*((Class)((extends)\s*(\w)+)?\s*((implements)\s* (\w)+)?(\s*(,)\s*(\w+))*\s*\{})

In pattern the definition of JClasModifiers is abstracted. Similarly we can use lower to higher level of abstractions to extract our desired artifacts. The specifications are also designed to represent the relationships between the extracted artifacts which are further used for recovering architecture of different software systems.

Similarly we can write following pattern specification to extract all procedures, functions and property procedure from source code of Visual basic.

Pattern: (VBproc|VBfun|VBprop)

The pattern specifications of VBproc, Vbfun, Vbprop are as given below in Pattern 1a, Patten 1b and Pattern 1c.

Pattern1a : ((Private|Public)\s*)?\s*(Static)?\bSub\b\s*(\w+).

Pattern1b: ((Private|Public)\s*)?\s*(Static)?\bFunction\b\s*(\w+).

Pattern1c: ((Private|Public)\s*)?\s*(Static)?\s*Property\s*(Get|Let|Set)\s* (\w+).

The legacy systems may have source code of million lines. The artifacts extraction speed is concerned while extracting artifacts from large systems. The Table given below shows the time taken by our tool for extracting artifacts from Tacacs source code.

Tacacs Source Code	Time Taken	No of artifacts Extracted
Scanning complete code	:57	19987
Include Files	0:0	153
Function calls	0:0	242
Comments	0:1	1708

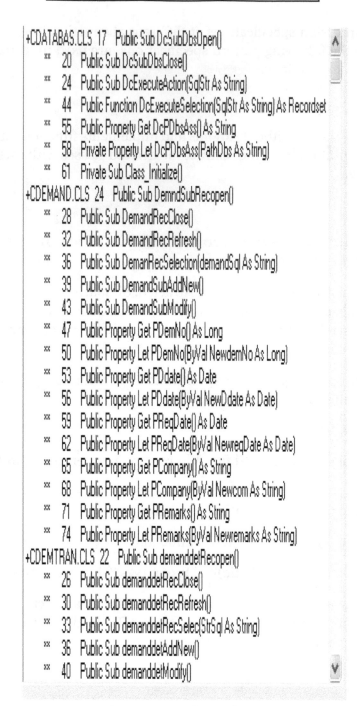

Figure: Extracted procedures

Software Blueprint

The goal of any software planning effort should be to analyze the business requirements and translate that understanding into a specification that facilitates the development process as efficiently as possible.

If you don't know where you're going, it is difficult to get there and impossible to know when you have arrived. Most planning efforts proceed by fanning out and mapping everything as they go, hoping that the end result will include a route to the ultimate destination. They craft their planning deliverables in ad hoc fashion as they go. The functional specification ends up becoming an apparently random maze designed to bewilder and befuddle the developers.

This problem is inevitable when you don't have a clear planning goal defined from the onset. The software blueprint defines a tangible goal for the planning process in the same way that a Form 1040 defines a tangible goal for the tax preparation process. It should provide developers with exactly the type of information they need to construct a program, in the same way that a house blueprint provides the construction crew with exactly the information they need to build a house.

While analogies and comparisons are never perfect, they do help make ideas more familiar and meaningful. House building is probably the most commonly cited analogy for software development. There certainly are a lot of similarities, but there are a lot of differences as well.

Software development is a very customized process. However, house building can also be highly customized. The elements that make up a house are fairly simple. Floors, walls, doors, and windows make up every house. Likewise, there is a fairly simple set of pieces that make up every software project. If we can arrange these pieces into a standard blueprint that organizes them, then that blueprint should be all we need to describe most software projects effectively for the builder's purposes.

A software blueprint is a single, simple, and standardized format to specify software requirements. Builders couldn't be expected to construct a new house without a blueprint, yet software developers are routinely asked to build software without an equivalent blueprint to work from.

Most software specifications do not even begin to serve as an adequate blueprint. They are designed to serve many purposes, but not specifically to meet the needs of the developers. They do not provide developers with the exact information they require, at the necessary level of detail and consistency, and in an easily accessible format.

If software were a house, here is how the usual planning and construction process might proceed:

1. The salesperson initiates contact with the buyer and tells the project manager what the buyers are prepared to spend.

2. The project manager has several meetings with the buyers. He gets a general idea of what they are looking for and prepares a Vision Document documenting the problems with their current house and specifying what size house the clients need. The Vision Document cites the projected cost (coincidently just a bit more than the buyers said they were willing to spend) and describes how much they will gain compared to their current home.

3. The homeowners think that sounds pretty good, so they meet with the house designer every day for the better part of a year discussing what kind of colors they like, what kind of dimmer switches annoy them, and the hours of the day when they use the bathroom and kitchen.

4. The house designer collects all the information, including tax returns, magazine pictures from Better Homes and Gardens, and poetry composed by the homeowners to describe their vision of the new house.

5. The house designer prepares some usage scenarios which summarize the times that the homeowners are likely to use the garage door opener as well as some transition diagrams illustrating in detail their expected traffic patterns in the new house. He bundles these up with the magazine pictures provided by the prospective owners, and hands all this to the construction supervisor.

6. The construction supervisor, already told what the house will consist of, what the buyers will pay, and when they need it completed, goes about the task of fabricating a construction plan and cost breakdown which reflect the timeline and total cost already predefined. The detailed estimate, tailored to meet the predetermined cost, reassures the steering team that their initial estimates were right on.

7. The construction supervisor goes about gathering a construction team whose members laugh or cry, according to their particular nature, when they are told what the house will include, what it will cost, and when they are expected to complete construction.

8. The construction supervisor hands off the house plan to the construction crew. In due course, the crew sets about to somehow build a "bedroom with two doors" and a kitchen that "radiates warmth" as they understand it from the documents they were given.

9. The management team, distracted with planning future houses, doesn't pay much attention to the builders for a few months. The homeowners are too busy at their current jobs to offer much information. After all, they already took too much time off for all that earlier planning.

10. The builders aren't sure where those two doors in the bedroom should be. They ask the planner and he tells them that the information is right there in the owner's childhood diary. The builders give up and put one into the hall and one into the bath.

11. Finally when the house is nearly complete, the homeowners make a walkthrough. They list about 179 first pass changes, citing the fact that it clearly says in the wife's diary that she always wanted a door to the patio from her bedroom. Oh, by the way, where IS the patio that was inferred by that passage?

12. The construction supervisor is sacked for not including the patio, and the crew, already far over budget and months late, works far into the night to make the changes.

That is pretty much the typical scenario in the software business. Needless to say, no home construction company could survive very long if it operated this way. In reality, the life expectancy for software firms is not high.

So how can this scenario occur so frequently in the software industry? In fairness, creating software is not as straightforward and clean-cut as building a house. There are many more variables and far fewer standard materials and methods. Yet, there are many basic lessons from home construction that seem to escape the notice of software builders.

First, you can't promise the customers exactly what they want for exactly what they would like to pay. Sure that may be a strategy for getting a sale, but not necessarily a formula for running a successful business.

Second, you can estimate the cost of a house pretty well just by knowing the square feet enclosed. Based on only that one metric, you can tell the owners within a narrow range what their house will cost, only adjusted for any high-quality extras they might want. There is no such square footage metric for software, so the estimation process is infinitely more difficult.

Third, you can't build a house based on traffic flow diagrams and room modeling charts that describe the house indirectly at best, with required details buried inconsistently among all the superfluous information. The builders of houses require a clear blueprint designed specifically to meet their needs. Yet in software development, more complex in many ways, we set about our jobs without an analogous blueprint.

Yet the level of complexity is really quite comparable. Software blueprints can be far more simple, standardized, clear, and efficient than the documents we normally produce in their place. What elements would a comparable software blueprint contain?

- A Data Dictionary to establish a clear, unambiguous vocabulary

- Mockups or prototypes to lay out the floor plan of the screens

- Pseudocode to unambiguously define operational logic

- Precise definitions of data elements so that the forms and databases can be constructed

- Logic to clearly define the rules for data translations

- Narratives to describe relevant background

With such a blueprint in hand, developers normally have all the information they need to produce software quickly and accurately the first time, with minimal input from the business experts. Builders of a house don't need to understand a lot about the day-to-day activities of the future owners. Likewise, software developers don't necessarily need to understand a lot about the client's business. The reason that many experts feel that greater understanding by developers is a requirement is because the developers usually do their own research or use their own judgment to compensate for incomplete project plans.

Obviously, you can't take disorganized output generated during the planning process and call that a blueprint. A blueprint has very specific characteristics. It distills other information and presents it in a logically complete and consistent format for use by the software builders.

Blueprint format has to be the expressed goal of all your efforts right from day one. The specific format of that blueprint must be clearly known from the start of the process, and all efforts should be dedicated to getting to that blueprint as efficiently as possible. You can't start with all the things you have been generating in the past and create a blueprint from it. Also, you can't get to a blueprint by accident. Nor can you create a good blueprint as an afterthought.

To produce a good software blueprint, you must engineer a planning process that begins to develop that blueprint from day one. The curious thing is that if you do so, that process can be considerably more simple and efficient than your current strategies that achieve far less useful results.

Software Framework

A software framework is a concrete or conceptual platform where common code with generic functionality can be selectively specialized or overridden by developers or users. Frameworks take the form of libraries, where a well-defined application program interface (API) is reusable anywhere within the software under development.

Certain features make a framework different from other library forms, including the following:

- Default Behavior: Before customization, a framework behaves in a manner specific to the user's action.

- Inversion of Control: Unlike other libraries, the global flow of control within a framework is employed by the framework rather than the caller.

- Extensibility: A user can extend the framework by selectively replacing default code with user code.

- Non-modifiable Framework Code: A user can extend the framework but not modify the code.

The purpose of software framework is to simplify the development environment, allowing developers to dedicate their efforts to the project requirements, rather than dealing with the framework's mundane, repetitive functions and libraries. For example, rather than creating a VoIP application from scratch, a developer using a prepared framework can concentrate on adding user-friendly buttons and menus, or integrating VoIP with other functions.

References

- Web-oriented-architecture-woa-30272: techopedia.com, Retrieved 16 April 2018

- Open-system-architecture-when-and-where-to-be-closed: insights.sei.cmu.edu, Retrieved 26 June 2018

- What-is-model-driven-architecture, analysis-and-design: selectbs.com, Retrieved 20 April 2018

- Architecture-models, software-architecture-design: tutorialspoint.com, Retrieved 14 June 2018

- Architectural-styles-for-software-design, software-engineering: tutorialride.com, Retrieved 10 May 2018

- Software-framework-14384: techopedia.com, Retrieved 14 May 2018

Software Maintenance

6

The modification of a software or software product for improvement of performance or correction of faults is known as software maintenance. In order to completely understand software maintenance, it is necessary to understand the processes related to it. The following chapter elucidates the varied processes and mechanisms associated with this area of study, such as backporting, software maintenance model, legacy modernization, etc.

Over a period of time, the developed software system may need modifications according to the changing user requirements. Such being the case, maintenance becomes essential. The software maintenance process comprises a set of software engineering activities that occur after the software has been delivered to the user.

Sometimes, maintenance also involves adding new features and functionalities (using latest technology) to the existing software system. The primary objective of software maintenance is to make the software system operational according to the user requirements and fix errors in the software. The errors arise due to nonfunctioning of the software or incompatibility of hardware with the software. When software maintenance is to be done on a small segment of the software code, software patches are applied. These patches are used to fix errors only in the software code that contains errors.

Software maintenance is affected by several constraints such as increase in cost and technical problems with hardware and software. This chapter discusses how software maintenance assists the present software system to accommodate changes according to the new requirements of users.

Basics of Software Maintenance

Software does not wear out or get tired. However, it needs to be upgraded and enhanced to meet new user requirements. For such modifications in the software system, software maintenance is performed. IEEE defines maintenance as 'a process of modifying a software system or component after delivery to correct faults, to improve performance or other attributes or to adapt the product to a changed environment.' The objective is to ensure that the software is able to accommodate changes after the system has been delivered and deployed.

To understand the concept of maintenance properly, let us consider an example of a car. When a car is 'used', its components wear out due to friction in the mechanical parts, unsuitable use, or by external conditions. The car owner solves the problem by changing its components when they become totally unserviceable and by using trained mechanics to handle complex faults during the car's lifetime. Occasionally, the owner gets the car serviced at a service station. This helps in preventing future wear and tear of the car. Similarly, in software engineering the software needs to be 'serviced' so that it is able to meet the changing environment (such as business and user needs) where it functions. This servicing of software is commonly referred to as software maintenance, which ensures that the software system continues to perform according to the user requirements even after the proposed changes have been incorporated. In addition, software maintenance serves the following purposes.

1. Providing continuity of service: The software maintenance process focuses on fixing errors, recovering from failures such as hardware failures or incompatibility of hardware with the software, and accommodating changes in the operating system and the hardware.

2. Supporting mandatory upgrades: Software maintenance supports upgradations, if required, in a software system. Upgradations may be required due to changes in government regulations or standards. For example, if a web-application system with multimedia capabilities has been developed, modification may be necessary in countries where screening of videos (over the Internet) is prohibited. The need for upgradations may also be felt to maintain competition with other software that exist in the same category.

3. Improving the software to support user requirements: Requirements may be requested to enhance the functionality of the software, to improve performance, or to customize data processing functions as desired by the user. Software maintenance provides a framework, using which all the requested changes can be accommodated.

4. Facilitating future maintenance work: Software maintenance also facilitates future maintenance work, which may include restructuring of the software code and the database used in the software.

Changing a Software System

As stated earlier, the need for software maintenance arises due to changes required in the software system. Once a software system has been developed and deployed, anomalies are detected, new user requirements arise, and the operating environment changes. This means that after delivery, software systems always evolve in response to the demands for change.

The concept of software maintenance and evolution of systems was first introduced by Lehman, who carried out several studies and proposed five laws based on these studies. One of the key observations of the studies was that large systems are never complete and continue to evolve. Note that during evolution, the systems become more complex, therefore, some actions are needed to be taken to reduce the complexity. The five laws stated by Lehman are discussed below:

1. Continuing change: This law states that change is inevitable, since systems operate in a dynamic environment, as the systems' environment changes, new requirements arise and the system must be modified. When the modified system is re-introduced into the environment, it requires further modifications in the environment. Note that if a system remains static, after a period of time it will not be able to serve the users' ever changing needs. This is because the system may become outdated after some time.

2. Increasing complexity: This law states that as a system changes, its structure degrades (often observed in legacy systems). To avoid this problem, preventive maintenance should be used, where only the structure of the software is improved without adding any new functionality to it. However, additional costs have to be incurred to reverse the effects of structural degradation.

3. Large software evolution: This law state that for large systems, software evolution is largely dependent on management decisions because of organizational factors, which are established earlier in the development process. This is true for large organizations, which have their own internal bureaucracies that control the decision-making process. The rate of change of the system in these organizations is governed by the organization's decision-making processes. This determines the gross trends of the system maintenance process and limits the possible number of changes to the system.

4. Organizational stability: This law states that changes to resources such as staffing have unnoticeable effects on evolution. For example, productivity may not increase by assigning new staff to a project because of the additional communication overhead. Thus, it can be said that large software development teams become unproductive because the communication overheads dominate the work of the team.

Conservation of familiarity: This law states that there is a limit to the rate at which new functionality can be introduced. This implies that adding a large increment of functionality to a system in one release, may certainly introduce new system faults. If a large increment is introduced, a new release will be required 'fairly quickly' to correct the new system faults. Thus, organizations should not budget for large functionality increments in each release without taking into account the need for fault repair.

Table Lehman Laws

Law	Description
Continuing change	The environment in which the software operates keeps on changing, therefore, the software must also be changed to work in the new environment.
Increasing complexity	The structure of the software becomes more complex with continuous change in software, therefore, some preventive steps must be taken to improve and simplify its structure.
Large software evolution	Software evolution is a self-regulating process. Software attributes such as size, time between releases, and the number of reported errors are almost constant for each system release.
Organizational stability	The rate with which the software is developed remains approximately constant and is independent of the resources devoted to the software development.
Conservation of familiarity	During the life of software, added to it in each release, may be introduced.

Lehman's observations have been accepted universally and are taken consideration when planning the maintenance process. However, it may be that one of the laws is ignored when some particular business decision is For example, it may be mandatory to carry out several major system changes in a single release for marketing and sales reasons.

Legacy System

The term 'legacy system' describes an old system, which remains in operation within an organization. These systems were developed according to the 'dated development practice' and-technology existing before the introduction of structured programming. Process models and basic principles such as modularity, coupling, cohesion, and good programming practice emerged too late for them. Thus, these systems were developed according to ad hoc processes and often used programming techniques, which were not amenable for developing large systems. The combination of employing dated processes, techniques, and technology resulted in undesirable characteristics in legacy systems.

Table: Legacy System Characteristics

Characteristics	Descriptions
High maintenance cost	Results due to combination of other system factors such as complexity, poor documentation, and lack of inexperienced personnel.
Complex software	Results due to structural degradation, which must have occurred over a legacy system's lifetime of change.
Obsolete support software	Support software may not be available for a particular platform or no longer be supported by its original vendor or any other organization.
Obsolete hardware	Legacy system's hardware may have been discontinued.
Lack of technical expertise	Original developers of a legacy system are unlikely to be involved with its maintenance today.
Business critical	Many legacy systems are essential for the proper working of the organizations which operate them.
Poorly understood	Documentation is often missing or inconsistent.
Poorly documented	As a consequence of system complexity and poor documentation, software maintainers often understand the legacy systems poorly.

Legacy systems are generally associated with high maintenance costs. The root cause of this expense is the degraded structure that results from prolonged maintenance. Systems with contrived structures are invariably complex and understanding them requires considerable effort. System understanding (a prerequisite for implementing changes) is particularly expensive, as it relies on individuals grasping a sufficient depth of understanding of the system.

Legacy systems were not designed to accommodate changes. This is because of the following reasons:

1. Short lifetime expectancy: At the time of their commission, it was not anticipated that legacy systems would be used for so many decades.

2. Failure of process models to treat evolution as an important activity: Evolution requirements, for example, can be extracted from business goals, but according to traditional practice, future requirements are largely ignored during the specification phase of the development.

3. Constraints present at the time of development: When legacy systems were developed, the memory and processing power were limited that constrained the software design decisions.

Techniques were used to make efficient use of these resources, but at the expense of maintainability it has been observed that to develop 'long-lived' software systems, ease of maintainability is a prerequisite.

Often organizations face a dilemma known as legacy dilemma, which states that 'a legacy system, which is business critical, must remain operational, in some form, within its organization. However, continued maintenance of the system is expensive and the scope for effectively implementing further change is heavily constrained. Moreover, the costs of replacing the system from scratch are prohibitively high.'

The Components of a Legacy System

The 'evolveability' of a legacy system is determined by the parts that constitute the legacy system.

Components of Legacy System

These parts can be categorized as given here:

1. Business: Represents a business perspective of legacy systems. Business goals are the long-term objectives for an organization, which heavily influence the evolveability of a legacy system. Business goals generate future requirements for the software systems that support the business. Note that if the business goals are thorough in nature, it is difficult to implement the changes. Also, thorough changes can only be accommodated after extensive rework.

2. Organizational: Includes both the development and operational organizations involved with the legacy system. The development organization is responsible for maintaining the system. Note that it is difficult to evolve a system if the individuals who mail1.tained the system retire or when poor documentation exists. The operational organization is the organization which is supported by the legacy system. That is, a legacy system provides services to its operational organization. An organization's attitude to change affects the system's evolveability. For example, workforces in some organizations are unwilling to accept change if it is imposed by the senior management.

3. Technical: Categorizes the legacy system into application software, system software, and hardware. When a system's hardware is no longer supported, it would be wise to replace the hardware instead of investing further. Also, the condition and quality of application software (including its documentation) is a significant factor in determining how a legacy system can evolve. For example, a contrived software architecture, or inconsistent documentation implies that the system cannot evolve readily.

There are four types of maintenance, namely, corrective, adaptive, perfective, and preventive. Corrective maintenance is concerned with fixing errors that are observed when the software is in use. Adaptive maintenance is concerned with the change in the software that takes place to make the software adaptable to new environment such as to run the software on a new operating system. Perfective maintenance is concerned with the change in the software that occurs while adding new functionalities in the software. Preventive maintenance involves implementing changes to prevent the occurrence of errors. The distribution of types of maintenance by type and by percentage of time consumed.

Corrective maintenance deals with the repair of faults or defects found in day-today system functions. A defect can result due to errors in software design, logic and coding. Design errors occur when changes made to the software are incorrect, incomplete, wrongly communicated, or the change request is misunderstood. Logical errors result from invalid tests and conclusions, incorrect implementation of design specifications, faulty logic flow, or incomplete test of data. All these errors, referred to as residual errors, prevent the software from conforming to its agreed specifications. Note that the need for corrective maintenance is usually initiated by bug reports drawn by the users.

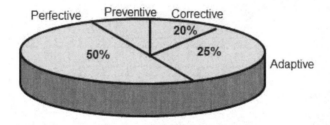

Types of Software Maintenance

In the event of a system failure due to an error, actions are taken to restore the operation of the software system. The approach in corrective maintenance is to locate the original specifications in order to determine what the system was originally designed to do. However, due to pressure from management, the maintenance team sometimes resorts to emergency fixes known as patching. Corrective maintenance accounts for 20% of all the maintenance activities.

Adaptive Maintenance

Adaptive maintenance is the implementation of changes in a part of the system, which has been affected by a change that occurred in some other part of the system. Adaptive maintenance consists of adapting software to changes in the environment such as the hardware or the operating system. The term environment in this context refers to the conditions and the influences which act (from outside) on the system. For example, business rules, work patterns, and government policies have a significant impact on the software system.

For instance, a government policy to use a single 'European currency' will have a significant effect on the software system. An acceptance of this change will require banks in various member countries to make significant changes in their software systems to accommodate this currency. Adaptive maintenance accounts for 25% of all the maintenance activities.

Perfective Maintenance

Perfective maintenance mainly deals with implementing new or changed user requirements. Perfective maintenance involves making functional enhancements to the system in addition to the activities to increase the system's performance even when the changes have not been suggested by faults. This includes enhancing both the function and efficiency of the code and changing the functionalities of the system as per the users' changing needs.

Examples of perfective maintenance include modifying the payroll program to incorporate a new union settlement and adding a new report in the sales analysis system. Perfective maintenance accounts for 50%, that is, the largest of all the maintenance activities.

Preventive Maintenance

Preventive maintenance involves performing activities to prevent the occurrence of errors. It tends to reduce the software complexity thereby improving program understandability and increasing software maintainability. It comprises documentation updating, code optimization, and code restructuring. Documentation updating involves modifying the documents affected by the changes in order to correspond to the present state of the system. Code optimization involves modifying the programs for faster execution or efficient use of storage space. Code restructuring involves transforming the program structure for reducing the complexity in source code and making it easier to understand.

Preventive maintenance is limited to the maintenance organization only and no external requests are acquired for this type of maintenance. Preventive maintenance accounts for only 5% of all the maintenance activities.

Software Maintenance Prediction

Since unexpected maintenance costs may lead to an unexpected increase in costs, it is important to predict the effect of modifications in the software system. Software maintenance prediction refers to the study of software maintainability, the modifications in the software system, and the maintenance costs that are required to maintain the software system. Various maintenance predictions and the questions associated with them.

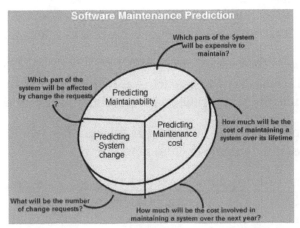

Various predictions are closely related and specify the following:

1. The decision to accept a system change depends on the maintainability of the system components affected by that change up to a certain extent.

2. Implementation of changes results in degradation of system structure as well as reduction in system maintainability.

3. Costs involved in implementing changes depend on the maintainability of the system components.

To predict the number of changes requested for a system, the relationship between the system and its external environment should be properly understood. To know the kind of relationship that exists, organizations should assess the following:

1. Number and the complexity involved in the system interface. More interfaces mean more complexity, which in turn means more demand for change.

2. Number of system (volatile) requirements. Changes required in organizational policies and procedures tend to be more volatile than the requirements based on a particular domain.

3. Number of business processes in which the system operates. More business processes implies more demands for system change.

To predict maintainability of a software system, it is important to consider the relationship among the different components and the complexity involved in them. Generally, it is observed that a software system having complex components is difficult and expensive to maintain. The complexity in a software system occurs due to the size of procedures and functions, the size and the number of modules, and the nested structures in the software code. On the other hand, a software system developed by using good programming practices reduces not only the complexity but also the effort required in software maintenance. As a result, such software systems minimize the maintenance cost. For maintaining the individual components in software systems, it is essential to identify the complexity measurements of components.

After a system has been put into operation, several process metrics are used to predict the software maintainability. Process metrics, which may be useful for assessing maintainability, are listed below.

1. Corrective maintenance: Sometimes, more errors are introduced rather than being repaired during the maintenance process. This shows decline in maintainability.

2. Average time required for impact analysis: Before starting the software maintenance process, it is essential to analyze the impact of modifications in the software system. This is known as impact analysis, which reflects the number of components affected by the change.

3. Number of outstanding change requests: If the number of outstanding change requests increases with time, it may imply decline in maintainability.

4. Average time taken to implement a change request: This involves activities· concerned with making changes to the system and its documentation rather than simply assessing the components which are affected. If the time taken to implement a change increases, it may imply a decline in maintainability.

Factors Affecting Software Maintenance

Many factors directly or indirectly lead to high maintenance costs. A software maintenance framework is created to determine the affects of these factors on maintenance. This framework comprises user requirements, organizational and operational environment, maintenance process, maintenance personnel, and the software product. These elements interact with each other based on three kinds of relationships, which are listed below.

Table Components of Software Maintenance Framework

Component	Features
User requirements	Request for additional functionality, error correction, capability, and improvement in maintainability.
	Request for non-programming related support.
Organizational environment	Change in business policies.
	Competition in market.
Operational environment	Hardware platform.
	Software specifications.
Maintenance process	Capturing requirements.
	Variation in programming and working practices.
	Paradigm shift.
	Error detection and correction.
Software product	Quality of documentation.
	Complexity of programs.
	Program structure.
Software maintenance team	Staff turnover.
	Domain expertise.

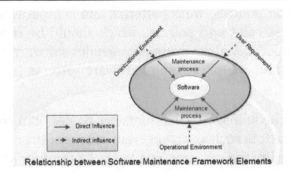

Relationship between Software Maintenance Framework Elements

1. Relationship of software product and environment: In this relationship, the software product changes according to the organizational and operational environment. However, it is necessary to accept only those changes which are useful for the software product.

2. Relationship of the software product and user: In this relationship, the software product is modified according to the new requirements of users. Hence, it is important to modify the software that is useful and acceptable to users after modification.

3. Relationship of software product and software maintenance team: In this 'relationship, the software maintenance team members act as mediators to keep track of the software product. In other words, the software maintenance team analyzes the modifications in other elements of software maintenance framework to determine their effect on the software product. These elements include user requirements, organizational and operational environments, and the software maintenance process. All these elements affect the modifications in software and are responsible for maintaining software quality.

Generally, users have little knowledge of the software maintenance process due to which they can be unsupportive to the software maintenance team. Also, users may have some misconceptions such as software maintenance is like hardware maintenance, changing software is easy, and changes cost too much and are time consuming.

If user requirements need major changes in the software, a lot of time may be consumed in implementing them. Similarly, users may opt for changes that are not according to the software standards or policies of a company. This situation creates a conflict between users and the software maintenance team.

To implement user requirements in software, the following characteristics should be considered.

1. Feasible: User requirements are feasible if the requested change is workable in the software system.

2. Desirable: Before implementing new changes, it is important to consider whether the user modification request is necessary.

3. Prioritized: In some cases, the user requirements may be both feasible and desirable. However, these requirements may not be of high priority at that time. In such a situation, the user requirements can be implemented later.

The working of software is affected by two kinds of environments, namely, organizational environment and operational environment. The organizational environment includes business rules, government policies, taxation policies, work patterns, and competition in the market. An organization has its own business rules and policies, which should be incorporated in the software maintenance process. The operational environment includes software systems (such as operating systems, database systems, and compilers) and hardware systems (such as processor, memory, and peripherals).

In both the environments, scheduling of the maintenance process can create problems. The scheduling is affected by various factors such as urgent requirement of the modified software, allocation of less amount of time to modify the software, and the lack of proper knowledge on how to implement user requirement in software.

Changes are implemented in the software system by following the software maintenance process (also known as software maintenance life cycle). The facets of a maintenance process which affect the evolution of software or contribute to high maintenance costs are listed below:

1. Error detection and correction: It has been observed that error-free software is virtually non-existent. That is, a software product tends to contain some kind of 'residual' errors.

If these errors are uncovered at a later stage of software development, they become more expensive to fix. The cost of fixing errors is even higher when errors are detected during the maintenance phase.

2. Difficulty in capturing change (and changing) requirements: Requirements and user problems become clear only when a system is in use. Also users may not be able to express their requirements in a form, which is understandable to the analyst or programmer.

3. Software engineering paradigm shift: Older systems that were developed prior to the advent of structured programming techniques may be difficult to maintain.

Software Product

The software developed for users can be for general use or specific use. For example, MSOffice is a software application that is generic in nature and may be used by a wide range of people. On the other hand, the payroll system may be customized according to the needs of the organization. However, the problem occurs when software is to be maintained. Generally, the aspects of a software product that contribute to the maintenance cost or challenge are listed below:

1. Difficulty of the application domain: The requirements of applications that have been widely used and well understood are less likely to undergo substantial modifications than those that have been recently developed.

2. Inflexibility in programs: While modifying software, it should be checked for the flexibility of change and reuse. This is because the inflexible software products are more prone to failures.

3. Quality of the documentation: Documentation is essential for understanding the requirements, software design, and how these requirements are converted into the software code. The unavailability of up-to-date systems documentation affects maintenance productivity adversely.

Software Maintenance Team

The group of individuals responsible for the software maintenance is referred to as the software maintenance team, which mayor may not comprise the development team that 'built' the software. Often, a separate maintenance team (comprising analysts, designers, and programmers) is formed to ensure that a system performs its functions properly. This team is employed as it has been observed that generally developers do not keep documentation up-to-date, leading to the need of more individuals or resources to tackle a problem. This results in a long time-gap between the time when a problem occurs and when it is fixed.

Various functions performed by the software maintenance team are listed below.

1. Locating information in system documentation

2. Keeping system documentation up-to-date

3. Improving system functionalities to adapt new environment

4. Enhancing system to perform new functions according to the user's needs

5. Detecting root cause of failures, if any

6. Handling changes made to the system.

The aspects of a maintenance team that lead to high maintenance costs are listed below:

1. Staff turnover: Generally, it is observed that when the staff turnover (the ratio of number of individuals that leave the organization during a specified period of time) is high, the software maintenance is not performed properly. This is because employees who originally worked on software products are replaced by new personnel who spend a substantial proportion of the maintenance effort in understanding the system.

2. Domain expertise: Sometimes, the maintenance team may have little or no knowledge about the system domain and the application domain they are working in. This problem is worsened if documentation is not maintained or is not up-to-date. All this may lead to delay in implementing the changes requested by the user.

Backporting

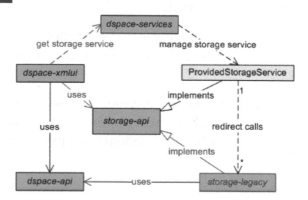

Backporting is a technique used to apply a security fix to a older version of the software component using the parts of the newer version of same software component. In some cases the environment may not support to apply a patch for a security weakness detected in the software, in such cases the parts of the code are taken from the new version of the software and applied to the older version which is vulnerable. Usually this process is done by the developers themselves or some third party and it involves changing only a few lines of codes or values of variables. Understand this very seriously and start to read about the other cyber security tips also. In nowadays world the technology changes at literally seconds, and you need to be informed.

To check if any one of your software component that is used on your servers is vulnerable to any security flaw, conduct a Vulnerability Assessment and check if there is a need for backporting any of your software components.

The tools that can be used to check for security weaknesses are:

• nmap

- SPARTA

nmap can be used to check for open ports on the server and the services running on those ports. It also identifies the version of service running which can be used to check if that version is vulnerable.

SPARTA also provides a detailed information about the open ports, the services running and their versions.

What to Backport

Candidates are commits which add

- Top-level classes, traits and objects
- Implemented methods to objects and classes

You can also add methods to sealed traits, but Migration Manager will complain (because of potential breakage when used from plain Java). It is possible to add exceptions, though, but usually it's not that important to include each and every potential backport.

Preparation

For each pending maintenance release, we keep a list of pull requests and commits which have accumulated in the development branch since the last maintenance release (e.g. #665). This list should be kept up-to-date. If a new pull request or bare commit comes in, make an educated guess whether its backportable (you don't need to attempt it right away), and if it is likely to not break compatibility, add it to the list.

Larger additions (e.g. IList) can be added as a bulk item.

Backport

Some general notes first: Backporting is not an exact science, and sometimes requires tradeoffs. When in doubt, don't backport. If necessary, don't backport a commit or a pull request in full, but only parts of it (but please make sure to document it in the commit message). Try to preserve the author of the original commit(s). cherry-pick does this automatically, but if you commit manually, you might need to specify -author. If you have to change the commit significantly, it's okay to have your name as author. In that case, please include the original author in the commit message, like so (e.g. 09324f1fb1), and document your changes:

Original commit by @<username>

<old-commit-message>

Changes to the original commit Backporting usually consists of these steps, depending on what you are backporting:

- A bare commit (not from a pull request): Just call git cherry-pick -edit <commit-id>. Add the following line at the end of the commit message:

Cherry-picking <commit-id>

- Multiple commits, if related, can be rolled into one backport commit (e.g. 2cac4469e8). You can use a sequence of git cherry-pick -no-commit commands to do that. After you're done, use git commit and try to find a commit message which roughly describes the common idea of all of the backported commits, but don't copy all original messages verbatim. Make sure to include all original commit IDs in the last line of the message.

- Commits from a pull request: Figure out which commits can be backported. If it's just a single one or multiple ones but not all of them, proceed like above. In the latter case, a good commit message is the title of the pull request.

For backporting a pull request in full, you can use GitHub to obtain the full diff by appending .diff to the pull request URL (e.g. 752.diff). Apply the patch to the code base with git apply -reject and manually merge the rejected parts.

When committing the backported patches, include the following line in the commit message (e.g. 18b86d36e5):

Cherry-picking pull request <pull-request> (<commit-id-1>, <commit-id-2>, ...)

In the rare event that a pull request contains commits by multiple different authors, you can still roll them into one: Either use the majority author, or list all authors in the commit message (whatever fits best).

- Bulk items: Copy whole the corresponding files in the maintenance branch. Write a commit message which looks like this (e.g. 1710912021) backport from Based on commit .

Once you're done, run the migration manager tests. If that works without problems, submit a pull request to the correct branch. Your help is much appreciated.

Debug Code

Debugging is the routine process of locating and removing computer program bugs, errors or abnormalities, which is methodically handled by software programmers via debugging tools. Debugging checks, detects and corrects errors or bugs to allow proper program operation according to set specifications.

Debugging is also known as debug.

Developing software programs undergo heavy testing, updating, troubleshooting and maintenance. Normally, software contains errors and bugs, which are routinely removed. In the debugging process, complete software programs are regularly compiled and executed to identify and rectify issues. Large software programs, which contain millions of source code lines, are divided into small components. For efficiency, each component is debugged separately at first, followed by the program as a whole.

Debugging Support in Eclipse

Eclipse allows you to start a Java program in *Debug mode*.

Eclipse provides a *Debug perspective* which gives you a pre-configured set of *views*. Eclipse allows you to control the execution flow via debug commands.

Setting Breakpoints

To define a breakpoint in your source code, right-click in the left margin in the Java editor and select *Toggle Breakpoint*. Alternatively you can double-click on this position.

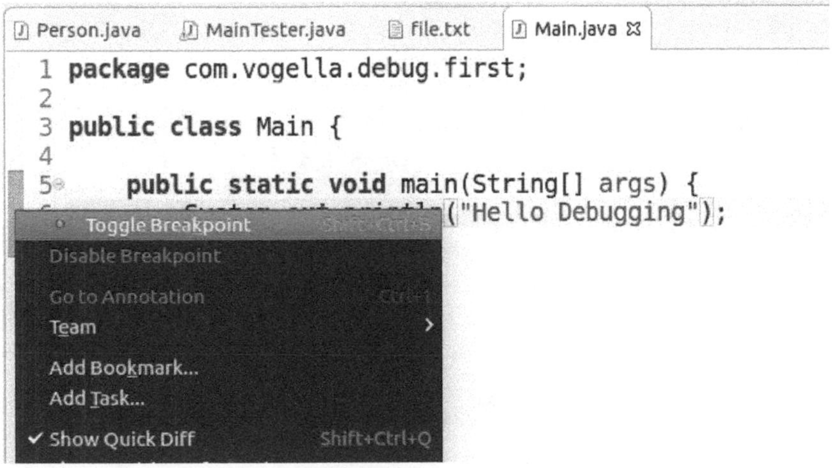

For example in the following screenshot we set a breakpoint on the line Counter counter = new Counter();.

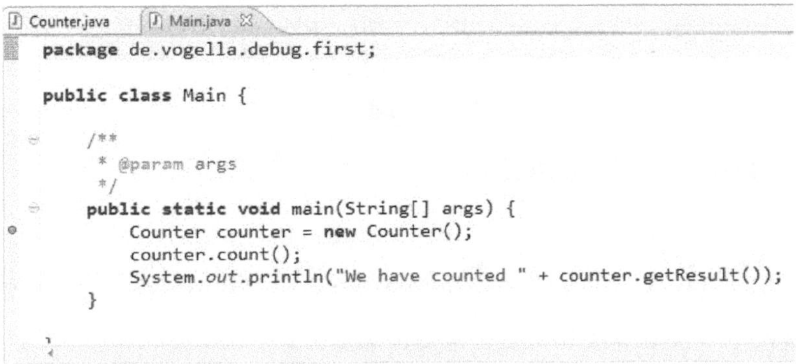

Starting the Debugger

To debug your application, select a Java file with a main method. Right-click on it and select Debug As Java Application.

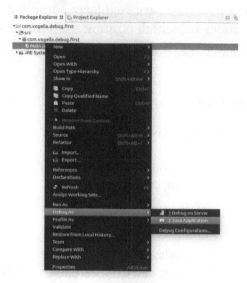

If you started an application once via the context menu, you can use the created launch configuration again via the Debug button in the Eclipse toolbar.

If you have not defined any breakpoints, program as normally. To debug the program you need to define breakpoints. Eclipse asks you if you want to switch to the *Debug perspective* once a stop point is reached. Answer *Yes* in the corresponding dialog. Afterwards Eclipse opens this *perspective*.

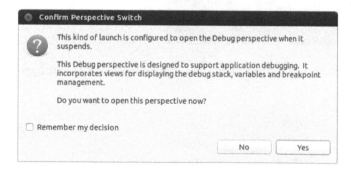

Controlling the Program Execution

Eclipse provides buttons in the toolbar for controlling the execution of the program you are debugging. Typically, it is easier to use the corresponding keys to control this execution.

You can use allow use shortcut key to step through your coding. The meaning of these keys is explained in the following table.

Table: Debugging key bindings / shortcuts	
Key	Description
F5	Executes the currently selected line and goes to the next line in your program. If the selected line is a method call the debugger steps into the associated code.
F6	F6 steps over the call, i.e. it executes a method without stepping into it in the debugger.
F7	F7 steps out to the caller of the currently executed method. This finishes the execution of the current method and returns to the caller of this method.
F8	F8 tells the Eclipse debugger to resume the execution of the program code until is reaches the next breakpoint or watchpoint.

The following picture displays the buttons and their related keyboard shortcuts.

The call stack shows the parts of the program which are currently executed and how they relate to each other. The current stack is displayed in the *Debug* view.

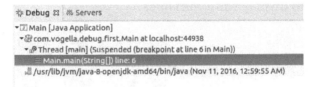

Breakpoints View and Deactivating Breakpoints

The *Breakpoints* view allows you to delete and deactivate *breakpoints* and *watchpoints*. You can also modify their properties.

To deactivate a breakpoint, remove the corresponding checkbox in the *Breakpoints* view. To delete it you can use the corresponding buttons in the view toolbar. These options are depicted in the following screenshot.

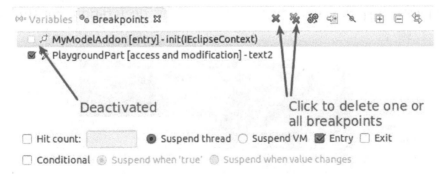

If you want to disable all breakpoints at the same time, you can press the Skip all breakpoints-button. If you press it again, your breakpoints are reactivated. This button is highlighted in the following screenshot.

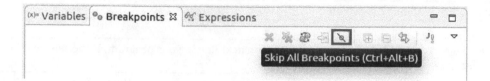

Evaluating Variables in the Debugger

The *Variables* view displays fields and local variables from the current executing stack. Please note you need to run the debugger to see the variables in this view.

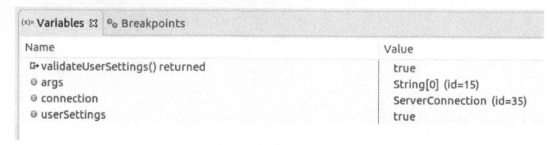

Use the drop-down menu to display static variables.

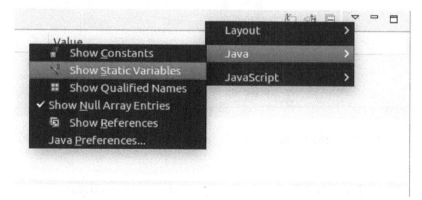

Via the drop-down menu of the Variables view you can customize the displayed columns.

For example, you can show the actual type of each variable declaration. For this select Layout > Select Column> Type.

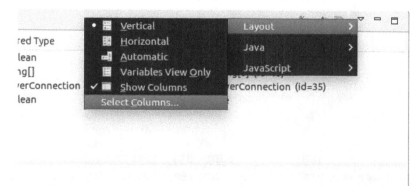

Changing Variable Assignments in the Debugger

The *Variables* view allows you to change the values assigned to your variable at runtime. This is depicted in the following screenshot.

Controlling the Display of the Variables with Detail Formatter

By default the *Variables* view uses the toString() method to determine how to display the variable.

You can define a *Detail Formatter* in which you can use Java code to define how a variable is displayed.

For example, the toString() method in the Counter class may show meaningless information, e.g. com.vogella.combug.first.Counter@587c94. To make this output more readable you can right-click on the corresponding variable and select the New Detail Formater entry from the context menu.

Afterwards you can use a method of this class to determine the output. In this example the getResult() method of this class is used. This setup is depicted in the following screenshot.

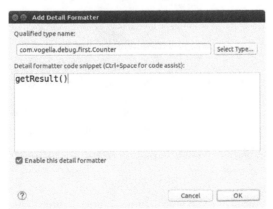

Advanced Debugging

Breakpoint Properties

After setting a breakpoint you can select the properties of the breakpoint, via right-click Breakpoint Properties. Via the breakpoint properties you can define a condition that restricts the activation of this breakpoint.

You can for example specify that a breakpoint should only become active after it has reached 12 or more times via the *Hit Count* property.

You can also create a conditional expression. The execution of the program only stops at the breakpoint, if the condition evaluates to true. This mechanism can also be used for additional logging, as the code that specifies the condition is executed every time the program execution reaches that point.

The following screenshot depicts this setting:

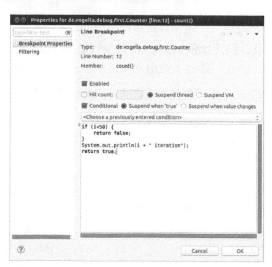

Watchpoint

A watchpoint is a breakpoint set on a field. The debugger will stop whenever that field is read or changed.

You can set a *watchpoint* by double-clicking on the left margin, next to the field declaration. In the properties of a *watchpoint* you can configure if the execution should stop during read access (Field Access) or during write access (Field Modification) or both.

Exception Breakpoints

You can set breakpoints for thrown exceptions. To define an exception breakpoint click on the Add Java Exception Breakpoint button icon in the *Breakpoints* view toolbar.

You can configure, if the debugger should stop at caught or uncaught exceptions.

Method Breakpoint

A method breakpoint is defined by double-clicking in the left margin of the editor next to the method header.

You can configure if you want to stop the program before entering or after leaving the method.

Breakpoints for Loading Classes

A class load breakpoint stops when the class is loaded.

To set a class load breakpoint, right-click on a class in the *Outline* view and choose the *Toggle Class Load Breakpoint* option.

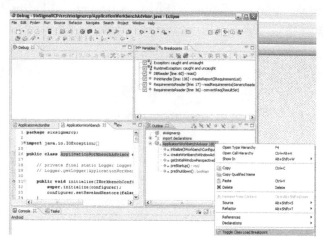

Alternative you can double-click in the left border of the Java editor beside the class definition.

Step Filter

You can define that certain packages should be skipped in debugging. This is for example useful if you use a framework for testing but don't want to step into the test framework classes. These packages can be configured via the Window Preferences Java Debug Step Filtering menu path.

Hit Count

For every breakpoint you can specify a hit count in its properties. The application is stopped once the breakpoint has been reached the number of times defined in the hit count.

Remote Debugging

Eclipse allows you to debug applications which runs on another Java virtual machine or even on another machine.

To enable remote debugging you need to start your Java application with certain flags, as demonstrated in the following code example.

```
java -Xdebug -Xnoagent \
-Djava.compiler=NONE \
-Xrunjdwp:transport=dt_socket,server=y,suspend=y,address=5005
```

In you Eclipse IDE you can enter the hostname and port to connect for debugging via the Run >Debug Configuration menu.

Here you can create a new debug configuration of the *Remote Java Application* type. This configuration allows you to enter the hostname and port for the connection as depicted in the following screenshot.

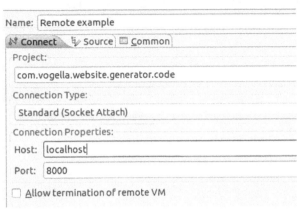

Remote debugging requires that you have the source code of the application which is debugged available in your Eclipse IDE.

Drop to Frame

Eclipse allows you to select any level (frame) in the call stack during debugging and set the JVM to restart from that point.

This allows you to rerun a part of your program. Be aware that variables which have been modified by code that already run will remain modified.

To use this feature, select a level in your stack and press the *Drop to Frame* button in the toolbar of the *Debug* view.

The following screenshot depicts such a reset. If you restart your for loop, the field result is not set to its initial value and therefore the loop is not executed as without resetting the execution to a previous point.

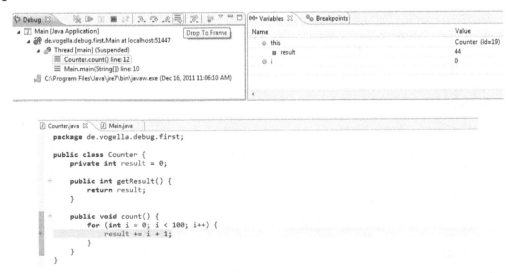

Creating Project for Debugging

To practice debugging create a new Java project called de.vogella.combug.first. Also create the package de.vogella.combug.first and create the following classes.

```java
package de.vogella.combug.first;

public class Counter {

  private int result = 0;

  public int getResult() {

    return result;

  }

  public void count() {

    for (int i = 0; i < 100; i++) {

      result += i + 1;

    }

  }

}

package de.vogella.combug.first;


public class Main {

  /**

    * @param args

    */

  public static void main(String[] args) {

    Counter counter = new Counter();

    counter.count();

    System.out.println("We have counted "

        + counter.getResult());

  }

}
```

Debugging

Set a breakpoint in the Counter class. Debug your program and follow the execution of the-count method.

Define a *Detailed Formatter* for your Counter which uses the getResult method. Debug your program again and verify that your new formatter is used.

Delete your breakpoint and add a breakpoint for class loading. Debug your program again and verify that the debugger stops when your class is loaded.

Hotfix

A hotfix is a software update designed to fix a bug or security hole in a program. Unlike typical version updates, hotfixes are urgently developed and released as soon as possible to limit the effects of the software issue. They are often released between incremental version updates.

You may receive a hotfix notification by email or as an alert in the program itself. It may be labeled as a "critical update" or "security update." Some applications allow you to update the software by simply clicking Update in the program. Other applications may require you to download the hotfix package and run the update as an executable file.

It is typically advisable to run a hotfix update as soon as possible to avoid problems with the software. However, any time you receive a hotfix notification, make sure it is legitimate and from the developer of the software before agreeing to install it. In most cases, you can check the software company's website to view the update history and release notes for the program.

Software Maintenance Model

Traditionally we use the term "software maintenance" for naming the discipline concerned with changes related to software system after delivery. An appreciation of this discipline is important especially because the cost is now extremely high. Safety and cost of software maintenance mean that there is an urgent need to find ways of reducing or eliminating maintenance problems. In this paper, we will discuss model of software maintenance process after delivery with qualified output and compared with other model.

Software maintenance process model is an abstract representation of the evolution of software to help analyze activities during software maintenance. Which use kind of maintenance model, should be aware of the characteristics of various models and, based on preservation of the environment to decide. The following analysis of several common models. Quickly modify model that the maintenance process is a "fire fighting" approach, which is the temporary custom software maintenance method, software problem should be solved as soon as possible, shouldn't analyze long-term effects on the implementation of changes.

Dr. Barry W. Boehm bases on economic models and principle, proposes maintenance process model. Boehm's theory is models and principles of economics can not only improve maintenance productivity, but also helps to understand the maintenance process.

Initially the model is put forward as a development model, because the software developers usually can't fully understand the requirements, can't build a perfect system, so it is suitable for maintenance. Made the basis of the model: the software life cycle of software changes implemented, is an iterative process, and to iteratively enhanced software system.

Software Maintenance Process

Software maintenance process shown in figure below.

- Preparation. Adequate preparation is a good start to maintenance. Including the designation of maintenance personnel, establish smooth communication channels to facilitate the maintenance, training, preparation and approval of "software maintenance plan" and so on maintenance. Including the designation of maintenance personnel, establish smooth communication channels to facilitate the maintenance, training, preparation and approval of "software maintenance plan" and so on.

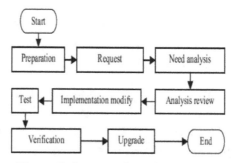

Figure: Software maintenance process

- Request: Software maintenance begins with a request to change the system, usually a request by the user, on-site maintenance engineers or developers to issue report card form.

- Need analysis: Responsible officer explain to human analysts, who analysis system change requests which means issues report card, including the issue positioning, issues related to the specific product and the corresponding change of scale, give a specific solution to issues related to documentation, test programs and strategies proposed and ultimately the formation of the problem analysis.

- Analysis review: The process is an important means to ensure maintenance of quality, can make early detection of problems and reduce the risk of maintenance problems later discovered. Analysts question the degree of difficulty according to the problem involves the size of the change and the problem-solving ability to grasp and other factors, to decide which assessment method.

- Implementations modify: According to one report to address personnel issues, problem analysis report and product manuals related to the modification of the product. It modifies the software, must first understand the program, help complete the requirements; also modify the program to understand the possible side effects, so that when changes in the program note; final report on the formation of a single software modifications.

- Test: Software is modified, the analytical report based on testers in the test program for testing. It's easy to introduce new errors and change, therefore the regression test, reduce side effects caused by change.

- Verification: After testing software changes before submission system upgrade, to go through the validation phase, the reviewers question whether the correct solution for the assessment. Verify the initiator for the managers, the purpose is to ensure the quality of software maintenance, can refer to the analysis phase of the evaluation methods for assessment.

- Upgrade: Software verification is complete in internal company, need publishing to user, upgrade system. Upgrade process from developers, engineers and users together.

Software Maintenance Process model

Software maintenance has seven phases, with each phase having input, process, control and output. The phases are problem identification, analysis, design, implementation, system test, acceptance test and delivery. Modification request (MR) constitutes the input to problem identification while validated MR is the final output of this first phase. The last phase of maintenance is delivery. Physical configuration Audit (PCA) plays an important part to make sure that the validated MR is fully achieved in the prior phases. Finally installation, training of users and version description document (VDD) is produced. Software maintenance process model is an abstract representation of the evolution of software to help analyze activities during software maintenance. Which use kind of maintenance model, should be aware of the characteristics of various models and, based on preservation of the environment to decide. The following analysis of several common models.

Quickly Modify Model

Quickly modify model that the maintenance process is a "fire fighting" approach, which is the temporary custom software maintenance method, software problem should be solved as soon as possible, shouldn't analyze long-term effects on the implementation of changes. Usually don't analyze the code to modify the structure of the ripple effect of the impact, even if the analysis is also very little written documentation. Quickly modify the model structure. In the right environment, this model is very effective. For example, if the system is developed and maintained by one person, this person is very familiar with the system, has the ability in the absence of detailed documentation in the case management system, whether changes can be made to determine how to modify and maintain work quickly and economic.

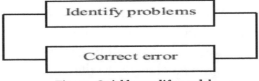

Figure: Quickly modify model

There are many customers in the business environment, this approach isn't reliable, but there are still many institutions using this model is due to software maintenance are time and resource constraints. For example, customers request the correction of an error, but are not willing to wait for software companies to change the cumbersome process and risk analysis. If the software rely on quick changes with a long time, it will accumulate a lot of problems, the software will become increasingly difficult to maintain, maintenance costs will increase, it will lose use of rapid change in the initial stages of the model to get any advantage. To address this problem, using the strategy is to quickly modify the model, into another, more sophisticated models, rapid changes in external pressure as an emergency to change the way modifications are completed, according to the model requires some fine measures.

Boehm Model

Dr. Barry W. Boehm bases on economic models and principle, proposes maintenance process model. Boehm's theory is models and principles of economics can not only improve maintenance productivity, but also helps to understand the maintenance process. Model structure show in figure below. Model maintenance process is divided into management decision-making to achieve change, software delivery and evaluation of four stages, expressed as a closed loop to maintain the process by promoting the maintenance management decision-making process. In management decision-making stage, use of specific strategies, and proposed a set of changes for cost-effective assessment to determine a set of approved changes and the implementation of changes to a dedicated budget.

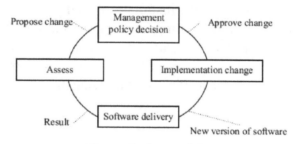

Figure: Boehm model

From the functional point of view of production, the model reflects the economics of investment and the relationship between earnings, reflecting a typical phases:

- Investment stage: This is a low input of resources and low-income stage, corresponding to an emergency there is a strong requirement to modify and enhance new software product;

- High-return stage: Institutions through software products have been growing returns, the initial problem is resolved. At this stage, resources and efficiency to the document, the agency's rapid growth in the accumulation of benefits;

- Effective reduction stage: At a certain point in time, the accumulation of effective growth rate gradually slows down. At the peak of the effectiveness of the product, to change to become less and less economic stage. Boehm model focuses on the management decision making, according to the approved changes to the implementation of changes to maintenance activities in the balance between investment and benefits from the perspective of economic interest to drive the software maintenance process. Based on this process, the organization can develop a reasonable maintenance strategy, maintenance efficiency to meet the organization to make decisions.

Iterative Enhancement Model

Initially the model is put forward as a development model, because the software developers usually cannot fully understand the requirements, cannot build a perfect system, so it is suitable for maintenance. Made the basis of the model: the software life cycle of software changes implemented, is an iterative process, and to iteratively enhanced software system.

Model requires a complete document, as the beginning of each round of iteration, is actually three stages of the cycle. According to the impact of the change request document, the first change of each phase (requirements, design, coding, testing and analysis of the document), full documentation of this change in the spread, and redesign systems.

According to safeguard the environment to find quick solutions. Usually use the "fastest" solution will lead to many problems, iterative model, other models of assimilation itself, it can be in a structured environment, the integrated model of rapid change, rapid change, identify problems, and Diego the next round generation to specifically address these issues. Process Model Metrics.

Metrics involves time, money and numbers. Process model metrics for software maintenance encourages keeping records of time spent on problem validation, document error rates, number of lines of corrective code added, error rates by priority and type (generated and corrected) and document changes. Document changes include VDDs, training manuals and operation guidelines.

Legacy Modernization

Legacy modernization, or software modernization is essentially to transport old software functionalities to a context that is compliant with up to date IT landscape potential.

As odd as it may sound, year to date, there are still thousands of companies at the global scale that have critical core business processes based on corporate software that dates back some 30 or even 50 years.

COBOL coding is easily a 30-year-old vintage specimen while IBM Mainframe software developed 50 years ago is still being directly used by clients on the manufacturer's latest hardware.

Benefits of Legacy Modernization

Having such old software tools supporting business operations potentially means incurring into multiple growing risks, costs as well as critical constraining factors. Here are some examples:

- Obsolescence

    o Losing Control: Having a part of one's core business dependent on some piece of code developed in some "old school" programming language that is no longer mastered by anyone alive has the power to render sleepless the more relaxed business managers.

    o No longer having whom to resort to: Having critical software that is either hardware or operating system dependent when those are no longer supported by their manufacturer or there is even no longer a manufacturer to resort to; well, hardly the position any business manager is eager to be in.

    o The missing component: The support infrastructure no longer exists. Some older software was developed having its backup process and policies dependent on either the backup hardware or the logic inherent to some specific backup product or solution. Most likely such backup product has already been discontinued which potentially renders restore activities unfeasible.

- Cost

  o Choosing the lesser problem: If a Legacy system is still around it usually means that it plays a critical role towards corporate core business. In most cases, replacing it comprehends significant costs both investment-wise as well as regarding potential operational stoppages and other related running costs. Still, doing nothing, although it may seem to save money in the short term, may represent an exponentially growing risk of not being able to work at all in the foreseeable time horizon.

  o OPEX and CAPEX: Having old systems running may imply investing in discontinued components stock such as backup tapes, hard disk drives, RAM memories or resorting to high-cost contractors that leverage their niche knowledge.

- Agility

  o Responsiveness: "Response Rate" is also one major factor that may lead to the need of modernizing old software. The initial standard Ethernet communication was around from under 10 Mbps (Mega Bits per Second, during the late 1980s) and later on 100 Mbps (during the 1990s). Currently, we can easily have 1/10Gb/s (Gigabits per second) as standard. So, if one speaks of a software tool that supports some critical operation with growing demand for software responsiveness in order to allow more I/O (input/output of processes data per time unit), the only way is to migrate or update the software.

  o Business Cycle: Being competitive in today's market requires the ability to promptly address an unforeseen demand and some Legacy Systems are not able to cope with such required flexibility. Most of today's Distribution Chains have minimized their warehouse offering due to inherent maintenance costs and risks associated with stored goods depreciation as well as potential incidents. So, upon a given urgent client request for material, those Distribution Chains will contact the factories not necessarily after the lowest price but in search for the one that is able to deliver the material in the shortest period of time. In such manner, the factory needs to have the flexibility to speed up production in order to be in the game.

- Integration

  o The ability to easily speak to others: IT has been growing in terms of platforms (like mobile and social networks) as well as complexity in terms of IT landscape components (cloud computing, distributed computing, other). Agile "Plugin" integrability is becoming a competitive edge in business terms and Legacy Systems were developed with the exact opposite mindset, of keeping core business processes isolated and in-house.

- Misalignment

  o The Law: In some cases, legislation or market regulation may imply the need of migrating an existing software so that it may comply with newly posed requirements.

o   The Market: Competition is another common compelling motivation towards Legacy Modernization. When competition gets ahead in the market by having more effective business support tools, the time has come to move forward or perish. In some cases, a new competitor while installing its business capacity resorts to modern software tools that allow running processes that deliver higher efficiency and therefore a competitive edge. That alone is enough to represent a shift in market share which starts a Legacy Modernization process.

Popular Approaches to Legacy Modernization

The entire topic poses such a complex multitude of potential impacts that several approaches and methodologies have been developed just to address it:

- Architecture Driven Modernization (ADM): Resorting to support infrastructure to mitigate the modernization complexity (virtualization is an example).

- The SABA Framework: Consists of planning ahead both the organizational as well as technical impacts; in fact, it is a best practice that if largely used would have minimized some headaches in big corporations.

- Reverse Engineering Model: Represents high costs and a very long project that may be undermined by technology pace.

- Visaggio's Decision Model (VDM): Consists of a decision model that aims at reaching the suitable software renewal processes at a component-level based for each case combining both the technological as well as the economic perspectives.

- Economic Model to Software Rewriting and Replacement Times (SRRT) – Similar to the above mentioned VDM model.

- DevOps Contribution: DevOps focus is to allow swift deployment of new software releases with an absolute minimum degree of bug or errors in total compliance with target operational IT environment. This, by itself, represents a major enabler factor to speed up Legacy Modernization processes.

Still basically, when considering Legacy Modernization there are three possible roads to choose from:

- Rewrite: Migrate the coding to a more recent development language. This option implies a high potential for underestimating both inherent costs and required time frame, therefore running into a never-ending story.

- Replace: Throw away the old system, replacing it with a new one. This option usually implies having to build an entirely new application ecosystems with semi off-the-shelf components that mimic or mirror some functionalities of the existing Legacy Systems, therefore usually meaning raising the complexity level without, most of the times, achieving 100% functionality compliance.

- Reuse: Find a manner to achieve portability of the Legacy System as is to an up to date IT environment. If applicable, this option allows a step-by-step approach where change is tested and fine-tuned.

Independently and prior to deciding which is the most suitable way to proceed, it is vital to have a clear picture about current status as well as of how well are the foundations established.

Getting Started with Legacy Modernization

Here are some steps that must be accomplished in order to layout a Legacy Modernization Process roadmap that results in added value:

- Clearly identify and map all IT Systems and inherent software applications within one's corporate landscape, regarding role, interactions (both amongst them as towards human users), their support platforms, resources and ageing status within the current technological standard.

- Clearly identify, list and mirror towards existing IT Systems and inherent software applications the corresponding corporate business processes.

- You must look at the business as well as IT and if the company does not have such culture and still considers IT "something annoying that we must have," you must need the unequivocal sponsorship of the board of management.

- Proceed with a dual approach perspective considering in one hand the IT Systems and inherent software applications technological ageing status versus current technological standard, and in the other hand matching them against corporate business processes evolutive roadmap.

- The overlapping of both timeline maps should allow a good perspective on required Legacy Modernization prioritization roadmap.

- Bear in mind that people cannot provide you what they do not have, meaning some process knowledge needs to be checked and cross-checked because most of the time although key users know how the process works and which steps it encompasses they do not know the logic behind it nor the implications in other business processes.

- Carefully cross check the Legacy Modernization prioritization roadmap with IT systems interdependencies and fine-tune the roadmap accordingly.

- Raise the core business potential impact while performing a risk assessment regarding each Legacy Modernization action and redefine the roadmap accordingly.

- Raise the budget impact of each Legacy Modernization action and redefine the roadmap accordingly.

- Prepare a final roadmap proposal and have it clearly conveyed (along with inherent risks and benefits) to all corporate stakeholders getting their buy-in.

- Have a clear failover strategy and make sure to also convey it in an assertive and crystal-clear manner.

IT systems are one of the main pillars of modern corporations and therefore Legacy Modernization deeply affects the company at all levels. It is something that just cannot be looked upon as the CIO's problem. It's either a benefit or potential catastrophe that mandates a corporate approach.

In some cases, the potential impact of attempting software migration bears such a risk that CIOs and top executives are left with the sole option of delaying those projects, hoping for technological evolution that enables lower cost and lower risk solutions.

Sometimes Waiting for the Next Big Thing has Proven to be the Wiser Option

Some seven years ago the evolution of virtual environments allowed some old, yet critical IT systems to be maintained as they were developed, just having them migrated to a virtual environment that basically holds them within a more secure and redundant "protective capsule." But, unfortunately, not all old software are good applicants for such process.

Risks, Challenges, and Benefits Derived from Legacy Modernization

Inherent risks to migrating Legacy Software include:

- The Challenge of Human Change Management: Humans deeply dislike change and need to be motivated, trained and coached towards it, which represents additional risk and cost.

- Old and New Cohabitation: Most corporations are not limited to one single Legacy System, and having the several existing ones migrated simultaneously is just not feasible due to the potentially catastrophic impact combined with the imminent coordination effort and costs. So, in most cases Legacy Modernization needs to be a corporate program that looks at each system required effort and time window as well as how to best articulate and prioritize the migration endeavor.

- Tailor-made Philosophy: Legacy applications were born in an era where the main concern of software engineers was to develop code in a way that better explored the specific platform (hardware and operating systems) where the application software would be running. This means that when migrating a Legacy System or application one extra care to be considered is how to tackle the assumptions that laid beneath the coding decisions taken to better explore specific platform functionalities that no longer exist, either having been discharged or become obsolete by new technology. One clear example relates to former 68000 CPU based hardware that would leverage RAM indexing in a manner that simply isn't relevant any longer; nevertheless, such strategic approach to coding may render ineffective a direct migration effort. Another example relates to the way in which former Novell Networks would allow information packages to flow. When Novell was heavily replaced on the 1990s, some applications would not work because they had been developed to have their I/O optimized according to such Network protocols.

- Integrability Cycles: In a corporate environment there are more systems "speaking" to each other than with humans. This means that one main concern when modernising a piece of Legacy software is to assure that I/O will obey by the data interchange rules and requirements posed by client applications and support resources (like databases).

- Hardcoded Business Processes: Let's consider tens of thousands or hundreds of thousands or even millions of lines of code that have been developed within a given logical architecture because it better addresses a given corporate process. Those lines of code have most likely been recurrently "enhanced" over several years via the intervention of the team that knew the underlying logic behind the entire software coding. To end this story let's consider that such team is gone and absolutely no documentation is available allowing to understand how the software matches the corporate process. It is a potential trial and error nightmare, aggravated by the fact that in most cases such Legacy Systems may not be replicated in "laboratory" therefore change needs to happen live, with the potential core business impact that derives from that.

Software Rot

Software rot refers to the slow degradation in the performance of computer software. Such software shows diminished responsiveness, lacks updates, may become faulty overtime owing to changes in the operating system it is running on and thus may need upgrading.

Software rot is also known as software erosion, code rot, software entropy, bit rot or software decay.

Software rot is generally categorized into two types:

- Dormant rot: Software that is not used on a consistent basis may eventually become useless as the rest of the application transforms. Variations in software environment as well as user demands play a role in the deterioration as well.

- Active rot: Without constant application of ideal mitigation procedures, software that has undergone constant modifications might lose its integrity gradually. However, most software requires constant updates as well as bug fixing. This may lead to an evolution process, which ultimately makes the program deviate from its original design. As a result of this constant evolution, the logic engineered by the original designers tends to be invalidated, presenting new bugs.

The main reasons behind software rot are as follows:

- Unused code

- Environment change

- Seldomly updated code

Fixing software rot is challenging; however, the following are some measures that can prevent or at least minimize the intensity of the rot:

- Introduce code reviews: Include code reviews as a compulsory step before the release. A clear set of coding guidelines, in addition to training coders for review using these guidelines, is essential.

- Create documentation: Include rules regarding commenting code in the coding guidelines, and make it mandatory for usage. This would force programmers to structure their comments in a consistent manner. This leads to an increase in readability across the code base.

- Mentor new programmers: When adding people to an existing team, make sure to appropriately initiate them in the code base.

- Hire the right ones: Hire the right people with the right set of skills specific for the requirement.

Example of Software Rot

Multi-process Firefox

When it was first written, Mozilla Firefox ran everything in a single process. After the release of Google Chrome, it was clear that a multi-process model allowed for better security and performance. Mozilla developers soon started planning to make Firefox multi-process. That was in 2007.

Almost a decade later, Mozilla finally began rollout of multi-process Firefox. This delay is not for want of trying. The teams at Mozilla are talented and driven. Still, Chrome was written from scratch in far less time than it has taken Firefox to change. There are two main reasons for this:

- Making a single process architecture multi-process means changing a *lot* of small things. Certain function calls have to be replaced with inter-process communication. Shared state must be wrapped in mutexes. Caches and local databases must handle concurrent access.

- Firefox needed to remain compatible with existing add-ons (or force devs to update their add-ons). Chrome got to create an extention API from scratch, avoiding such constraints.

It gets worse. These constraints are at odds with each other: Overhaul the internal architecture, but alter public-facing APIs as little as possible. It's no wonder Mozilla needed 10 years to accomplish this feat.

Event-driven Apache

When Apache httpd was first written, it used a process-per-connection model. One process would listen on port 80, then accept() and fork(). The child process would then read() and write() on the socket. When the request was finished, the child would close() the socket and exit().

This architecture had the advantage of being simple, easy to implement on many platforms, and... not much else. It was absolutely terrible for performance, especially when handling long-lived connections. To be fair: this *was* 1995. And Apache soon moved to a threaded model, which did help performance. Still, it couldn't handle 10,000 simultaneous connections. A connection-per-thread architecture takes 1,000 threads to service 1,000 concurrent connections. Each thread has its own stack and state, and must be scheduled by the operating system. It makes for a bad time.

In contrast, Nginx used a reactor pattern from the start. This allowed it to handle more concurrent connections and rendered it immune to slowloris attacks.

Nginx was first released in 2007, and its performance advantage was apparent. Years before the release of Nginx, the Apache devs had begun re-architecting httpd to perform better. The event MPM shipped with Apache 2.2 in 2005. Still, there were teething issues. Most importantly, the event MPM broke compatibility with popular modules like mod_php. It wasn't until 2012 that

Apache 2.4 shipped with it as the default. While far better than the previous prefork and worker MPMs, the worker MPM didn't acheive parity with Nginx. Instead, it used separate thread pools for listening/accepting connections and processing requests. The architecture is roughly equivalent to running a load balancer or reverse proxy in front of a worker MPM httpd.

CPython GIL

Python is a nice programming language. It's expressive, easy to learn (at least as programming languages go), and it's supported on a wide variety of platforms. But for the past two decades, the most popular implementation of Python has had one major problem: it can't easily take advantage of multiple CPU cores.

The cause of Python's lack of parallelism is its global interpreter lock, or GIL.

In CPython, the global interpreter lock, or GIL, is a mutex that prevents multiple native threads from executing Python byte codes at once. This lock is necessary mainly because CPython's memory management is not thread-safe. (However, since the GIL exists, other features have grown to depend on the guarantees that it enforces).

Originally, the GIL wasn't a big deal. When Python was created, multi-core systems were rare. And a GIL is simple to write and easy to reason about. But today, even wristwatches have multi-core CPUs. The GIL is an obvious and glaring defect in what is otherwise a pleasant language. Despite CPython's popularity, despite the project's capable developers, despite sponsors such as Google, Microsoft, and Intel, fixing the GIL isn't even on the roadmap.

In conclusion, even when given talented engineers, plenty of money, and clear vision, mature software can be extremely difficult to change. Cases that disprove software rot don't seem to exist. There are plenty of old software projects, but they haven't had to adapt much. I'd love to find good counterexamples, as the current evidence paints a bleak picture for the long-term future of software.

References

- Software-maintenance, software-engineering: ecomputernotes.com, Retrieved 11 April 2018

- Types-of-software-maintenance, software-engineering: Retrieved 25 May 2018

- Backporting-what-is-it-and-how-it-is-done: gotowebsecurity.com, Retrieved 14 March 2018

- Debugging-16373: techopedia.com, Retrieved 31 March 2018

- Legacy-modernization-software-systems-explained: bmc.com, Retrieved 11 April 2018

User Interface Design

User interface design refers to the design of user interfaces for software and machines, such as computers, appliances and electronic devices for optimizing usability and the user experience. This chapter discusses in detail about GUI, graphic control elements, HTML, cascading style sheets, client-side scripting, etc. for a deeper understanding of user interface design.

Graphical User Interface

A graphical user interface (GUI) is a type of user interface that allows users to navigate around a computer or device and complete actions via visual indicators and graphical icons.

All major operating systems such as Windows, Mac, iOS, and Android have a graphic interface where you can click on an icon to complete an action such as opening an application, viewing a menu or navigating through your device.

Initially, GUI's were developed for use with a mouse and keyboard but are now widely used in many handheld mobile devices, such as smartphones and tablets and which uses a combination of technologies to provide a platform for interaction.

Unlike a command line operating system or CUI, GUI operating systems are much easier to learn and use for beginners because commands do not need to be memorized and users don't need any knowledge of program languages.

There was no single inventor of the GUI and its history is linked with some of the most famous names in computing, most notably Apple who first implemented it into its Lisa and Macintosh computers.

GUI's have evolved dramatically over the years and continues with the rise in speech recognition and natural language processing technology which controls many devices through voice assistants

The first graphical user interface was developed in 1981 at Xerox PARC by Alan Kay, Douglas Engelbart alongside other researchers who realized that having a graphical representation of an operating system would make it more accessible to the masses.

The first commercial use of a GUI was in the Apple Lisa computer in 1983. Before this, computers such as MS-DOS and Linux used command-line UIs, as their usage was limited to advanced business users rather than consumers.

A year later, the Apple Macintosh became the most popular commercial computer with a GUI. Microsoft's followed suit in 1985 with Windows 1.0, although Windows 2.0 was a significant improvement when it was launched in 1997. It wasn't until 1995 and the launch of Windows 95 that Microsoft caught up with Apple's commercial success in the world of GUI systems.

Benefits of a Graphical User Interface

The major benefit of a GUI is that systems using one are accessible to people of all levels of knowledge, from an absolute beginner to an advanced developer or other tech-savvy individuals. They make it simple for anyone to open menus, move files, launch programs or search the internet without having to tell the computer via the command line to carry out a function.

GUIs also provide instant feedback. Clicking an icon will open it up, for example, and this can be seen in real-time. Using a command line interface, you won't know whether it's a valid entry until you hit return; if it's not valid, nothing will happen.

Disadvantages of Using a Graphical User Interface

Because the elements are graphics rather than text, GUIs can use a lot more processing power compared to a standard text-based UI.

Additionally, advanced users can find GUIs frustrating, because often a chain of actions will have to happen (such as opening up a menu, navigating to the file you want to open, clicking it) before the process is complete. With a text or command-line UI, one single line can be inputted and it will be actioned.

Uses of Graphical User Interface

GUIs are used for the majority of computer operating systems, mobile operating systems and software in existence. Although some operating systems, such as Linux, still use command-line interfaces, this makes them less mainstream because they are only suitable for those who have an in-depth knowledge of commands.

Graphic Control Elements

When designing your interface, try to be consistent and predictable in your choice of interface elements. Whether they are aware of it or not, users have become familiar with elements acting in a certain way, so choosing to adopt those elements when appropriate will help with task completion, efficiency, and satisfaction.

Interface elements include but are not limited to:

- Input Controls: checkboxes, radio buttons, dropdown lists, list boxes, buttons, toggles, text fields, date field
- Navigational Components: breadcrumb, slider, search field, pagination, slider, tags, icons
- Informational Components: tooltips, icons, progress bar, notifications, message boxes, modal windows
- Containers: accordion

Input Controls

Checkboxes allow the user to select one or more options from a set. It is usually best to present checkboxes in a vertical list. More than one column is acceptable as well if the list is long enough that it might require scrolling or if comparison of terms might be necessary.

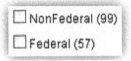

Radio Buttons

Radio buttons are used to allow users to select one item at a time.

Dropdown Lists

Dropdown lists allow users to select one item at a time, similarly to radio buttons, but are more compact allowing you to save space. Consider adding text to the field, such as 'Select one' to help the user recognize the necessary action.

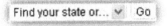

List Boxes

List boxes, like checkboxes, allow users to select a multiple items at a time,but are more compact and can support a longer list of options if needed.

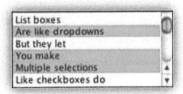

Buttons

A button indicates an action upon touch and is typically labeled using text, an icon, or both.

Dropdown Button

The dropdown button consists of a button that when clicked displays a drop-down list of mutually exclusive items.

Toggles

A toggle button allows the user to change a setting between two states. They are most effective when the on/off states are visually distinct.

Text Fields

Text fields allow users to enter text. It can allow either a single line or multiple lines of text.

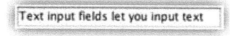

Date and Time Pickers

A date picker allows users to select a date or time. By using the picker, the information is consistently formatted and input into the system.

Navigational Components

Search Field

A search box allows users to enter a keyword or phrase (query) and submit it to search the index with the intention of getting back the most relevant results. Typically search fields are single-line text boxes and are often accompanied by a search button.

Breadcrumb

Breadcrumbs allow users to identify their current location within the system by providing a clickable trail of proceeding pages to navigate by.

Pagination

Pagination divides content up between pages, and allows users to skip between pages or go in order through the content.

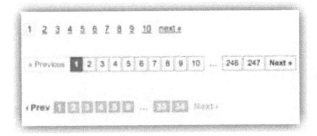

Tags

Tags allow users to find content in the same category. Some tagging systems also allow users to apply their own tags to content by entering them into the system.

Sliders

A slider, also known as a track bar, allows users to set or adjust a value. When the user changes the value, it does not change the format of the interface or other info on the screen.

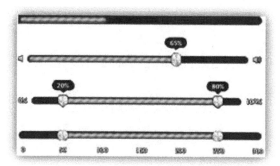

Icons

An icon is a simplified image serving as an intuitive symbol that is used to help users to navigate the system. Typically, icons are hyperlinked.

Image Carousel

Image carousels allow users to browse through a set of items and make a selection of one if they so choose. Typically, the images are hyperlinked.

Information Components

Notifications

A notification is an update message that announces something new for the user to see. Notifications are typically used to indicate items such as, the successful completion of a task, or an error or warning message.

Progress Bars

A progress bar indicates where a user is as they advance through a series of steps in a process. Typically, progress bars are not clickable.

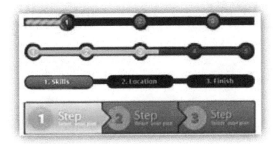

Tool Tips

A tooltip allows a user to see hints when they hover over an item indicating the name or purpose of the item.

Message Boxes

A message box is a small window that provides information to users and requires them to take an action before they can move forward.

Modal Window (Pop-up)

A modal window requires users to interact with it in some way before they can return to the system.

Containers

Accordion

An accordion is a vertically stacked list of items that utilizes show or hide functionality. When a label is clicked, it expands the section showing the content within. There can have one or more items showing at a time and may have default states that reveal one or more sections without the user clicking.

Hyper Text Markup Language

First developed by Tim Berners-Lee in 1990, HTML is short for HyperText Markup Language. HTML is used to create electronic documents (called pages) that are displayed on the World Wide

Web. Each page contains a series of connections to other pages called hyperlinks. Every web page you see on the Internet is written using one version of HTML code or another.

HTML code ensures the proper formatting of text and images so that your Internet browser may display them as they are intended to look. Without HTML, a browser would not know how to display text as elements or load images or other elements. HTML also provides a basic structure of the page, upon which Cascading Style Sheets are overlaid to change its appearance. One could think of HTML as the bones (structure) of a web page, and CSS as its skin (appearance).

Appearance of an HTML tag

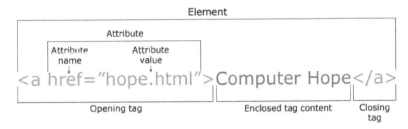

As seen above in the above HTML tag example, there are not many components. Almost all HTML tags have an opening tag that contains the name with any attributes and a close tag that contains a forward slash and the name of the tag that is being closed. For tags that do not have a closing tag like the <img> tag, it is best practice to end the tag with a forward slash.

Each tag is contained within a less than and greater than angle brackets and everything between the opening and closing tag is displayed or affected by the tag. In the above example, the <a> tag is creating a link called "Computer Hope" that is pointing to the hope.html file.

Appearance of HTML

The following is an example of a basic web page written in HTML as well as a description of each section and its function.

<!DOCType HTML PUBLIC "-//W3C//DTD HTML 4.01 Transitional//EN" "https://www.w3.org/TR/html4/loose.dtd">

<html lang="en"><head>

<title>Example page</title>

<meta http-equiv="Content-Type" content="text/html; charset=windows-1252">

</head>

<body>

<h1>This is a heading</h1>

<p>This is an example of a basic HTML page.</p>

</body></html>

The example above contains the key ingredients to a basic web page. The first line (Doc Type) describes what version of HTML the page was written in so that an Internet browser can interpret the text that follows. Next, the HTML opening tag lets the browser know that it is reading HTML code. The HTML tag is followed by the head section which contains information about the page such as its title, meta tags, and where to locate the CSS file. The body section is all content that is viewable on the browser. For example, all the text you see here is contained within the body tags. Finally, closing tags wrap each element for proper syntax.

HTML5

HTML5 is the update made to HTML from HTML4 (XHTML follows a different version numbering scheme). It uses the same basic rules as HTML4, but adds some new tags and attributes which allow for better semantics and for dynamic elements that are activated using JavaScript. New elements include section, <article>, <aside>, <audio>, <bdi>, <canvas>, <datalist>, <details>, <embed>, <figure>, <figcaption>, <footer>, <header>, <keygen>, <mark>, <meter>, <nav>, <output>, <progress>, <rp>, <rt>, <ruby>, <time>, <track>, <video>, and <wbr>. There are also new input types for forms, which include tel, search, url, email, datetime, date, month, week, time, datetime-local, number, range, and color.

With the increasing movement to keep structure and style separate, a number of styling elements have been removed along with those that had accessibility issues or saw very little use. These following elements should no longer be used in HTML code: <acronym>, <applet>, <basefont>, <big>, <center>, <dir>, <font>, <frame>, <frameset>, <noframes>, <strike>, and <tt>. HTML5 also simplifies the doctype declaration to the tag in the following box.

<!doctype html>

Appearance of HTML5

As shown below the HTML5 code is very similar to the earlier HTML4 example, but is much cleaner with the revised doctype tag.

<!doctype html>

<html>

<head>

<meta charset="utf-8">

<title>Example page</title>

</head>

<body>

<h1>This is a heading</h1>

<p>This is an example of a basic HTML page.</p>

</body>

</html>

Ways to Create and View HTML

Because HTML is a markup language it can be created and viewed in any text editor as long as it is saved with a .htm or .html file extension. However, most find it easier to design and create web pages in HTML using an HTML editor.

Once the HTML file is created it can be viewed locally or uploaded to a web server to be viewed online using a browser.

File Extensions Used with HTML

HTML files use either the .htm or .html file extension. Older versions of Windows (Windows 3.x) only allow three-letter file extensions, so they used .htm instead of .html. However, both file extensions have the same meaning, and either may be used today. That being said, we recommend sticking to one naming convention as certain web servers may prefer one extension over the other.

Cascading Style Sheets

CSS stands for Cascading Style Sheets and it is the language used to style the visual presentation of web pages. CSS is the language that tells web browsers how to render the different parts of a web page.

Every item or element on a web page is part of a document written in a markup language. In most cases, HTML is the markup language, but there are other languages in use such as XML. Throughout this guide we will use HTML to demonstrate CSS in action, just keep in mind that the same principles and techniques apply if you're working with XML or a different markup language.

Difference Between CSS and HTML

The first thing to understand when approaching the topic of CSS is when to use a styling language like CSS and when to use a markup language such as HTML.

- All critical website content should be added to the website using a markup language such as HTML.

- Presentation of the website content should be defined by a styling language such as CSS.

Blog posts, page headings, video, audio, and pictures that are not part of the web page presentation should all be added to the web page with HTML. Background images and colors, borders, font size, typography, and the position of items on a web page should all be defined by CSS.

It's important to make this distinction because failing to use the right language can make it difficult to make changes to the website in the future and create accessibility and usability issues for website visitors using a text-only browser or screen reader.

CSS Syntax

CSS syntax includes selectors, properties, values, declarations, declaration blocks, rulesets, at-rules, and statements.

- A selector is a code snippet used to identify the web page element or elements that are to be affected by the styles.

- A property is the aspect of the element that is to be affected. For example, color, padding, margin, and background are some of the most commonly used CSS properties.

- A value is used to define a property. For example, the property color might be given the value of red like this: color: red;.

- The combination of a property and a value is called a declaration.

- In many cases, multiple declarations are applied to a single selector. A declaration block is the term used to refer to all of the declarations applied to a single selector.

- A single selector and the declaration block that follows it in combination are referred to as a ruleset.

- At-rules are similar to rulesets but begin with the @ sign rather than with a selector. The most common at-rule is the @media rule which is often used to create a block of CSS rules that are applied based on the size of the device viewing the web page.

- Both rulesets and at-rules are CSS statements.

An Example of CSS Syntax

Let's use a block of CSS to clarify what each of these items is:

```
h1 {
    color: red;
    font-size: 3em;
    text-decoration: underline;
}
```

In this example, h1 is the selector. The selector is followed by a declaration block that includes three declarations. Each declaration is separated from the next by a semicolon. The tabs and line breaks are optional but used by most developers to make the CSS code more human-readable.

By using h1 as the selector, we are saying that every level 1 heading on the web page should follow the declarations contained in this ruleset.

The ruleset contains three declarations:

- color:red;

- font-size: 3em;

- text-decoration: underline;

color, font-size, and text-decoration are all properties. There are literally hundreds of CSS properties you can use, but only a few dozen are commonly used.

We applied the values red, 3em, and underline to the properties we used. Each CSS property is defined to accept values formatted in a specific way.

For the color property we can either use a color keyword or a color formula in Hex, RGB, or HSL format. In this case, we used the color keyword red. There are a few dozen color keywords available in CSS3, but millions of colors can be accessed with the other color models.

We applied the value of 3em to the property font-size. There are a wide range of size units we could have used including pixels, percentages, and more.

Finally, we added the value underline to the property text-decoration. We could have also used overline or line-through as values for text-decoration. In addition, CSS3 allows for the use of the linc-styles solid, double, dotted, dashed, and wavy was well the specification of text-decoration colors. We could have applied all three values at once by using a declaration like this:

text-decoration: blue double underline;

That rule would cause the h1 in our initial example to be underlined with a blue double line. The text itself would remain red as defined in our color property.

Preparing HTML Markup for Styling

CSS should be used to add content to a web page. That task is best handled by markup languages such as HTML and XML. Instead, CSS is used to pick items that already exist on a web page and to define how each item should appear.

In order to make it as easy as possible to select items on a web page, identifiers should be added to elements on the webpage. These identifiers, often called hooks in the context of CSS, make it easier to identify the items that should be affected by the CSS rules.

Classes and IDs are used as hooks for CSS styles. While the way CSS renders is not affected by the use of classes and hooks, they give developers the ability to pinpoint HTML elements that they wish to style.

Classes and IDs aren't interchangeable. It's important to know when to use each.

Using Classes

Use classes when there are multiple elements on a single web page that need to be styled. For example, let's say that you want links in the page header and footer to be styled in a consistent manner, but not the same way as the links in the body of the page. To pinpoint those links you could add a class to each of those links or the container holding the links. Then, you could specify the styles using the class and be sure that they would only be applied to the links with that class attribute.

Using IDs

Use IDs for elements that only appear once on a web page. For example, if you're using an HTML unordered list for your site navigation, you could use an ID such as nav to create a unique hook for that list.

Here's an example of the HTML and CSS code for a simple navigation bar for a basic e-commerce site:

```
<style>
    #nav {

        background: lightgray;

        overflow: auto;

        }

    #nav li {

        float: left;

        padding: 10px;

        }

    #nav li:hover {

        background: gray;

        }

</style>
<ul id="nav">

    <li><a href="">Home</a></li>

    <li><a href="">Shop</a></li>

    <li><a href="">About Us</a></li>

    <li><a href="">Contact Us</a></li>

</ul>
```

That code would produce a horizontal navigation menu with a light gray background beginning from the left-hand side of the page. Each navigation item will have 10 pixels of spacing on all sides and the background of each item will become darker when you allow your mouse to hover over it.

Any additional lists on the same web page would not be affected by that code.

```
#example-nav {

background: lightgray;

overflow: auto;

}

#example-nav li {

float: left;
```

```
padding: 10px;

}

#example-nav li:hover {

background: gray;

}
```

When not to use Hooks

You don't have to add a class or ID to an HTML element in order to style it with CSS. If you know you want to style every instance of a specific element on a web page you can use the element tag itself.

For example, let's say that you want to create consistent heading styles. Rather than adding a class or ID to each heading it would be much easier to simply style all heading elements by using the heading tag.

```
<style>
    ul {
        list-style-type: upper-roman;
        margin-left: 50px;
        }
    p {
        color: darkblue
        }
</style>
<p>Some paragraph text here. Two short sentences.</p>
<ul>
<li>A quick list</li>
<li>Just two items</li>
</ul>
<p>Additional paragraph text here. This time let's go for three sentenc-
es. Like this.</p>
```

That code would render like this.

.code_sample ul {

```
list-style-type: upper-roman;

margin-left: 50px;

}

.code_sample p {

color: darkblue

}
```

Some paragraph text here. Two short sentences.

- A quick list
- Just two items

Additional paragraph text here. This time let's go for three sentences. Like this.

- Another list
- Still just two items

In this case, even though we only wrote the style rules for ul and p elements once each, multiple items were affected. Using element selectors is a great way to create an attractive, readable, and consistent website experience by creating consistent styling of headings, lists, and paragraph text on every page of the website.

Best Practices for Preparing Your Markup for Styling

Now that you know how classes, IDs, and element tags can be used as hooks for CSS rulesets, how can you best implement this knowledge to write markup that makes it easy to pinpoint specific elements?

- Apply classes liberally and consistently. Use classes for items that should be aligned in one direction or the other, and for any elements that appear repeatedly on a single web page.
- Apply IDs to items that appear only once on a web page. For example, use an ID on the div that contains your web page content, on the ul that that contains the navigation menu, and on the div that contains your web page header.

Ways of Linking CSS Rules to an HTML Document

There are three ways of adding CSS rules to a web page:

- Inline styles
- Internal stylesheets
- External stylesheets

In the vast majority of cases, external stylesheets should be used. However, there are instances where inline styles or internal stylesheets may be used.

Inline Styles

Inline styles are applied to specific HTML elements. The HTML attribute style is used to define rules that only apply to that specific element. Here's a look at the syntax for writing inline styles:

```
<h1 style="color:red; padding:10px; text-decoration:underline;">Example
Heading</h1>
```

That code would cause just that heading to render with red underlined text and 10 pixels of padding on all sides. There are very few instances where inline styles should be used. In nearly all cases they should be avoided and the styles added to a stylesheet.

Internal Stylesheets

An internal stylesheet is a block of CSS added to an HTML document head element. The style element is used between the opening and closing head tags, and all CSS declarations are added between the style tags.

We can duplicate the inline styles from the code above in an internal stylesheet using this syntax:

```
<head>

    <style>

        h1 {

            color: red;

            padding: 10px;

            text-decoration: underline;

            }

    </style>

</head>

<body>

    <h1>Example Heading</h1>

</body>
```

That code would produce the same results as the inline styles. However, the benefit to using internal stylesheets rather than inline styles is that all h1 elements on the page will be affected by the styles.

External Stylesheets

External stylesheets are documents containing nothing other than CSS statements. The rules defined in the document are linked to one or more HTML documents by using the link tag within the head element of the HTML document.

To use an external stylesheet, first create the CSS document.

```
/*************************************************
Save with a name ending in .css such as styles.css
*************************************************/
h1 {

    color: red;

    padding: 10px;

    text-decoration: underline;

    }
```

Now that we have an external stylesheet with some styles, we can link it to an HTML document using the link element.

```
<head>

<link rel="stylesheet" type="text/css" href="styles.css">

</head>

<body>

    <h1>Example Heading</h1>

</body>
```

When this HTML document is loaded the link tag will cause the styles in the file styles.css to be loaded into the web page. As a result, all level 1 heading elements will appear with red text, underlined, and with 10 pixels of padding applied to every side.

When to use Each Method

In nearly all cases external stylesheets are the proper way to style web pages. The primary benefit to using external stylesheets is that they can be linked to any number of HTML documents. As a result, a single external stylesheet can be used to define the presentation of an entire website.

Internal stylesheets may be used when designing a simple one-page website. If the website will never grow beyond that single initial page using an internal stylesheet is acceptable.

Inline styles are acceptable to use in two instances:

1. When writing CSS rules that will only be applied to a single element on a single web page.

2. When applied by a WYSIWYG editor such as the tinyMCE editor integrated into a content management system such as WordPress.

In all other cases, inline styles should be avoided in favor of external stylesheets.

Working of CSS

When writing CSS, there are many times that rules are written that conflict with each other. For example, when styling headers, all of the following rules may apply to an h1 element.

- An element-level rule creating consistent h1 rendering across all pages of the website.

- A class-level rule defining the rendering of h1 elements occurring in specific locations – such as the titles of blog posts.

- An id-level element defining the rendering of an h1 element used in just one place on a one or more web pages – such as the website name.

How can a developer write rules that are general enough to cover every h1 yet specific enough to define styles that should only appear on specific instances of a given element?

CSS styles follow two rules that you need to understand to write effective CSS. Understanding these rules will help you write CSS that is broad when you need it to be, yet highly-specific when you need it to be.

The two rules that govern how CSS behaves are inheritance and specificity.

Cascading Inheritance

Why are CSS styles called cascading? When multiple rules are written that conflict with each other, the last rule written will be implemented. In this way, styles cascade downward and the last rule written is applied.

Let's look at an example. Let's write two CSS rules in an internal stylesheet that directly contradict each other:

```
<head>
    <style>
        p {color: red;}
        p {color: blue;}
    </style>
</head>
<body>
<p>What color will the text of this paragraph be?</p>
</body>
```

The browser will cascade through the styles and apply the last style encountered, overruling all previous styles. As a result, the heading is blue.

```
.code_sample_p {color: red;}
```

```
.code_sample_p {color: blue;}
```

What color will the text of this paragraph be?

This same cascading effect comes into play when using external stylesheets. It's common for multiple external stylsheets to be used. When this happens, the style sheets are loaded in the order they appear in the HTML document head element. Where conflicts between stylesheet rules occur, the CSS rules contained in each stylesheet will overrule those contained in previously loaded stylesheets. Take the following code for example:

```
<head>

<link rel="stylesheet" type="text/css" href="styles_1.css">

<link rel="stylesheet" type="text/css" href="styles_2.css">

</head>
```

The rules in styles_2.css will be applied if there are conflicts between the styles contained in these two stylesheets.

Inheritance of styles is another example of the cascading behavior of CSS styles.

When you define a style for a parent element the child elements receive the same styling. For example, if we apply color styling to an unordered list, the child list items will display the same styles.

```
<head>
  <style>
    ul {color: red;}
  </style>
</head>
<body>
  <ul>
    <li>Item 1</li>
    <li>Item 2</li>
  </ul>
</body>
```

Here's how that code would render.

```
.code-sample-ul {color: red;}
```

- Item 1
- Item 2

Not every property passes from a parent to its child elements. Browsers deem certain properties as non-inherited properties. Margins are one example of a property that isn't passed down from a parent to a child element.

Specificity

The second rule that determines which rules are applied to each HTML element is the rule of specificity.

CSS rules with more specific selectors will overrule CSS rules with less specific selectors regardless of which occurs first. As we discussed, the three most common selectors are element tags, classes, and ids:

- The least specific type of selector is the element level selector.

- When a class is used as a selector it will overrule CSS rules written with the element tag as the selector.

- When an ID is used as a selector it will overrule the CSS rules written with element or class selectors.

Another factor that influences specificity is the location where the CSS styles are written. Styles written inline with the style attribute overrule styles written in an internal or external stylesheet.

Another way to increase the specificity of a selector is to use a series of elements, classes, and IDs to pinpoint the element you want to address. For example, if you want to pinpoint unordered list items on a list with the class "example-list" contained with a div with the id "example-div" you could use the following selector to create a selector with a high level of specificity.

```
div#example-div > ul.example-list > li {styles here}
```

While this is one way to create a very specific selector, it is recommended to limit the use of these sorts of selectors since they do take more time to process than simpler selectors.

Once you understand how inheritance and specificity work you will be able to pinpoint elements on a web page with a high degree of accuracy.

Client-side Scripting

All websites run on three components: the server, the database, and the client. The client is simply the browser a person is using to view a site, and it's where client-side technology is unpacked and processed. The server is at a remote location anywhere in the world—housing data, running a site's back-end architecture, processing requests, and sending pages to the browser. The client is anywhere your users are viewing your site: mobile devices, laptops, or desktop computers. Server-side scripting is executed by a web server; client-side scripting is executed by a browser.

Client-end scripts are embedded in a website's HTML markup code, which is housed on the server in a language that's compatible with, or compiled to communicate with, the browser. The browser temporarily downloads that code, and then, apart from the server, processes it. If it needs to request additional information in response to user clicks, mouse-overs, etc. (called "events"), a request is sent back to the server.

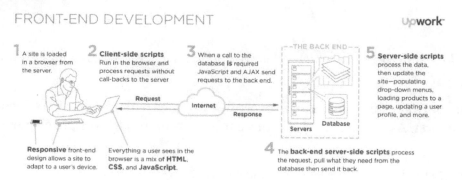

Client-side scripting is always evolving—it's growing simpler, more nimble, and easier to use. As a result, sites are faster, more efficient, and less work is left up to the server.

Working of Client-side Scripting

There is overlap between the two technologies as they work in tandem, but there are core differences. Server-side scripting works in the back end of a site, which the user doesn't see. It creates a scaffolding for the site to access its database, all the behind-the-scenes mechanics that organize and power a website. Client-side code, however, handles what the user does see.

- Scripts are embedded within and interact with the HTML of your site, selecting elements of it, and then manipulating those elements to provide an interactive experience.

- Scripts interact with a cascading style sheet (CSS) file that styles the way the page looks.

- It dictates what work the server-side code is going to have to accomplish (where utility should be built around these front-end functions), and returns data that's pulled from the site in a way that's readable by the browser. For example: If there's a form for updating a profile, the back end is built to pull specific data from the database to populate that form, while front-end scripts populate the form with that information.

- Scripts put less stress on the server because they don't require processing on the server once they're downloaded, just when post-backs are made. "Post-backs" perform specific call-and-answers with the server-side code, and respond to the user immediately.

Client-side Programming Languages and Frameworks

Now that you've got a broad view of what front-end technology is and does, here's a look at some of the most widely used scripting languages and front-end frameworks. Languages are almost always used in the context of their frameworks, which make quick work of complicated code with libraries of pre-packaged, shareable code, and lots of add-ons. Your developer may use one or a combination of these when building the front end of your site.

- HTML and CSS: These are the core building blocks of any site. HTML dictates a site's organization and content. CSS comprises the code for every graphic element—from backgrounds to fonts—that make up the look and feel of a website. Learn more about HTML and markup languages.

- JavaScript: JavaScript is client-side scripting. The most widely used client-side script—nearly every site's front end is a combination of JavaScript and HTML and CSS. JavaScript is fueled by an array of excellent frameworks that simplify it and give it more agility.

JavaScript Frameworks

- AngularJS: An incredibly robust JavaScript framework for data-heavy sites

- JQuery, jQuery Mobile: A fast, small, JS object library that streamlines how JavaScript behaves across different browsers

- Node.js: A server-side platform that uses JavaScript, and is changing the way real-time applications can communicate with the server for faster response times and a more seamless user experience. It works with another JavaScript framework, Express.js, to build server-side Web applications.

- A mobile-first framework that uses HTML, CSS, and JavaScript to facilitate rapid responsive app development

- React, for user interface design

- Express.js, Backbone.js, Ember.js, MeteorJS, and more

- TypeScript: A compile-to-JavaScript language that is a superset of JavaScript, created by Microsoft

- AJAX (JavaScript + XML)—a technology that allows specific parts of a site to be updated without a full-page refresh by asynchronously connecting to the database and pulling JSON– or XML-based chunks of data.

- VBScript & JScript are Microsoft's front-end scripts that run on the ASP.NET framework. JScript is Microsoft's reverse-engineered version of JavaScript.

- ActionScript, which creates animated interactive web applications for Adobe Flash Play

- Java (as "applets") snippets of back-end code that run independently with a run-time environment in the browser

Client-side Scripting Breakthrough

An important breakthrough that changed the hard-and-fast rules for client side vs. server side? AJAX. The old standard was that server-side processing and page post-backs were used when the browser needed to interact with things on the server, like databases. AJAX, with its asynchronous calls to the server, can pull the data instantly and efficiently, without requiring a post-back.

Another major boost is jQuery, a fast, small, and feature-rich JavaScript library with an easy-to-use API that works across a multitude of browsers. Like code libraries do, jQuery changed the way that millions of people write JavaScript, simplifying a number of other client-side scripts like AJAX at the same time.

Asynchronous JavaScript and XML

AJAX stands for Asynchronous JavaScript and XML. AJAX is a new technique for creating better, faster, and more interactive web applications with the help of XML, HTML, CSS, and Java Script.

- Ajax uses XHTML for content, CSS for presentation, along with Document Object Model and JavaScript for dynamic content display.

- Conventional web applications transmit information to and from the sever using synchronous requests. It means you fill out a form, hit submit, and get directed to a new page with new information from the server.

- With AJAX, when you hit submit, JavaScript will make a request to the server, interpret the results, and update the current screen. In the purest sense, the user would never know that anything was even transmitted to the server.

- XML is commonly used as the format for receiving server data, although any format, including plain text, can be used.

- AJAX is a web browser technology independent of web server software.

- A user can continue to use the application while the client program requests information from the server in the background.

- Intuitive and natural user interaction. Clicking is not required, mouse movement is a sufficient event trigger.

- Data-driven as opposed to page-driven.

Rich Internet Application Technology

AJAX is the most viable Rich Internet Application (RIA) technology so far. It is getting tremendous industry momentum and several tool kit and frameworks are emerging. But at the same time, AJAX has browser incompatibility and it is supported by JavaScript, which is hard to maintain and debug.

AJAX is Based on Open Standards

AJAX is based on the following open standards –

- Browser-based presentation using HTML and Cascading Style Sheets (CSS).

- Data is stored in XML format and fetched from the server.

- Behind-the-scenes data fetches using XMLHttpRequest objects in the browser.

- JavaScript to make everything happen.

Before 2005, communication between client-side and server-side was harder to establish. Developers use hidden iframes to populate the server data to the client-side. But in 2005, James Garrett write an article named AJAX: a new approach to Web applications. The key technology is used in AJAX is XMLHttpRequest(XHR), firstly invented by Microsoft and then use by other browsers. XHR has capabilities to retrieve data from server-side and populate on client-side with the help of existing technologies. Before 2005, developers use different technologies for communication with server-side such as Java Applets or Flash movies.

XMLHttpRequest Object

Internet Explorer 5 was the first browser who introduced XHR (XMLHttpRequest) object in the internet world. Internet Explorer includes ActiveX object in MSXML library. Internet Explorer has three version of XHR object :

1. MSXML2.XMLHttp

2. MSXML2.XMLHttp.3.0

3. MSXML2.XMLHttp.6.0

Create XHR Object for Internet Explorer 7+

```
// function for create XHR for IE 7+
function createXHR(){
  if(typeof arguments.callee.activeXString != 'string'){
    var ver = [
      "MSXML2.XMLHttp.6.0",
      "MSXML2.XMLHttp.3.0",
      "MSXML2.XMLHttp"
    ];

    for(var i=0;  i<ver.length;i++){
      try{
        new ActiveXObject(ver[i]);
        argument.callee.activeXString = ver[i];
        break;
      }catch(ex){
        //skip
      }
    }
  }
}
```

```
return new ActiveXObject(argument.callee.activeXString);
}
```

Elaboration of above Code

1. This function tries to create most latest version of XHR available on Internet Explorer.

2. In this function, firstly we can check the type of arguments.callee.activeXstring. If type of this activeXstringis not string, then we create an array of latest version of XHR includes in MSXML for Internet Explorer.

3. After that we apply the forloop to assign the latest version of XHR to arguments.callee. activeXstring.

4. At the last line of that function we return a new instance of ActiveXObject with latest version of XHR.

```
return new ActiveXObject(argument.callee.activeXString);
```

All modern browser including IE 7+, Google Chrome, Safari, Firefox supports the native XHR object. Native XHR object can be created by using XMLHttpRequest constructor.

```
var xhr = new XMLHttpRequest();
```

Create XHR Object for Earlier Version of Internet Explorer

The above function is best suited for the greater version than IE 7. If you want to create an XML-HttpRequest object for the pervious version of IE, extend the above function to check the support of native XMLHttpRequest in the Internet Explorer.

```
function createXHR(){
    if (typeof XMLHttpRequest != "undefined"){
        return new XMLHttpRequest();
    }else if(typeof ActiveXObject != "undefined"){){
        if(typeof arguments.callee.activeXString != 'string'){
            var ver = [
                "MSXML2.XMLHttp.6.0",
                "MSXML2.XMLHttp.3.0",
                "MSXML2.XMLHttp"
            ];

            for(var i=0; i<ver.length;i++){
```

```
    try{

      new ActiveXObject(ver[i]);

      argument.callee.activeXString = ver[i];

      break;

    }catch(ex){

    //skip

  }

 }

 }

  return new ActiveXObject(argument.callee.activeXString);

}else{

  throw new Error("No XHR object available.");

}

}
```

Elaboration of above Code

1. This function checks if the browser supports the native XHR than return the new instance of XMLHttpRequestconstructor.

2. If browser supports ActiveX then set latest version of XMLHttpRequest by MSXML.

3. In the last check if browser neither support native XHR nor ActiveX , so throw an error with "No XHR Supports" message.

Syntax of XMLHttpRequest

`xhr.open(method:string,url:string,asynchronous:boolean)`

To start with the XMLHttpRequest object, first call the open() method of XHR. It has three arguments :

1. method (GET, POST, DELETE)

2. url(requested URL)

3. true(asynchronous or synchronous)

Example:

`xhr.open("get", "data.json", true);`

Examples

1. We call the open() method of an XHR object to prepare the request to be sent only. We cannot call the XHR request by using open() method only.

2. In this method, the first parameter is for Http Request methods like GET, PUT, POST, DELETE etc. As per Http standards, use these methods in capital letters, otherwise, some browser behaves unexpectedly like Firefox.

3. Second parameter in open() method is URL. If you use same domain URL, your call goes smoothly otherwise if you use cross-domain URL, you fight with cross-origin like errors.

4. The last parameter has the main power. The last parameter will be decided that your request goes as an asynchronous type or synchronous type. By default, it sets as an asynchronous type.

Above line of code just prepare the request which sent to the server. For sending the XHR request we use send() method.

```
xhr.send(null);
```

In the send() method, we can send data as the parameter or null because this argument is required for some browsers. If you don't have data to send, set this argument to null.

```
xhr.open("get", "data.json", true);
xhr.send(null);
```

Above request is an asynchronous type of request. So, we cannot wait for the response to this request. With the response, we have some data with relevant properties :

1. responseText

2. responseXML

3. status

4. statusText

responseText:

responseText has the text value which returned as the body of response.

responseXML:

responseXML returns with value when content-type set to text/xml or application/xml otherwise it gives null value.

status:

This property sends HTTP status of the response.

statusText:

This property sends the HTTP status text of the response.

```
var xhr = new XMLHttpRequest();

xhr.open("GET", "data.json",true);

xhr.send(null);


if((xhr.status>= 200 && xhr.status<300) || xhr.status === 304){

  alert(xhr.responseText);

}else{

  alert("Some problem "+ xhr.status);

}
```

Elaboration of above Code

1. In the first line, we create an XMLHttpRequest instance by the using of XMLHttpRequest()

   ```
   var xhr = new XMLHttpRequest();
   ```

2. In the next line, we can prepare the request to be send by send() method

   ```
   xhr.open("GET", "data.json", true);
   ```

3. In the next line of code, we can send the request by send() method.

   ```
   xhr.send(null);
   ```

4. After we get the response, check the status code. On the basis of status code, we retrieve the data or error. If status code is equal to or greater than 200 and less than 300 or 304. We alert the responseText, otherwise alert the status code of error.

```
if((xhr.status>=  200  &&  xhr.status<300)  ||  xhr.status  ===  304){
alert(xhr.responseText);  }else{         alert("Some problem "+ xhr.sta-
tus);}
```

Phases of Request/Response Cycle (ReadyState)

1. 0—Uninitialized—open() is not called yet.

2. 1—Open—open() method called but send () method not called.

3. 2—Send—send() method waiting for response.

4. 3—Receiving—Some response data received.

5. 4—Completed—All response data is received and available for use.

Readystate Event

When the phases of readyState changes from one phase to another readystatechange event are fired. We can use onreadystatechange event handler to handle the phases of readyState. For front-end developers, only last phase is important because at this phase all data is received and available for use.

```javascript
var xhr = new XMLHttpRequest();

xhr.onreadystatechange = function(){

  if(xhr.readyState === 4){

    if((xhr.status>= 200 && xhr.status<300) || xhr.status === 304){

      alert(xhr.responseText);

     }else{

      alert("Some problem "+ xhr.status);

    }

  }

};


xhr.open("GET", "data.json",true);

xhr.send(null);
```

Elaboration of above Code

In the above code, we implement one enhancement is that we can check the readyState phase of XMLHttpRequest. We apply the check if readyState is 4, then we implement and put logic on retrieved data.

```javascript
xhr.readyState === 4
```

Abort the XMLHttpRequest

We can use abort() method to cancel the asynchronous XMLHttpRequestbefore response is received.

```javascript
xhr.abort();
```

Model–view Controller

We've seen how GUI programs are structured around a view tree, and how input events are handled by attaching listeners to views. This is the start of a separation of concerns – output handled by views, and input handled by listeners.

But we're still missing the application itself – the backend that actually provides the information to be displayed, and computes the input that is handled.

The model-view-controller pattern, originally articulated in the Smalltalk-80 user interface, has strongly influenced the design of UI software ever since. In fact, MVC may have single-handedly inspired the software design pattern movement; it figures strongly in the introductory chapter of the seminal "Gang of Four" book (Gamma, Helm, Johnson, Vlissides, Design Patterns: Elements of Reusable Software).

MVC's primary goal is separation of concerns. It separates the user interface frontend from the application backend, by putting backend code into the model and frontend code into the view and controller. The original MVC also separated input from output; the controller is supposed to handle input, and the view is supposed to handle output. We'll see that this separation is less effective in practice, however.

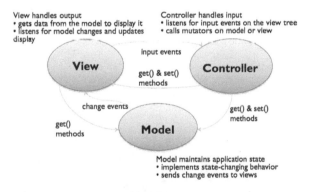

The model is responsible for maintaining application-specific data and providing access to that data. Models are often mutable, and they provide methods for changing the state safely, preserving its representation invariants. OK, all mutable objects do that. But a model must also notify its clients when there are changes to its data, so that dependent views can update their displays, and dependent controllers can respond appropriately. Models do this notification using the listener pattern, in which interested views and controllers register themselves as listeners for change events generated by the model.

View objects are responsible for output. A view occupies some chunk of the screen, usually a rectangular area. Basically, the view queries the model for data and draws the data on the screen. It listens for changes from the model so that it can update the screen to reflect those changes.

Finally, in the original MVC pattern, the controller handles the input. It receives keyboard and mouse events, and instructs the model to change accordingly. But we'll see below that the separation of concerns in this part of the pattern between the view and the controller has not really worked out well in practice.

In principle, the model-view separation has several benefits. First, it allows the interface to have multiple views showing the same application data. For example, a database field might be shown in a table and in an editable form at the same time. Second, it allows views and models to be reused in other applications. The model-view pattern enables the creation of user interface toolkits, which are libraries of reusable interface objects.

A simple example of the MVC pattern is a text field widget (this is Java Swing's text widget). Its model is a mutable string of characters. The view is an object that draws the text on the screen (usually with a rectangle around it to indicate that it's an editable text field). The controller is an object that receives keystrokes typed by the user and inserts them in the string. Note that the controller may signal a change in the view (here, moving the cursor) even when there is no change in the underlying model.

Instances of the MVC pattern appear at many scales in GUI software. At a higher level, this text field might be part of a view (like the address book editor), with a different controller listening to it (for text-changed events), for a different model (like the address book). But when you drill down to a lower level, the text field itself is an instance of MVC.

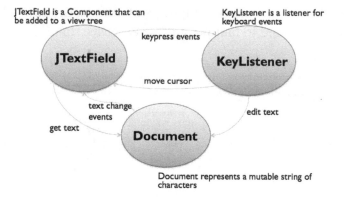

Here's a larger example, in which the view is a filesystem browser (like the Mac Finder or Windows Explorer), the model is the disk filesystem, and the controller is an input handler that translates the user's keystrokes and mouse clicks into operations on the model and view.

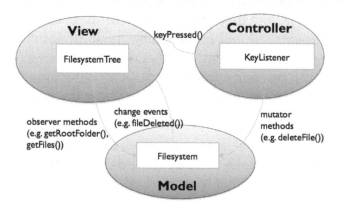

The original MVC pattern has a few problems when you try to apply it, which boil down to this: you can't cleanly separate input and output in a graphical user interface. Let's look at a few reasons why.

First, a controller often needs to produce its own output. The view must display affordances for the controller, such as selection handles or scrollbar thumbs. The controller must be aware of the screen locations of these affordances. When the user starts manipulating, the view must modify its appearance to give feedback about the manipulation, e.g., painting a button as if it were depressed.

Second, some pieces of state in a user interface don't have an obvious home in the MVC pattern. One of those pieces is the selection. Many UI components have some kind of selection, indicating the parts of the interface that the user wants to use or modify. In our text box example, the selection is either an insertion point or a range of characters.

Which object in the MVC pattern should be responsible for storing and maintaining the selection? The view has to display it, e.g., by highlighting the corresponding characters in the text box. But the controller has to use it and modify it. Keystrokes are inserted into the text box at the location of the selection, and clicking or dragging the mouse or pressing arrow keys changes the selection.

Perhaps the selection should be in the model, like other data that's displayed by the view and modified by the controller? Probably not. Unlike model data, the selection is very transient, and belongs more to the frontend (which is supposed to be the domain of the view and the controller) than to the backend (the model's concern). Furthermore, multiple views of the same model may need independent selections. In Emacs, for example, you can edit the same file buffer in two different windows, each of which has a different cursor.

So we need a place to keep the selection, and similar bits of data representing the transient state of the user interface. It isn't clear where in the MVC pattern this kind of data should go.

In principle, it's a nice idea to separate input and output into separate, reusable classes. In reality, it isn't always feasible, because input and output are tightly coupled in graphical user interfaces. As a result, the MVC pattern has largely been superseded by what might be called Model-View, in which the view and controllers are fused together into a single class, often called a component or a widget.

Most of the widgets in a GUI toolkit are fused view/controllers like this; you can't, for example, pull out the scrollbar's controller and reuse it in your own custom scrollbar. Internally, the scrollbar probably follows a model-view-controller architecture, but the view and controller aren't independently reusable.

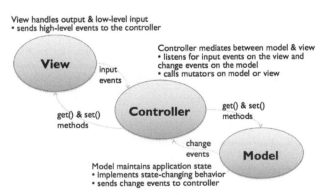

Partly in response to this difficulty, and also to provide a better decoupling between the model and the view, some definitions of the MVC pattern treat the controller less as an input handler and more as a mediator between the model and the view.

In this perspective, the view is responsible not only for output, but also for low-level input handling, so that it can handle the overlapping responsibilities like affordances and selections.

But listening to the model is no longer the view's responsibility. Instead, the controller listens to both the model and the view, passing changes back and forth. The controller receives high-level input events from the view, like selection-changed, button-activated, or textbox-changed, rather than low-level input device events. The Mac Cocoa framework uses this approach to MVC.

References

- What-is-a-graphical-user-interface, operating-systems-30248: itpro.co.uk, Retrieved 19 May 2018

- How-to-and-tools, user-interface-elements: usability.gov, Retrieved 30 June 2018

- How-scripting-languages-work: upwork.com, Retrieved 14 March 2018

- What-is-ajax: tutorialspoint.com, Retrieved 23 May 2018

- Ajax-asynchronous-javascript-and-xml-1914: medium.com, Retrieved 13 April 2018

Software Requirements

Software requirements is an area of software engineering concerned with the establishment of the needs of the user that can be solved by software. It involves activities that can be grouped under analysis, elicitation, specification and management. The varied aspects of software requirements have been introduced in this chapter, such as requirement gathering, requirement analysis and software requirements specification.

In the software development process, requirement phase is the first software engineering activity. This phase is a user-dominated phase and translates the ideas or views into a requirements document. Note that defining and documenting the user requirements in a concise and unambiguous manner is the first major step to achieve a high-quality product.

The requirement phase encompasses a set of tasks, which help to specify the impact of the software on the organization, customers' needs, and how users will interact with the developed software. The requirements are the basis of the system design. If requirements are not correct the end product will also contain errors. Note that requirements activity like all other software engineering activities should be adapted to the needs of the process, the project, the product and the people involved in the activity. Also, the requirements should be specified at different levels of detail. This is because requirements are meant for people such as users, business managers, system engineers, and so on. For example, business managers are interested in knowing which features can be implemented within the allocated budget whereas end-users are interested in knowing how easy it is to use the features of software.

Requirement is a condition or capability possessed by the software or system component in order to solve a real world problem. The problems can be to automate a part of a system, to correct shortcomings of an existing system, to control a device, and so on. IEEE defines requirement as:

1) A condition or capability needed by a user to solve a problem or achieve an objective.

2) A condition or capability that must be met or possessed by a system or system component to satisfy a contract, standard, specification, or other formally imposed documents.

3) A documented representation of a condition or capability as in (1) or (2).'

Requirements describe how a system should act, appear or perform. For this, when users request for software, they provide an approximation of what the new system should be capable of doing. Requirements differ from one user to another and from one business process to another.

Guidelines for Expressing Requirements

The purpose of the requirements document is to provide a basis for the mutual understanding between the users and the designers of the initial definition of the software development life cycle (SDLC) including the requirements, operating environment and development plan.

The requirements document should include the overview, the proposed methods and procedures, a summary of improvements, a summary of impacts, security, privacy, internal control considerations, cost considerations, and alternatives. The requirements section should state the functions required in the software in quantitative and qualitative terms and how these functions will satisfy the performance objectives. The requirements document should also specify the performance requirements such as accuracy, validation, timing, and flexibility. Inputs, outputs, and data characteristics need to be explained. Finally, the requirements document needs to describe the operating environment and provide (or make reference to) a development plan.

There is no standard method to express and document requirements. Requirements can be stated efficiently by the experience of knowledgeable individuals, observing past requirements, and by following guidelines. Guidelines act as an efficient method of expressing requirements, which also provide a basis for software development, system testing, and user satisfaction. The guidelines that are commonly followed to document requirements are listed below:

1. Sentences and paragraphs should be short and written in active voice. Also, proper grammar, spelling, and punctuation should be used.

2. Conjunctions such as 'and' and 'or' should be avoided as they indicate the combination of several requirements in one requirement.

3. Each requirement should be stated only once so that it does not create redundancy in the requirements specification document.

Types of Requirements

Requirements help to understand the behavior of a system, which is described by various tasks of the system. For example, some of the tasks of a system are to provide a response to input values, determine the state of data objects, and so on. Note that requirements are considered prior to the development of the software. The requirements, which are commonly considered, are classified into three categories, namely, functional requirements, non-functional requirements, and domain requirements.

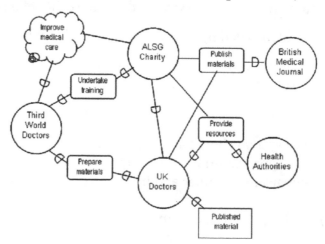

IEEE defines functional requirements as 'a function that a system or component must be able to perform.' These requirements describe the interaction of software with its environment and specify the inputs, outputs, external interfaces, and the functions that should be included in the software. Also, the services provided by functional requirements specify the procedure by which the software should react to particular inputs or behave in particular situations.

To understand functional requirements properly, let us consider the following example of an on-line banking system:

1. The user of the bank should be able to search the desired services from the available ones.

2. There should be appropriate documents' for users to read. This implies that when a user wants to open an account in the bank, the forms must be available so that the user can open an account.

3. After registration, the user should be provided with a unique acknowledgement number so that he can later be given an account number.

The above mentioned functional requirements describe the specific services provided by the on-line banking system. These requirements indicate user requirements and specify that functional requirements may be described at different levels of detail in an online banking system. With the help of these functional requirements, users can easily view, search and download registration forms and other information about the bank. On the other hand, if requirements are not stated properly, they are misinterpreted by software engineers and user requirements are not met.

The functional requirements should be complete and consistent. Completeness implies that all the user requirements are defined. Consistency implies that all requirements are specified clearly without any contradictory definition. Generally, it is observed that completeness and consistency cannot be achieved in large software or in a complex system due to the problems that arise while defining the functional requirements of these systems. The different needs of stakeholders also prevent the achievement of completeness and consistency. Due to these reasons, requirements may not be obvious when they are,'first specified and may further lead to inconsistencies in the requirements specification.

The non-functional requirements (also known as quality requirements) are related to system attributes such as reliability and response time. Non-functional requirements arise due to user requirements, budget constraints, organizational policies, and so on. These requirements are not related directly to any particular function provided by the system.

Non-functional requirements should be accomplished in software to make it perform efficiently. For example, if an aeroplane is unable to fulfill reliability requirements, it is not approved for safe operation. Similarly, if a real time control system is ineffective in accomplishing non-functional requirements, the control functions cannot operate correctly.

The description of different types of non-functional requirements is listed below:

1. Product requirements: These requirements specify how software product performs. Product requirements comprise the following.

2. Efficiency requirements: Describe the extent to which the software makes optimal use of resources, the speed with which the system executes, and the memory it consumes for its operation. For example, the system should be able to operate at least three times faster than the existing system.

3. Reliability requirements: Describe the acceptable failure rate of the software. For example, the software should be able to operate even if a hazard occurs.

4. Portability requirements: Describe the ease with which the software can be transferred from one platform to another. For example, it should be easy to port the software to a different operating system without the need to redesign the entire software.

5. Usability requirements: Describe the ease with which users are able to operate the software. For example, the software should be able to provide access to functionality with fewer keystrokes and mouse clicks.

6. Organizational requirements: These requirements are derived from the policies and procedures of an organization. Organizational requirements comprise the following.

7. Delivery requirements: Specify when the software and its documentation are to be delivered to the user.

8. Implementation requirements: Describe requirements such as programming language and design method.

9. Standards requirements: Describe the process standards to be used during software development. For example, the software should be developed using standards specified by the ISO and IEEE standards.

10. External requirements: These requirements include all the requirements that affect the software or its development process externally. External requirements comprise the following.

11. Interoperability requirements: Define the way in which different computer based systems will interact with each other in one or more organizations.

12. Ethical requirements: Specify the rules and regulations of the software so that they are acceptable to users.

13. Legislative requirements: Ensure that the software operates within the legal jurisdiction. For example, pirated software should not be sold.

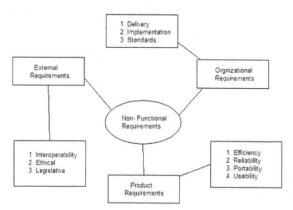

Non-functional requirements are difficult to verify. Hence, it is essential to write non-functional requirements quantitatively, so that they can be tested. For this, non-functional requirements metrics are used. These metrics are listed in Table.

Metrics for Non-functional Requirements

Features	Measures
Speed	Processed transaction/second
	User/event response time
	Screen refresh rate
Size	Amount of memory (KB)
	Number of RAM chips.
Ease of use	Training time
	Number of help windows
Reliability	Mean time to failure (MTTF)
	Portability of unavailability
	Rate of failure occurrence
Robustness	Time to restart after failure
	Percentage of events causing failure
	Probability of data corruption on failure
Portability	Percentage of target-dependent statements
	Number of target systems

Requirements which are derived from the application domain of the system instead from the needs of the users are known as domain requirements. These requirements may be new functional requirements or specify a method to perform some particular computations. In addition, these requirements include any constraint that may be present in the existing functional requirements. As domain requirements reflect the fundamentals of the application domain, it is important to understand these requirements. Also, if these requirements are not fulfilled, it may be difficult to make .the system work as desired.

A system can include a number of domain requirements. For example, it may comprise a design constraint that describes the user interface, which is capable of accessing all the databases used in a system. It is important for a development team to create databases and interface designs as per established standards. Similarly, the requirements of the user such as copyright restrictions and security mechanism for the files and documents used in the system are also domain requirements. When domain requirements are not expressed clearly, it can result in the following difficulties.

Problem of understandability: When domain requirements are specified in the language of application domain (such as mathematical expressions), it becomes difficult for software engineers to understand them.

Problem of implicitness: When domain experts understand the domain requirements but do not express these requirements clearly, it may create a problem (due to incomplete information) for the development team to understand and implement the requirements in the system.

Information about requirements is stored in a database, which helps the software development team to understand user requirements and develop the software according to those requirements.

Requirements Engineering Process

This process is a series of activities that are performed in the requirements phase to express requirements in the Software Requirements Specification (SRS) document. It focuses on understanding the requirements and its type so that an appropriate technique is determined to carry out the Requirements Engineering (RE) process. The new software developed after collecting requirements either replaces the existing software or enhances its features and functionality. For example, the payment mode of the existing software can be changed from payment through hand-written cheques to electronic payment of bills.

An RE process is shown, which comprises various steps including feasibility study, requirements elicitation, requirements analysis, requirements specification, requirements validation, and requirements management.

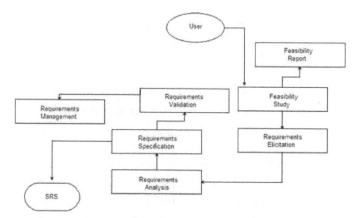

The requirements engineering process begins with feasibility study of the requirements. Then requirements elicitation is performed, which focuses on gathering user requirements. After the requirements are gathered, an analysis is performed, which further leads to requirements specification. The output of this is stored in the form of software requirements specification document. Next, the requirements are checked for their completeness and correctness in requirements validation. Last of all, to understand and control changes to system requirements, requirements management is performed.

Requirement Gathering

Requirements elicitation (also known as Requirements Gathering or Capture) is the process of generating a list of requirements (functional, system, technical, etc.) from the various stakeholders (customers, users, vendors, IT staff, etc).

The process is not as straight forward as just asking the stakeholders what they want they system to do, as in many cases, they are not aware of all the possibilities that exist, and may be limited by their immersion in the current state. For example asking people in the 19th Century for their requirements for a self-propelled vehicle, would have just resulted in the specification for a faster horse-drawn carriage rather than an automobile.

Techniques used for Requirements Elicitation

- Interviews: These are an invaluable tool at the beginning of the process for getting background information on the business problems and understanding a current-world perspective of what the system being proposed needs to do. You need to make sure that your interviews cover a diverse cross-section of different stakeholders, so that the requirements are not skewed towards one particular function or area.

- Questionnaires: One of the challenges with interviews is that you will only get the information that the person is consciously aware of. Sometimes there are latent requirements and features that are better obtained through questionnaires. By using carefully chosen, probing questions (based on the information captured in prior interviews), you can drill-down on specific areas that the stakeholders don't know are important, but can be critical to the eventual design of the system.

- User Observation: One of the best ways to determine the features of a system, that does not result in "paving the cowpath" (i.e. building a slightly improved version of the current state) is to observe users actually performing their daily tasks, and ideally recording the actions and activities that take place. By understanding the holistic context of how they perform the tasks, you can write requirements that will reinvent the processes rather than just automating them, and will ensure that usability is paramount.

- Workshops: Once you have the broad set of potential requirements defined, you will need to reconcile divergent opinions and contrasting views to ensure that the system will meet the needs of all users and not just the most vocal group. Workshows are a crucial tool that can be used to validate the initial requirements, generate additional detail, gain consensus and capture the constraining assumptions.

- Brainstorming: This is a powerful activity, which can be performed either in the context of a workshop or on its own. By considering different parts of the system and considering 'what-if' scenarios, or 'blue-sky' ideas, you can break out of the context of the current-state and consider visionary ideas for the future. Tools such as whiteboards or mind-mapping software can be very helpful in this phase.

- Role Playing: In situations where the requirements depend heavily on different types of user, formal role-playing (where different people take on the roles of different users in the system/process) can be a good way of understanding how the different parts of the system need to work to support the integrated processes (e.g in an ERP system).

- Use Cases & Scenarios: Once you have the high-level functional requirements defined, it is useful to develop different use-cases and scenarios that can be used to validate the functionality in different situations, and to discover any special exception or boundary cases that need to be considered.

- Prototyping: There is truth to the saying "I don't know what I want, but I know that I don't want that!". Often stakeholders won't have a clear idea about what the requirements are, but if you put together several different prototypes of what the future could be, they will know which parts they like. You can then synthesize the different favored parts of the prototypes to reverse-engineer the requirements.

Ways to Capture the Information

There are many different ways to capture the information, from a simple Word document, spreadsheet or presentation to sophisticated modeling diagrams. We recommend that the initial high-level brainstorming and requirements discovery be done on a whiteboard to foster collaboration. Once the initial ideas have crystallized, we recommend using a formal Requirements Management System to record the information from the whiteboard and drill-down the functional requirements in smaller focus-groups to arrive at the use-cases and system requirements.

Common Mistakes

Be careful to avoid making these mistakes:

- Basing a solution on complex or cutting-edge technology and then discovering that it cannot easily be rolled out in the 'real world'.

- Not prioritising the requirements, for example, 'must have', 'should have', 'could have' and 'would have' - known as the MoSCoW principle.

- Insufficient consultation with real users and practitioners.

- Solving the 'problem' before you know what the problem is.

- Lacking a clear understanding and making assumptions rather than asking.

Requirements gathering is about creating a clear, concise and agreed set of customer requirements that allow you to provide what the customer wants.

Requirement Analysis

Requirements analysis as the process of studying user needs to arrive at a definition of a system, hardware or software requirements. The process of studying and refining system, hardware or software requirements.' Requirements analysis helps to understand, interpret, classify, and organize the software requirements in order to assess the feasibility, completeness, and consistency of the requirements. Various other tasks performed using requirements analysis are listed below:

1. To detect and resolve conflicts that arise due to unclear and unspecified requirements.

2. To determine operational characteristics of the software and how they interact with the environment.

3. To understand the problem for which the software is to be developed.

4. To develop an analysis model to analyze the requirements in the software.

Software engineers perform analysis modeling and create an analysis model to provide information of 'what' software should do instead of 'how' to fulfill the requirements in software. This model emphasizes information such as the functions that software should perform, behavior it should exhibit, and constraints that are applied on the software. This model also determines the relationship of one component with other components. The clear and complete requirements specified in the analysis model help the software development team to develop the software according to those requirements. An analysis model is created to help the development team to assess the quality of the software when it is developed. An analysis model helps to define a set of requirements that can be validated when the software is developed.

Let us consider an example of constructing a study room, where the user knows the dimensions of the room, the location of doors and windows, and the available wall space. Before constructing the study room, he provides information about flooring, wallpaper, and so on to the constructor. This information helps the constructor to analyze the requirements and prepare an analysis model that describes the requirements. This model also describes what needs to be done to accomplish those requirements. Similarly, an analysis model created for the software facilitates the software development team to understand what is required in the software and then they develop it.

In Figure the analysis model connects the system description and design model. System description provides information about the entire functionality of the system, which is achieved by implementing the software, hardware and data. In addition, the analysis model specifies the software design in the form of a design model, which provides information about the software's architecture, user interface, and component level structure.

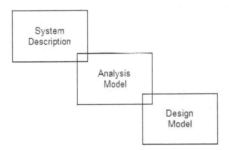

The guidelines followed while creating an analysis model are listed below:

1. The model should concentrate on requirements in the problem domain that are to be accomplished. However, it should not describe the procedure to accomplish the requirements in the system.

2. Every element of the analysis model should help in understanding the software requirements. This model should also describe the information domain, function, and behavior of the system.

3. The analysis model should be useful to all stakeholders because every stakeholder uses this model in his own manner. For example, business stakeholders use this model to validate requirements whereas software designers view this model as a basis for design.

4. The analysis model should be as simple as possible. For this, additional diagrams that depict no new or unnecessary information should be avoided.

Also, abbreviations and acronyms should be used instead of complete notations. The choice of representation is made according to the requirements to avoid inconsistencies and ambiguities. Due to this, the analysis model comprises structured analysis, object-oriented modeling, and other approaches. Each of these describes a different manner to represent the functional and behavioral information. Structured analysis expresses this information through data-flow diagrams whereas object-oriented modeling specifies the functional and behavioral information using objects. Other approaches include ER modeling and several requirements specification languages and processors.

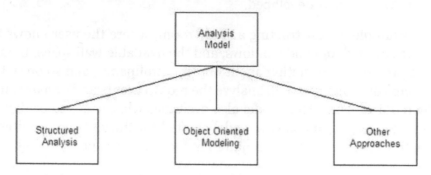

Structured Analysis

Structured analysis is a top-down approach, which focuses on refining the problem with the help of functions performed in the problem domain and data produced by these functions. This approach facilitates the software engineer to determine the information received during analysis and to organize the information in order to avoid the complexity of the problem. The purpose of structured analysis is to provide a graphical representation to develop new software or enhance the existing software.

IEEE defines a data-flow diagram (also known as bubble chart and work flow diagram) as, 'a diagram that depicts data sources, data sinks, data storage and processes performed on data as nodes and logical flow of data as links between the nodes.' DFD allows the software development team to depict flow of data from one process to another. In addition, DFD accomplishes the following objectives.

1. It represents system data in a hierarchical manner and with required levels of detail.

2. It depicts processes according to defined user requirements and software scope.

A DFD depicts the flow of data within a system and considers a system as a transformation function that transforms the given inputs into desired outputs. When there is complexity in a system, data needs to be transformed using various steps to produce an output. These steps are required to refine the information. The objective of DFD is to provide an overview of the transformations that occur in the input data within the system in order to produce an output.

A DFD should not be confused with a flowchart. A DFD represents the flow of data whereas a flowchart depicts the flow of control. Also, a DFD does not depict the information about the procedure to be used for accomplishing the task. Hence, while making a DFD, procedural details about the processes should not be shown. DFD helps the software designer to describe the transformations taking place in the path of data from input to output

A DFD consists of four basic notations (symbols), which help to depict information in a system. These notations are listed in Table.

Table DFD Notations

Name	Notation	Description
External entity		Represents the source or destination of data within the system. Each external entity is identified with a meaningful and unique name.
Data flow		Represents the movement of data from its source to destination within the system.
Data store		Indicates the place for storing information within the system.
Process		Shows a transformation or manipulation of data within the system. A process is also known as bubble.

While creating a DFD, certain guidelines are followed to depict the data-flow of system requirements effectively. These guidelines help to create DFD in an understandable manner. The commonly followed guidelines for creating DFD are listed below:

1. DFD notations should be given meaningful names. For example, verbs should be used for naming a process whereas nouns should be used for naming external entity, data store, and data-flow.

2. Abbreviations should be avoided in DFD notations.

3. Each process should be numbered uniquely but the numbering should be consistent.

4. ADFD should be created in an organized manner so that it is easily understood.

5. Unnecessary notations should be avoided in DFD in order to avoid complexity.

6. ADFD should be logically consistent. For this, processes without any input or output and any input without output should be avoided.

7. There should be no loops in a DFD.

8. ADFD should be refined until each process performs a simple function so that it can be easily represented as a program component.

9. A DFD should be organized in a series of levels so that each level provides more detail than the previous level.

10. The name of a process should be carried to the next level of DFD.

11. The data store should be depicted at the context level where it first describes an interface between two or more processes. Then, the data store should be depicted again in the next level of DFD that describes the related processes.

There are various levels of DFD, which provide details about the input, processes, and output of a system. Note that the level of detail of process increases with increase in level(s). However, these levels do not describe the system's internal structure or behavior. These levels are listed below.

1. Level 0 DFD: This shows an overall view of the system. Level a DFD is also known as context diagram.

2. Level 1 DFD: This elaborates level a DFD and splits the process into a detailed form.

3. Level 2 DFD: This elaborates level 1 DFD and displays the process(s) in a detailed form.

4. Level 3 DFD: This elaborates level 2 DFD and displays the process(s) in a detailed form.

To understand various levels of DFD, let us consider an example of a banking system. This DFD represents how a 'user' entity interacts with a 'banking system' process and avails its services. The Level 0 DFD depicts the entire banking system as a single process. There are various tasks performed in a bank such as transaction processing, pass book entry, registration, demand draft creation, and online help. The data-flow indicates that these tasks are performed by both the user and the bank. When the user performs a transaction, the bank verifies whether the user is registered in the bank.

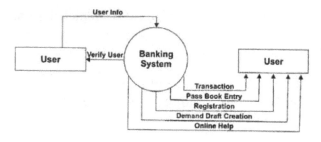

Level 0 DFD of a Banking System

The Level a DFD is expanded in Level 1 DFD. In this DFD, the 'user' entity is related to several processes in the bank, which include 'register', 'user support', and 'provide cash'. Transaction can be performed only if the user is already registered in the bank. Once the user is registered, he can perform a transaction by the processes, namely, 'deposit cheque', 'deposit cash' and 'withdraw cash'. Note that the line in the process symbol indicates the level of process and contains a unique identifier in the form of a number. If the user is performing transaction 'deposit cheque', the user needs to provide a cheque to the bank. The user's information such as name, address, and account number is stored in 'user-detail' data store, which is a database. If cash is to be deposited and withdrawn, then the information about the deposited cash is stored in 'cash-detail' data store. The user can get a demand draft created by providing cash to the bank. It is not necessary for the user to be registered in that bank to have a demand draft. The details of amount of cash and date are stored in 'DD-detail' data store. Once the demand draft is prepared its receipt is provided to the user. The 'user support' process helps users by providing answers to their queries related to the services available in the bank.

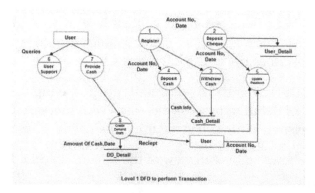

Level 1 DFD to perform Transaction

Level 1 DFD can be further refined into Level2 DFD for any process of a banking system that has detailed tasks to perform. For instance, Level2 DFD can be prepared to deposit a cheque, deposit cash, withdraw cash, provide user support, and to create a demand draft. However, it is important to maintain the continuity of information between the previous levels (Level0 and Level1) and Level2 DFD. As mentioned earlier, the DFD is refined until each process performs a simple function, which is easy to implement.

Let us consider the 'withdraw cash' process to illustrate Level2 DFD. The information collected from Level1 DFD acts as an input to Level 2 DFD. To withdraw cash, the bank checks the status of balance in the user's account (as shown by 'check account status' process) and then allots a token (shown as 'allot token' process). After the user withdraws cash, the balance in user's account is updated in the 'user-detail' data store and a statement is provided to the user.

If a particular process of Level2 DFD requires elaboration, then this level is further refined into Level3 DFD. Let us consider the process 'check account status' to illustrate Level3 DFD. To check the account status, the bank fetches the account detail (shown as 'fetch account detail' process) from the 'account-detail' data store. After fetching the details, the balance is read (shown as 'read balance' process) from the user's account. Note that the requirements engineering process of DFDs continues until each process performs a function that can be easily implemented as an individual program component.

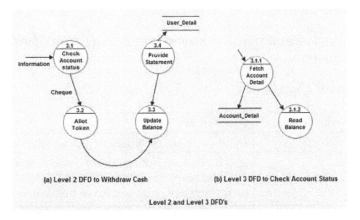

(a) Level 2 DFD to Withdraw Cash   (b) Level 3 DFD to Check Account Status

Level 2 and Level 3 DFD's

Although data-flow diagrams contain meaningful names of notations, they do not provide complete information about the structure of data-flows. For this, a data dictionary is used, which is a repository that stores description of data objects to be used by the software. A data dictionary stores an organized collection of information about data and their relationships, data-flows, data types, data stores, processes and so on. In addition, it helps users to understand the data types and processes defined along with their uses. It also facilitates the validation of data by avoiding duplication of entries and provides the users with an online access to definitions.

A data dictionary comprises the source of data, which are data objects and entities as well as the elements listed below:

1. Name: Provides information about the primary name of the data store, external entity, and data-flow.

2. Alias: Describes different names of data objects and entities used.

3. Content description: Provides information about the content with the help of data dictionary notations (such as '=', '+', and "* *").

4. Supplementary information: Provides information about data types, values used in variables, and limitation of these values.

5. Where-used/how-used: Lists all the processes that use data objects and entities and how they are used in the system. For this, it describes the inputs to the process, output from the process, and the data store.

Object-oriented Modeling

Nowadays, an object-oriented approach is used to describe system requirements using prototypes. This approach is performed using object-oriented modeling (also known as object-oriented analysis), which analyzes the problem domain and then partitions the problem with the help of objects. An object is an entity that represents a concept and performs a well-defined task in the problem domain. For this, an object contains information of the state and provides services to entities, which are outside the object(s). The state of an object changes when it provides services to other entities.

The object-oriented modeling defines a system as a set of objects, which interact with each other by the services they provide. In addition, objects interact with users through their services so that they can avail the required services in the system.

To understand object-oriented analysis, it is important to understand various concepts used in an object-oriented environment.

Table Object-oriented Concepts

Object-Oriented Concept	Description
Object	An instance of a class used to describe the entity.
Class	A collection of similar objects, which encapsulates data and procedural abstractions in order to describe their states and operations to be performed by them.
Attribute	A collection of data values that describe the state of a class.
Operation	Also known as methods and services, provides a means to modify the state of a class.
Superclass	Also known as base class; is a generalization of a collection of classes related to it.
Subclass	A specialization of superclass and inherits the attributes and operations from the superclass.
Inheritance	A process in which an object inherits some or all the features of a superclass.
Polymorphism	An ability of objects to be used in more than one form in one or more classes.

Generally, it is considered that object-oriented systems are easier to develop and maintain. Also, it is considered that the transition from object-oriented analysis to object-oriented design can be done easily. This is because object-oriented analysis is resilient to changes as objects are more stable than functions that are used in structured analysis. Note that object-oriented analysis comprises a number of steps, which include identifying objects, identifying structures, identifying attributes, identifying associations, and defining services.

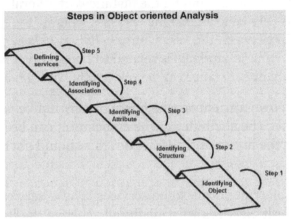

While performing an analysis, an object encapsulates the attributes on which it provides the services. Note that an object represents entities in a problem domain. The identification of the objects starts by viewing the problem space and its description. Then, a summary of the problem space is gathered to consider the 'nouns'. Nouns indicate the entities used in problem space and which will further be modeled as objects. Some examples of nouns that can be modeled as objects are structures, events, roles, and locations.

Structures depict the hierarchies that exist between the objects. Object modeling applies the concept of generalization and specialization to define hierarchies and to represent the relationships between the objects. As mentioned earlier, superclass is a collection of classes which can further be refined into one or more subclasses. Note that a subclass can have its own attributes and services apart from the attributes and services inherited from its superclass. To understand generalization and specialization, consider an example of class 'car'. Here, 'car' is a superclass, which has attributes such as wheels, doors, and windows. There may be one or more subclasses of a superclass. For instance, a superclass 'car' has subclasses 'Mercedes' and 'Toyota', which have the inherited attributes along with their own attributes such as comfort, locking system, and so on.

It is essential to consider the objects that can be identified as generalization so that the classification of structure can be identified. In addition, the objects in the problem domain should be determined to check whether they can be classified into specializations. Note that the specialization should be meaningful for the problem domain.

Attributes add details about an object and store the data for the object. For example, the class 'book' has attributes such as author name, ISBN, publisher and author. The data about these attributes is stored in the form of values and are hidden from outside the objects. However, these attributes are accessed and manipulated by the service functions used for that object. The attributes to be considered about an object depend on the problem and the requirements for that attribute. For example, while modeling the student admission system, attributes such as age and qualification are required for the object 'student'. On the other hand, while modeling for hospital management system, the attribute 'qualification' is unnecessary and requires other attributes of class 'student' such as gender, height, and weight. In short, it can be said that while using an object, only the attributes that are relevant and required by the problem domain should be considered.

Associations describe the relationships among the instances of several classes. For example, an instance of class 'university' is related to an instance of class 'person' by 'educates' relationship. Note that there is no relationship between the 'class 'university' and class 'person'. However, only the instance(s) of class 'person' (that is, student) is related to class 'university'. This is similar to entity relationship modeling, where one instance can be related by 1:1, l: M, and M: M relationships.

An association may have its own attributes, which mayor may not be present in other objects. Depending on the requirements, the attributes of the association can be 'forced' to belong to one or more objects without losing the information. However, this should not be done unless the attribute itself belongs to that object.

As mentioned earlier, an object performs some services. These services are carried out when an object receives a message for it. Services are a medium to change the state of an object or carry out a process. These services describe the tasks and processes provided by a system. It is important to consider the 'occur' services in order to create, destroy, and maintain the instances of a class. To identify the services, the system states are defined and then the external events and the required responses are described. For this, the services provided by objects should be considered.

Software Requirements Specification

A System Requirements Specification (SRS) (also known as a Software Requirements Specification) is a document or set of documentation that describes the features and behavior of a system or software application. It includes a variety of elements that attempts to define the intended functionality required by the customer to satisfy their different users.

In addition to specifying how the system should behave, the specification also defines at a high-level the main business processes that will be supported, what simplifying assumptions have been made and what key performance parameters will need to be met by the system.

Main Elements

Depending on the methodology employed (agile vs waterfall) the level of formality and detail in the SRS will vary, but in general an SRS should include a description of the functional requirements, system requirements, technical requirements, constraints, assumptions and acceptance criteria. Each of these is described in more detail below:

- **Business Drivers:** It describes the reasons why the customer is looking to build the system. The rationale for the new system is important as it will guide the decisions made by the business analysts, system architects and developers. Another compelling reason for documenting the business rationale behind the system is that the customer may change personnel during the project. Documentation which clearly identifies the business reasons for the system will help sustain support for a project if the original sponsor moves on. The drivers may include both problems (reasons why the current systems/processes are not sufficient) and opportunities (new business models that the system will make available). Usually a combination of problems and opportunities are needed to provide motivation for a new system.

- **Business Model:** It describes the underlying business model of the customer that the system will need to support. This includes such items as the organizational context, current-state and future-state diagrams, business context, key business functions and process flow diagrams. This section is usually created during the functional analysis phase.

- **Functional and System Requirements:** It usually consists of a hierarchical organization of requirements, with the business/functional requirements at the highest-level and the detailed system requirements listed as their child items. Generally the requirements are written as statements such as "System needs the ability to do x" with supporting detail and information included as necessary.

- **Business and System Use Cases:** It usually consists of a UML use case diagram that illustrates the main external entities that will be interacting with the system together with the different use cases (objectives) that they will need to carry out. For each use-case there will be formal definition of the steps that need to be carried out to perform the business objective, together with any necessary pre-conditions and post-conditions. The business use cases are usually derived from the functional requirements and the system use cases are usually derived from the system requirements.

- **Technical Requirements:** It is used to list any of the "non-functional" requirements that essentially embody the technical environment that the product needs to operate in, and include the technical constraints that it needs to operate under. These technical requirements are critical in determining how the higher-level functional requirements will get decomposed into the more specific system requirements.

- System Qualities: It is used to describe the "non-functional" requirements that define the "quality" of the system. These items are often known as the "-ilities" because most of them end in "ility". They included such items as: reliability, availability, serviceability, security, scalability, maintainability. Unlike the functional requirements (which are usually narrative in form), the system qualities usually consist of tables of specific metrics that the system must meet to be accepted.

- Constraints and Assumptions: It outlines any design constraints that have been imposed on the design of the system by the customer, thereby removing certain options from being considered by the developers. Also this section will contain any assumptions that have been made by the requirements engineering team when gathering and analyzing the requirements. If any of the assumptions are found to be false, the system requirements specification would need to be re-evaluated to make sure that the documented requirements are still valid.

- Acceptance Criteria: It describes the criteria by which the customer will "sign-off" on the final system. Depending on the methodology, this may happen at the end of the testing and quality assurance phase, or in an agile methodology, at the end of each iteration. The criteria will usually refer to the need to complete all user acceptance tests and the rectification of all defects/bugs that meet a pre-determined priority or severity threshold.

Alternatives

In agile methodologies such as extreme programming or scrum formal, static documentation such as a software requirements specification (SRS) are usually eschewed in favor of a more lightweight documentation of the requirements, namely by means of user stories and acceptance tests.

This approach requires that the customer is easily accessible to provide clarification on the requirements during development and also assumes that the team members responsible for writing the user stories with the customer will be the developers building the system. A more formal approach may be needed if the customer is inaccessible and a separate team of business analysts will be developing the requirements.

In Rapid Application Development (RAD) methodologies such as DSDM or Unified Process (RUP, AUP) the requirements specification is often kept at a higher-level with much of the detailed requirements embodied in prototypes and mockups of the planned system. These prototypes are a more visual way to represent the requirements and help the customer more easily comprehend what is planned (and therefore provide more timely feedback).

References

- Software-requirement, software-engineering: ecomputernotes.com, Retrieved 16 April 2018
- Requirements-gathering: inflectra.com, Retrieved 25 June 2018
- Requirements-gathering: projectsmart.co.uk, Retrieved 14 July 2018
- Requirements-analysis, software-engineering: ecomputernotes.com, Retrieved 10 July 2018
- Requirements-definition: inflectra.com, Retrieved 30 June 2018

Permissions

All chapters in this book are published with permission under the Creative Commons Attribution Share Alike License or equivalent. Every chapter published in this book has been scrutinized by our experts. Their significance has been extensively debated. The topics covered herein carry significant information for a comprehensive understanding. They may even be implemented as practical applications or may be referred to as a beginning point for further studies.

We would like to thank the editorial team for lending their expertise to make the book truly unique. They have played a crucial role in the development of this book. Without their invaluable contributions this book wouldn't have been possible. They have made vital efforts to compile up to date information on the varied aspects of this subject to make this book a valuable addition to the collection of many professionals and students.

This book was conceptualized with the vision of imparting up-to-date and integrated information in this field. To ensure the same, a matchless editorial board was set up. Every individual on the board went through rigorous rounds of assessment to prove their worth. After which they invested a large part of their time researching and compiling the most relevant data for our readers.

The editorial board has been involved in producing this book since its inception. They have spent rigorous hours researching and exploring the diverse topics which have resulted in the successful publishing of this book. They have passed on their knowledge of decades through this book. To expedite this challenging task, the publisher supported the team at every step. A small team of assistant editors was also appointed to further simplify the editing procedure and attain best results for the readers.

Apart from the editorial board, the designing team has also invested a significant amount of their time in understanding the subject and creating the most relevant covers. They scrutinized every image to scout for the most suitable representation of the subject and create an appropriate cover for the book.

The publishing team has been an ardent support to the editorial, designing and production team. Their endless efforts to recruit the best for this project, has resulted in the accomplishment of this book. They are a veteran in the field of academics and their pool of knowledge is as vast as their experience in printing. Their expertise and guidance has proved useful at every step. Their uncompromising quality standards have made this book an exceptional effort. Their encouragement from time to time has been an inspiration for everyone.

The publisher and the editorial board hope that this book will prove to be a valuable piece of knowledge for students, practitioners and scholars across the globe.

Index

Printed in the USA
CPSIA information can be obtained
at www.ICGtesting.com
JSHW051425221024
72173JS00006B/1399

9 781682 857465